Organization Design

SECOND EDITION

Organization Design
A guide to building effective organizations

Patricia Cichocki
with Christine Irwin

KoganPage

LONDON PHILADELPHIA NEW DELHI

First published in Great Britain and the United States in 2011 by Kogan Page Limited
Second edition, 2014

Apart from any fair dealing for the purposes of research or private study, or criticism or review, as permitted under the Copyright, Designs and Patents Act 1988, this publication may only be reproduced, stored or transmitted, in any form or by any means, with the prior permission in writing of the publishers, or in the case of reprographic reproduction in accordance with the terms and licences issued by the CLA. Enquiries concerning reproduction outside these terms should be sent to the publishers at the undermentioned addresses:

2nd Floor, 45 Gee Street
London EC1V 3RS
United Kingdom
www.koganpage.com

1518 Walnut Street, Suite 1100
Philadelphia PA 19102
USA

4737/23 Ansari Road
Daryaganj
New Delhi 110002
India

© Patricia Cichocki, 2011, 2014

The right of Patricia Cichocki to be identified as the author of this work has been asserted by her in accordance with the Copyright, Designs and Patents Act 1988.

ISBN   978 0 7494 7059 3
E-ISBN   978 0 7494 7060 9

British Library Cataloguing-in-Publication Data

A CIP record for this book is available from the British Library.

Library of Congress Cataloging-in-Publication Data

Cichocki, Patricia.
    Organization design / Patricia Cichocki, Christine Irwin. – 2nd Edition.
        pages cm
    Summary: "With the rate of change in organizations at an all-time high, the need for strong organization design has never been more pressing. Organization Design provides a complete road map to design and delivery and covers all the critical areas including downsizing, outsourcing, job design, change management and re-structuring. This thoroughly revised edition is a practical toolkit to take organization designers from start to finish, outlining the basic theory, providing a step-by-step approach to implementation, and offering solutions to the recurring challenges that will inevitably be met along the way"-- Provided by publisher.
        ISBN 978-0-7494-7059-3 (pbk.) – ISBN 978-0-7494-7060-9 (ebk)   1. Organizational change–Management.   2. Organizational change–Planning.   3. Strategic planning.   4. Organizational effectiveness.   5. Organizational change.   I. Irwin, Christine.   II. Title.
    HD58.9.C499 2014
    658–dc23
                                                                                                2013049649

Typeset by Graphicraft Limited, Hong Kong
Print production managed by Jellyfish
Printed and bound in by CPI Group (UK) Ltd, Croydon CR0 4YY

'No matter how many communes anybody invents,
the family always creeps back.'
Margaret Mead

To my family – Jan, Daniel and Philip.
Patricia

CONTENTS

LIST OF FIGURES

LIST OF TABLES

LIST OF TOOLS

ABOUT THE AUTHORS

Patricia Cichocki

Patricia is an expert in organization design and change: consulting and coaching internationally, working with clients in the commercial, government, and non-profit sectors. She has a particular interest in trust and control as levers for organization's design and development. Her experience was honed at Barclays Bank PLC as a senior line manager and consultant working on complex global strategy, design and change programmes in business and IT. She is adept at managing the practicalities of embedding organization design and the importance of pragmatic design to meet strategic aims. Patricia has a Master's in Consulting and Change with Distinction from HEC Paris and the University of Oxford and a BSc (Hons) in Geography from University College London. She is a member of the Organization Design Forum in Europe and the United States and was a founding Board Director and current member of the Change Leaders, the global community of practice dedicated to helping organizations positively address the human side of change. Patricia can be contacted by email at **patricia@designtochange.com**

Christine Irwin

Christine retired in 2011 after a 35-year career which saw her become one of the UK's leading practitioners in organization design and implementation. Her professional life spanned working inside major corporates in financial services, manufacturing and retail; and as an external consultant to clients in manufacturing, business-to-business retail, financial services, central government, and the charities sector. She relished developing and sharing her knowledge with others. The first edition of *Organization Design: A guide to building effective organizations* is just part of that legacy. During her working life she was an active member of the Organization Design Forum in the United States where she served as an elected board member from 2001 to 2010; and a member of the Organisation Development Innovation Network. She holds an MBA with Distinction from Manchester Business School and a BSc (Hons) in Operational Research from the University of Leeds.

FOREWORD

For years practitioners and managers looked at work structure as the reporting relationships and the boxes on the organization chart. This has changed in recent years. Today, it would be hard to find anyone in a complex organization to refute the importance and integral nature of an organization's structure to its mission or competitive advantage. Cichocki and Irwin have moved us further along a path of skill development and enlightenment about the critical nature of organization design and its contribution to organization effectiveness. They provide us a map and compass to widen the vista of organization design and take us on a journey beginning with strategic design thinking and preparation to defining activities for successful design outcomes. This book positions organization design as a key success factor for any business improvement, cultural shift or transformation effort. The book highlights the notion that a well-designed organization has a unique form related to its needs and that a well-designed organization unlocks the potential of the organization.

Regardless of the organization design methods you have championed or used in the past, this book will add immensely to your organization design portfolio. Too often because we are more familiar with one methodology than another we put lots of energy into one approach and ignore or minimize the benefits of others. We look to find the right design and it is always harder than we anticipate. The current volatile business environment makes it difficult to design an organization for the future. The result is sometimes less than optimal. There are so many scenarios or alternatives possible. Understanding the context and need, finding the right mix and balance of alternatives and selecting a final design is the core of *Organization Design: A guide to building effective organizations*. The authors draw upon their experience in organizations and put forth a strong organization model – the Organization Design Compass and the OPTIMAL Way. The Compass is used not only to guide the mapping of design options but to frame debates throughout design. The contribution of this book is immense.

The writing is clear, the ideas holistic and the set up user-friendly. The book outlines a four-part process but provides the flexibility of starting at any point and exploring each quadrant as the thinking evolves within the organization, whether it is the broader organization, a business unit or team. The building blocks are ideas from which to formulate appropriate ideas for many situations and can be applied across a broad spectrum of organization size or organization unit. Simple tools and templates are provided to support the process during each phase of design. Each chapter is laid out to move through the process in an organized, modular fashion that is easy to chunk into manageable periods of time.

The book is important to anyone serious about organization design and about ensuring organizations have the practical 'know how' to follow through on any type of design or redesign. Whether you are an organization designer, line manager, HR professional, Organization Development/ Organization Effectiveness specialist, Finance or IT specialist or senior leader you will reap benefit.

As the authors note, 'A great wind is blowing and that gives you either imagination or a headache. Organization design can ease the headache and stimulate the imagination to build a more effective organization for the future'. We can all thank Cichocki and Irwin for sharing their experience and know how in ways that will undoubtedly improve our work in building effective organizations.

Mila N Baker

Academic Chair and Director, M.S. Human Resource Management;
Director, Leadership and Human Capital, New York University

ACKNOWLEDGEMENTS

This book draws heavily on the first edition which I (Patricia) co-authored with Christine Irwin. It was a product of our many years of experience, education and collaboration with others. We have been fortunate to learn from many professional and academic colleagues across the globe. Our thanks go to all the people and organizations that we have worked with, for and alongside. In particular, we thank our colleagues, past and present from Barclays Bank PLC where we met and both learned so much; and to our clients at Design to Change. We also thank two international communities of practice: 'the Change Leaders' and 'the Organization Design Forum' whose members have provided us with a great deal of knowledge, stimulation, challenge, and friendship over many years. We acknowledge our debt to them for the generous sharing of their experiences and techniques that have so enriched our work.

The second edition was produced by me (Patricia). I want to acknowledge Christine's assistance and encouragement over many years working together, as well as her continued support to me in her retirement. A book is a major design project; with all the time, change, mess and emotion that entails. It would not be accomplished without a good team and support behind it. Thank you to all the people who have helped me make the second edition a reality; by giving permission for materials, providing suggestions and feedback along the way or by reviewing and commenting on drafts. In particular, I have really appreciated the feedback from readers and users of the first edition which has helped me in this refinement. To my publishers, Kogan Page, thank you for your continued support. To try to name all the people and organizations that have helped and inspired me would risk insulting those I omit. I thank you all.

Introduction

> *The law of the survival of the fittest is as inexorable for organizations as it is in nature. For survival, for continual growth and development, in organizations as with individuals, it helps to know what you would like to be before you try to become it. Analysis of the ideal, of what should be, when compared with the reality of what is, may be disillusioning, but it is the proper starting point for improvement and for planned change. ...In pursuing an optimal structure, organizations have normally followed an implicit re-formulation of Ockham's Razor – 'as simple as you can, as complex as you must' ...or to put it another way, the designer of organizational structures needs to tread a tight-rope stretched between the pressures for uniformity on the one hand and diversity on the other.* (CHARLES HANDY)

Not long after I started my first job, I picked up *Understanding Organizations* by Charles Handy (1993) to accompany me on a train journey. In it I read the quote above. I was hooked. The power of design to enable change and balance the many tight-ropes in leading organizations has fascinated me ever since. The world for people and organizations is constantly changing. The jobs and ways of working that my ancestors and predecessors in work held are in many aspects, unrecognizable to me. The computers that I worked with as an undergraduate and in my earlier career have long been dusty museum pieces. My children are emerging into a world of work that will change many times throughout their careers.

Organization design has again become a hot topic recently with leaders, the HR community and with academia, because organizations are becoming more complex. A working knowledge of organization design has become an essential personal competency for successful senior leaders.

Organization design sets out to answer the question, 'What is the optimal form for a group to fulfil its purpose and strategy so it can reach its intended outcomes?' The resulting configuration is the organization design. Form is much more than structure. Redrawing the organization's structure alone is not organizational design. If insufficient change is made across various dimensions of an organization and without appropriate balance then the desired transformation will not be made.

Increased complexity is drawing people back to organization design. That design should provide sufficient framework to support the organization as it evolves and adapts to enable it to achieve its reason for being. It is about defining the important things, and keeping balance, not about defining every last detail. Good organizational design will secure flexibility and adaptability for future growth, sustainability, and success in twenty-first-century organizations.

McKinsey asserted in 2013 that disruptive technologies are bringing advances that will transform life, business, and the global economy; they are relentless, far reaching, touching all sorts of organizations. They listed 12 disruptive technologies: mobile internet; automation of knowledge work; the internet of things; cloud technology; advanced robotics; autonomous and near-autonomous vehicles; next-generation genomics; energy storage; 3D printing; advanced materials; advanced oil and gas exploration and recovery; and renewable energy. Their reach will be widespread. Some of the biggest opportunities and challenges for business leaders will arise from new tools that could transform how work is done. These tools could redefine jobs as tasks are augmented by, or transferred to, machines, requiring new skills for workforces. It will impact the leadership and the design of organizations, globally. The environment and the organization are becoming more integrated, volatile, uncertain, complex and ambiguous.

And any change occurs unevenly across industries and across the globe. Growth for some; decline for others; change for all. Change is the only constant. In the midst of all that change some things still hold true. There are people and organizations. An organization is simply 'a group of people with a shared purpose'. The forms they take to accomplish their purpose needs thinking through if they are to maximize their efforts. Design is one of the enduring concepts for people to think through how to achieve their shared purpose and fulfil their ambitions.

> Design is a powerful agent for change. Through a process that involves problem-solving and an in-depth understanding of human wants and needs, present and future, designers bring technological, scientific and social revolutions to life.
>
> (World Economic Forum Global Agenda Council on Design Innovation, 2012)

To design is to act like a designer, think like a designer, create like a designer, producing designs and end products. For organization design the end result is not gardens, cars, houses, nor the Olympic Games opening ceremony:

it is organizations. To design organizations is to act like a designer, think like a designer, create like a designer, producing designs and transformed organizations.

Over the years, I have observed that whenever and wherever organization design is carried out: many new people get involved who are undertaking organization design for the first time; they come from a range of different backgrounds, experiences, geographies and often organizations; and they lack a common understanding of what it means to design. They often don't bring a 'design mindset' and they lack a framework to share, understand, and use. Organization design is for too many, a mystery and the results too often a disappointment. Yet, there are many pieces of the jigsaw around, if you know where to look.

As with other types of design; good organization design is the big deal that separates the OK from the great. You know a well-designed organization when you come into contact with one. There is a shared purpose and the organization is structured with interdependent and coordinated parts forming a coherent and systematic whole. Everything works well and in harmony; people know what has to be achieved collectively and individually; the purpose, strategy, and goals are shared and unambiguous; it is good to do business with as a customer or supplier; if you are an employee you feel valued and productive. Organization design is the art, the science and the business of building effective organizations. It is a deep expertise and competence, consisting of knowledge from theory and experience.

> Many of my clients tell me that they find it increasingly difficult to operate within outdated or dysfunctional structures. My prevailing impression is that organizations either overlook the importance of organizational design or simply don't know what to do.
>
> (Gill Corkindale, 2011)

This book is for anyone who needs to know how to design an organization. It is a guide for designers and those that want to learn about designing organizations. I imagine you, the reader, are a leader or the type of person that leaders turn to, to remodel their organization. I imagine too that you are experienced in your own sphere, but looking to develop or extend your skills to organization design so you can powerfully transform organizations. You may work within an organization or as an external advisor. You are probably interested in how organizations work, what makes them more effective, and why some are better at delivering their required results than others. You are probably good at balancing hard and soft skills and comfortable taking multiple perspectives.

People looking for practical guidance on how to build effective organizations come from diverse backgrounds and many different roles. You may come from: strategic HR; strategic planning; portfolio, programme or project management; leadership or line management; internal or external consultancy; change management; organization development; organization effectiveness; business process and IT management; corporate restructuring; in fact any area or team that gets involved in start-ups, reorganizations, mergers and acquisitions, divestitures or changes to supply chains. You may also be seeking to learn or teach practical organization design; or support organization design work with your specialist expertise. I hope that if you are a more experienced designer, you too will find new ideas, fresh inspiration, insight, and the articulation of areas rarely covered. The book will also be of interest to CEOs, HR Directors, academics, students and others; who need a broad awareness of organization design.

If you are new to organization design, whatever your business challenges, when asked to design your organization (in part or as a whole) you need to know how to carry out that challenge. You may need to know, what to do, how to do it, where to start, who to involve and when to do it. How do you respond when your business asks demanding questions of you? How much of the organization needs to change? What skills do we need to do this? What needs doing when? What is different about an organization design project from other types of projects? Carrying out an organization design is never the same twice. Context, the scale of the challenge and the business issues and risks posed, mean that even for experienced practitioners organization design is never routine. You may be concerned to understand the impact of the designs you devise and make sure they have the right buy-in and agreements. The implications of getting it wrong can be hugely detrimental to the organization, its people, its customers, and other stakeholders.

All organizations can benefit from understanding organization design whether they are: commercial or public; local or global; physical or virtual; based in China or in Chicago; a part of a larger organization; the whole of an organization or across a supply chain. Most organization design tasks cover part of a broader organization, say: a business unit, a functional unit, a department, a team, or a company. The task could be reorganizing a part of the organization to deliver a set of processes or functions, setting up an operational shared service centre or setting up a new section. It is more unusual to design a large, enterprise-wide organization, because these changes happen less frequently. However, the same thought process is required and the achievement of successful outcomes can be just as satisfying. As Frank Lloyd Wright advised, 'regard it as just as desirable to build a chicken house as to build a cathedral'. Throughout this book I have in mind the design of a medium-size organization (rather than a very small team or an organization of tens of thousands), but it could be in any industry or geography.

This book is a practical guide to building effective organizations through organization design. In this edition, I will share with you what I have learned about an 'organization design mindset and framework'. There is a practical process; a robust, broad-based model; and a set of tools and techniques that all link together; with a common lexicon that makes organization design easier. A suite that is accessible for anyone or any team getting involved in organization design. Like programme and project methodologies it can be used by all and work with different design and change approaches and organizational contexts. The suite was largely developed when I worked with my former business partner, Christine Irwin, prior to her retirement.

Our expertise had been developed as practitioners, with a deep understanding of organization design and change theory. To echo Isaac Newton, if we have seen farther it is by standing on the shoulders of giants. I will share relevant theory and experience along the way. The frameworks used throughout the book are ours; assembled from many techniques used over the years; drawn from solid organization design theories from research, academia, and other practitioners and melded into a comprehensive, practical whole.

This book has a rich source of ideas to help you get started to work with others to design and build effective organizations. There is a map and compass to guide you on your way. Despite the mystery and intrigue that surrounds organization design, it is very achievable. Mastery and intent are on the horizon.

How the book is structured

Parts One and Two together provide you with the knowledge of how to establish and run an organization design programme. Part Three covers how to respond to three perennial challenges in designing organizations.

Part One: Understanding organization design

Like any good guidebook, it starts with some background. This part covers the foundations of organization design for the rest of the book:

- Putting organization design in context: organization design requires participants to think and engage like a designer. Five questions are answered: What is design? What is an organization? What is organization design? Why does organization design matter? Why design an organization?

- Familiarize yourself with the Organization Design Compass and OPTIMAL Way: designers use models and process in their work; there is considerable variation in how they do so.
    Organization design models and process as concepts are explored. The authors' model, 'the Organization Design Compass' and their process, 'the OPTIMAL Way' are introduced.
    Variations in how you can use them in design work are discussed.

- Some essential building blocks: designers deliberately generate ideas and options to create insight and concepts. Chapter 3 introduces you to archetypes, metaphors and three frameworks that are established ways for organization designers to think through their ideas, create insight, diagnose and learn. When designing, they will help you create different concepts.

Part Two: Designing your organization the OPTIMAL Way

Part Two presents step-by-step, chapter-by-chapter, the use of the OPTIMAL Way. It shows you how to design an organization in a systematic way, gaining buy-in, making well-informed decisions, and delivering a high-level design blueprint ready for more detailed design and implementation. It is shown as a participative process (that can be varied and used with more or less engagement). Throughout Part Two, there is a comprehensive toolset that will help you explore all aspects of the Organization Design Compass. There are techniques that will help you gain insight and design together with examples and case studies to bring each step to life. You will see how to carry out an organization design, what some of the outputs look like, what outcomes you can achieve along the way. Part Two covers:

- Outlining your brief.
- Pulling together your programme.
- Taking stock of the change required.
- Identifying the assessment criteria.
- Mapping the design options.
- Assessing the alternatives.
- Laying out the way forward.
- Taking the OPTIMAL Way forward.

Part Three: Dealing with recurring challenges

Part Three covers how to respond to some challenges that organization designers face time and time again, whatever the organization and methodology used. This part is aimed at more advanced practitioners and/or those seeking specific guidance. It is assumed that those reading this part have an understanding of at least one organization design model and familiarity with organization design processes; here the Organization Design Compass and OPTIMAL Way are referenced. Designers are frequently asked:

- How to maintain design integrity over time? Chapter 11 suggests the use of a design authority to help maintain organization design integrity. It explains organization design integrity. It explains what a design authority is and how it helps maintain integrity.
- How to choose between options when the environment is very uncertain? Chapter 12 explains how designers can use scenario thinking to get valuable insight in highly complex or uncertain conditions. It shows you how to build scenarios; describes how scenario planning can help your strategic thinking and inform designs; and provides tools and techniques for scenario testing which can provide insight into how different designs may work.

- How to assess the level of capability development over time? Understanding the capabilities an organization has access to, is key to designing and changing organizations. Sometimes it is important to set and monitor defined interim and/or final levels for targeted capabilities, either for an organization as a whole or for particular areas or groups of people. Chapter 13 shows you how you can tailor and use a capability maturity assessment framework to assess the maturity of an organization's target capabilities: either at a point in time or periodically. Two case studies demonstrate this.

What has changed in this edition

The second edition has a greater emphasis on how organization designers can learn from design in general and from acting and thinking like a designer. The main enhancements are the inclusion of:

- Key points – at the chapter openers.
- Greater clarity on what design and designing is.
- Greater clarity on what an organization is and the importance of its purpose.
- Deeper insight into why organizations are designed.
- Discussion on different ways to carry out design work.
- Greater clarity on how the OPTIMAL Way process can be tailored.
- An increased range of archetypes.
- Further resources to get insight, for example metaphors and positive deviance.
- A richer source of references and direction for further guidance.
- Further examples to reinforce points, spanning geography and sectors.

In addition, some tools and tables have been simplified.

PART ONE
Understanding organization design

Putting organization design in context

01

> *When the wind of change blows, some build walls, others build windmills.* **(ANONYMOUS)**

KEY POINTS

Organization design is:

- the process of designing an organization and the resulting configuration;
- a discipline, a framework and mindset that aims to create value;
- powerful because it holds the key to change.

Organization design matters because it:

- positively impacts performance;
- ensures resources are more effectively used;
- enables a culture of accountability;
- translates strategy into action;
- can allow organizations to fulfil their strategic intent;
- helps organizations deal with change;
- allows for adaptation without creating chaos;
- reduces risk.

▶

◀

What drives an organization to carry out a design?

- Defining or redefining the organizational purpose.

- Establishing or re-establishing the organization's strategy.

- There are significant changes to operations.

- Faced with sustained evolution.

- The organization is not performing as expected.

- Cost cutting, a new leader making changes or adopting 'best practices' are other reasons that drive re-designs but be cautious if they aren't supporting the context and strategy.

Organization design: a guide to building effective organizations. What does that mean? Why should you be interested? How does organization design help you decide whether a wall or a windmill is right for your organization? The aim of this chapter is to answer the question, 'Why design an organization'? This chapter covers what design is, what an organization is, what organization design is, why organization design matters, and why design an organization. Organization design is complex, with many facets: an understanding of all of these will help you carry out work in this arena and explain it to others. It is important to understand why organization design matters for many stakeholders and in particular the strategic leadership of an organization and the triggers that make organization design an appropriate intervention rather than other transformation approaches. There is increasing recognition that organization design matters, as Tom Jasinski, AVP, Organization Effectiveness at MetLife Inc, New York said in 2009, 'In good times or in bad, organization design matters!' This is because executed well, organization design can powerfully deliver business results and translate strategy into action. In addition, organization design matters because organizations have to deal with more significant and frequent change, the impact of which has higher visibility to organizations' stakeholders. By reading this chapter you should gain an insight into the strategic context for organization design that will help frame the rest of this book.

Let's look at organization design in context (see Figure 1.1). It is a dynamic model; the major links are shown. Organization design is a critical business activity establishing the framework by which an organization serves its customers and interfaces with the market. An organization is influenced by

FIGURE 1.1   Organization design in context

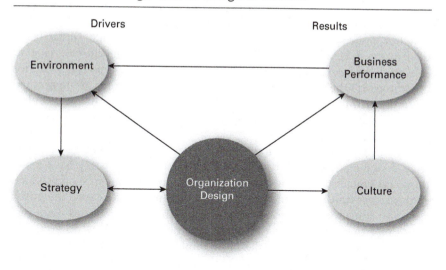

its external environment and it influences its environment (Daft, 2007). Strategy is the organization's choices on how it achieves its vision. Organization design is the vehicle through which the business strategy is executed (Galbraith, 1973, 1995) and it translates strategy into results both directly and via changing culture (Salz, 2013).

> Paradoxically, the most important aspect of delivering cultural change is not to focus explicitly on changing the culture, but rather to focus on what the exact nature of the change is (a problem that needs fixing), how it will be achieved, and how the existing culture will facilitate or resist the required change. This subtle and important difference is often misunderstood.
>
> (Salz, 2013)

Culture in turn also drives performance (Heskett, 2011 and Sackman and Stiftung, 2006). Organization design is thus a cornerstone of competitive advantage and performance. It is one of the few levers senior leaders can directly manage to help them achieve competitive advantage in an extremely challenging global marketplace (Nadler and Tushman, 1997).

What is design?

This may seem a basic question, but many people who are asked to work on organization design programmes are not trained in design or its concepts. The understanding of design outside design circles is still immature. Take a minute and think what does design mean for you.

When asked this question, people often describe the designed artefact, the end product: the iPhone, the Guggenheim in Bilbao, or the Ferrari (probably a red one). In organizational terms, people commonly describe the published organization chart. Maybe you also think of the blueprints that are produced for how the product or building will look. Those blueprints might be sketches, models, and videos of the whole or parts of the design. Design is not the frippery. It is much more than fonts, logos, posters, and clothes. As Steve Jobs said, 'In most people's vocabularies, design means veneer. It's interior decorating. It's the fabric of the curtains or the sofa. But to me, nothing could be further from the meaning of design. Design is the fundamental soul of a human-made creation that ends up expressing itself in successive outer layers of the product or service.'

Take five minutes, write down what you would have to consider if you were designing a garden. If you did this, you would probably have many things on your list. There is a lot more to design than the finished product. And is it ever finished? Good designs are powerful. Think of something that you love; something that you engage with, with strong emotions – not just something that you like or that you take for granted. Why do you love that tablet or that car so much? Now think about the car-washing kit or kitchen gadget that lies at the back of the garage or drawer – used once and never picked up again and maybe replaced by another item that fulfils the same function. As a customer why do you keep going back to the same company over and over again, when there are other companies out there that offer the same products or services and maybe even cost less? It is not blind loyalty; there are some companies that have an appeal, their products and services are pleasing to use and you have come to know and enjoy dealing with these companies. As an employee, why have you enjoyed working in some companies or one department but not another even when the work was similar? Design sets apart the OK from the great. Quality and function alone are not enough; it is the overall design of a thing that is a key differentiator. Something that is well-designed is easy to use and it works, but above that it taps into our emotions and we enjoy it. MIT, Harvard, McKinsey, P&G, Dell, Samsung and Harley-Davidson are among the many businesses moving to design to help navigate the present and the future. It is why in the United Kingdom and in Europe governments are embracing design to help redesign basic social services.

Design is both a noun and a verb. The term encompasses both the artefact and the process of designing that artefact (Walls *et al*, 1992). It is the design and designing. It is what designers produce and what and how they do it. But it is more than that; it is a discipline, a framework and a mindset. Design is the artefact and the supporting deliverables. It is the end result in whole or in part and the interim products and information about it; the ideas and concepts, sketches, details, features, plans and blueprints. It is how it looks and feels for the people who use it.

Design is a process – it is designing. Designing involves:

- in-depth research and analysis of many factors, such as: the intent; the context – constraints, boundaries and opportunities; it looks at the people, customers, clients and other stakeholders' needs;

- searching for insight and foresight;
- exploring concepts: using the insight, foresight, research and analysis to generate concepts that can be communicated and tested, combined and recombined;
- creating 'solutions' by combining systems of concepts to make a whole and exploring their arrangement; evaluating these, refining and reiterating;
- realizing the idea and delivering the end result; producing plans at a level of detail that it can be constructed or implemented.

Design is a discipline, a framework and mindset that aims to create value. To design is to think like a designer and act like a designer. It is a way of thinking and acting that follows a loose framework where insights are collected from a variety of sources that ultimately guide activities toward a solution. The design mindset includes some core tenets:

- Action orientation – taking lots of small practical steps forward.
- A learner's mindset – accepting that the first solution is rarely (if ever) the right solution and that introducing new things requires iteration. It uses divergent and convergent thinking at different stages to explore widely and then narrow in.
- Encouraging disparate viewpoints and getting a holistic perspective on problems and solutions. The design process is a communication process; it is about having the right people, right information, right interactions, right knowledge, right conversation, and right outcomes. Most of the methodologies and tools are about making that happen; they are the design of interactions.

Design is messy: it is non-linear. It involves engaging, discussing, thinking, iterating, reiterating, testing, learning, evolving, and making choices and decisions. A challenge, when people are new to design or working on a design, is the rush to find the perfect design and move on to action. A good designer doesn't use one lens or only one view but is a *bricoleur* who understands that design is its own practice. Much like the artist or the scientist – the designer has skills, methods, processes, tools and techniques that not only can, but require the ability, to use different lenses and approaches.

Design is powerful because it holds the key to change. It has a set of tools, techniques and methods that can guide people towards a much better way of doing things. Designers, by the very nature of their professional practice, are change agents who solve complex problems. Good designers have the ability to:

- tolerate ambiguity that shows up in viewing design as inquiry or as an iterative loop of divergent-convergent thinking;
- maintain sight of the big picture by including systems thinking;
- handle uncertainty;

- handle the tensions and paradoxes that need balancing to create the desired effects;
- make decisions;
- think as part of a team – they need to work with others;
- think and communicate in the several languages of design.

What is an organization?

An organization is a group of people brought together for a purpose and arranged to form a systematic whole with interdependent and coordinated underlying parts. The *Oxford English Dictionary* defines an organization as 'an organized body of people with a particular purpose, as a business, government department, charity, etc' and 'the action or process of organizing, ordering, or putting into systematic form; the arrangement and coordination of parts into a systematic whole; frequently in social organization'. So an organization has both an expressed purpose and an established mechanism for achieving it.

An organization has an expressed purpose; it is not simply a group of people. It is something that exists beyond the people and that can hold a broader purpose even as the individuals come and go. The purpose of the group drives everything. Profit (if that is a requirement) is an outcome and a metric. The critical factor is that there is an intentionally established purpose (Katz, 1966). Indeed, groups of people require (in a socio-psychological sense) that sense of purpose (what they are there to do).

An organization has an established mechanism for achieving its purpose. It is arranged to form a systematic whole with interdependent and coordinated underlying parts. Buchanan and Huczynski (2007) described organizations as 'a social arrangement for achieving controlled performance in pursuit of collective goals'. An organization has a boundary that defines its scope, the 'territory' that it controls and regulates. There is a dynamic interchange across the boundary between an organization and its environment. As it pursues its purpose, it has work to do for that purpose, and resources to deploy.

There are different types of organizations. For instance, Tom Burns (1963) suggested two 'ideal types' of organizational structure: mechanistic and organismic (organic). The mechanistic organization type adopts this form because of the relatively stable environmental conditions that exist – these are more defined and more hierarchical. The organic organizations, on the other hand, have adapted to meet unstable environmental conditions – these are harder to define upfront and more horizontal. Commercial companies are organizations that exist to deliver their goods and services to customers and make profit for their shareholders and owners. The public sector has organizations (in the UK there are hospitals, National Health Service Trusts, government departments, and local authorities) that exist to deliver services and to provide government administration. The same is true for not-for-profit organizations like charities and religious groups.

An organization can be a few people or a million plus. The National Health Service in the UK employs more than 1.7 million people, Walmart 2.1 million worldwide and the Chinese People's Liberation Army 3.2 million (BBC, 2012). Some religious organizations have over a billion members.

Organizations are all created for a purpose; choices are made about their structure, the number of people needed, and their skills, how work is organized; how tasks are performed, how they are run and what they value. This also holds equally true of organizations without a physical presence for instance, social networks and communities of practice. An organization can refer to an entire enterprise including its many sub-units or just a part of a larger organization.

What is organization design?

Organization design is the art, the science and the business of building effective organizations. 'Organization design' is both a verb and a noun. It is both the process of designing an organization and the deliverables. The organization design process aims is to identify the optimal form for a group to fulfil its purpose and strategy so it can reach its intended outcomes. The resulting configuration is the organization design – the concepts, outlines and blueprints for the future organization and ultimately the changed organization. Organization design is a discipline, a framework and mindset that aims to create value. It is powerful because it holds the key to change. There are models; tools and techniques that help design organizations.

As with other types of design, good organization design is the big deal that separates the OK from the great. As with other design professions, theories and lessons from existing practice can guide you. In this book, we will show you how to think like a designer and build effective organizations, through organization design. McKinsey & Company (2010) found that redesign strategies that focused on changing mindsets and on how the new organizational model would work, not just how it would look were much more likely to be successful. This echoes Steve Jobs's words, 'Design is not just what it looks like and feels like. Design is how it works'.

Why does organization design matter?

The nature of the change is not smooth; it is bumpy, discontinuous, emergent, episodic, fluctuating between big and small; revolutionary and evolutionary. Together with the dizzying pace of change in organizations this further complicates the already difficult existence of the leader and manager. The pace will increase yet further, and so will the volume of information individuals must manage. It will be essential for organizations to separate the critical from the irrelevant and quickly. Leaders need to align ongoing change to a clear vision of the future and a shared purpose. Change without purpose causes confusion, worry, and mental exhaustion.

Organization design matters because it powerfully delivers results: it positively impacts an organization's business performance. There is a whole body of research showing that good organization design is important for many reasons. Benefits are multiplied and enhanced significantly when the organization is planned and managed as an integrated whole with parts working together to support the organization's overall goals. A well-designed organization has a unique form related to its needs: although building this requires long-term commitment to put it in place, it cannot be copied easily. A well-designed organization unlocks the potential of the organization, its employees, and other resources: it runs smoothly. As Bryan and Joyce (2007) said, 'Redesigning an organization to take advantage of today's sources of wealth creation isn't easy but there can be no better use of a CEO's time.'

Organization design matters because it can lead to significant returns for any organization in any sector because resources are more effectively used. In the commercial sector, it delivers improved financial performance, improved competitive advantage, and significant returns on investment. Organization design is an important leadership function: one that is critical to encouraging ethical behaviour as well as the pursuit of shareholder value. Research by Capelle Associates Inc across 210 Canadian companies in 2000 found a statistically significant relationship between organization design and employee satisfaction, customer satisfaction, and financial performance. Companies with a stronger focus on organization design had better organizational performance on all three factors. Companies with weaker focus on organization design tended to have poorer performance on all three factors. Capelle found governance was similarly correlated against the three factors. You will see later in the book that governance forms an intrinsic part of our organization design model, the Organization Design Compass. Organization design impacts culture, which in turn plays a strong role in organization success. Strategy, values, leadership styles, organizational behaviour, work organization, structures, and rules all contribute to the culture. Good organization design practice aligns all of these and so creates a strong and healthy culture.

Organization design matters because it enables a culture of accountability, as employees understand the organization's goals, and how they support these via their team's and their own accountabilities and authorities. There is clarity: demarcating the areas of ownership and control; employees feel well led. There are improvements to productivity and reduced waste because the organization and its people's goals are properly aligned. It creates an environment where people can actively contribute and work effectively. This results in higher employee satisfaction. Because employees are better enabled to deliver high-quality services and products, they can better meet customer expectations leading to increased customer satisfaction. Suppliers up and downstream also find a well-designed organization easier to work with.

Organization design matters because it translates strategy into action. Many recent studies have shown that between 70 and 90 per cent of organizations that have formulated strategies, failed to execute them. The ability to execute strategy is widely acknowledged to be one of the ultimate differentiators and the ultimate challenge in today's business environment. But even where organizations are very good at strategy development, executives fail to enable the ownership, passion, and excitement that they feel about the journey ahead to be transferred to their team, and their teams, and their teams. Everyone in the organization needs to be able to describe the strategy and explain what part they play in achieving it. Can you imagine the impact of being able to do this in your own organization? Can you imagine being able to make conscious choices as to how your organization responds, within a framework that contributes to the whole organization's success? Organization design can create the infrastructure to enable a strategy to be operationalized and for the organization to maximize their contribution.

Organization design matters because it can allow organizations to fulfil their strategic intent and be what they need to be, for instance: innovative, flexible, more responsive, and attractive to talent. Innovative because certain designs encourage innovation and shorten development cycles without compromising growth. Flexible and able to respond to changing customer needs while bolstering organizational efficiency and effectiveness: because designs can create a well-aligned, flexible, and productive organization, that is able to meet the demands of a shifting marketplace. More responsive: because organization design can enable quicker decision-making as some designs help accelerate information flow and streamline decision-making. Attractive to talent: through the provision of opportunities for personal growth by allowing people to take on different, challenging roles within the same organization. In contrast in a poorly designed organization, productivity and performance issues are evident. Great mission, great people, and great leadership all help but without a good organization design, the organization and its people will not perform at their best.

Organization design matters because it helps organizations deal with change and change is becoming more frequent and significant. Numerous academic and consultants' studies have found that the pace of change has never been greater than in the current business environment and there is a consensus that the change, being triggered by internal or external factors, comes in all shapes, forms and sizes and, therefore, affects all organizations in all sectors and industries. 'Corporations once built to last like pyramids are now more like tents. Tomorrow they're gone or in turmoil' – Peter F Drucker. The CIPD/Said Business School, Oxford study 'Organizing for Success in the Twenty-First Century' (2002–05) showed that on average, UK big companies were experiencing major change about once every three years with more frequent localized changes. As economies become global, firms must respond to heightened competition, changing economic fortunes and shifting regulatory requirements. Today, organizations are either constantly reorganizing or it can feel as if they are. The level and amount of change in organizations continues to accelerate rapidly while the complexity of issues that people are required to engage with continues to grow. This is being felt across all types of organizations whether they are businesses, government, or not-for-profits. Organization design matters because it is more widely recognized as a suitable response to change and essential to good change, particularly by senior leaders. As HR becomes increasingly more strategic, with a seat at many senior leadership tables, the requirement for an organization design intervention is more likely to be recognized. In addition, changes from the 1990s generated by business re-engineering and later SAP implementations both have elements of organization design within them.

Organization design matters because it identifies who will make decisions, shape outcomes, and lead the change process, which allows for adaptation without creating chaos. Organization design matters because it reduces risk. Organizations are more open to external scrutiny and at the first signs of problems, commentary is available across the globe via the internet. Past misdemeanours by organizations and their supply chains are reflected in increased regulation, legislation and fines from local and global bodies. The banking crisis led to the recognition of the lack of oversight in that industry. Elsewhere think of BP in the Gulf of Mexico, GlaxoSmithKline in China, and Primark in Bangladesh.

Why design an organization?

Organization design is not the only response to change. Some proponents in recent years have argued that there has been a reduced need for organizational restructuring and design because soft evolutionary changes that operate in isolation can be used instead. There are those that argue that because organizations are so complex there is no time to design and the focus should be on adaptation and evolution, 'sense and respond'. However, interest in design is renewing and growing; within academia, professional groups and from leaders and practitioners in organizations.

Stéphane Girod's unpublished research report for the Accenture Institute for High Performance explains why. He found that when for instance, the context is changing, the industry is changing and the organization is changing internally; evolutionary adaptive processes are not enough, organization design is called for. Girod looked at 50 of the largest American industrial multinational enterprises ranked by *Fortune* between 1985 and 2004 and found that in a context of rising internationalization, that while evolutionary adaptive processes have certainly flourished within them, they had kept using and even increasingly used restructuring. Girod's statistical analysis indicated that multinational enterprises used restructuring when they faced a double increasing complexity caused by their strategic changes. He concurred with Henderson, Miller and Hambrick (2006) that the dynamic nature of environments such as internationalization requires more frequent restructurings due to the more frequent misalignments between the environment, strategy and structure.

In part, organization design, can suffer from a bad reputation because:

- What is labelled as design is nothing more than a redrawing of a structure chart without consideration of the other elements of the organization and often with no design thinking.
- It is carried out without an understanding of design. There is limited organization design training or practical information available and accessible. In this book we hope to partly plug that.
- It is carried out with an understanding of design but remotely by groups who don't live with consequences.
- It is done in too little or too much detail.

Some aspects of organization change take longer than others – simply restructuring and ignoring the other aspects is risky. Salz (2013) commented on the number of Barclays restructures (more than 8 in 10 years):

> While most companies reorganise from time to time, it is inherently difficult to develop robust governance and control structures in organisations that undergo frequent structural change, as different operating models require different enablers (eg, management information flows between Group Centre and business units), which require time to be put in place.

Organization design is not about designing everything to a minute detail. Organizations face too much complexity and inherently 'wicked problems' to make that meaningful. Organization design, done well is about having sufficient frameworks to move forward, some plans and directions, to allow the people within it to work towards the purpose and strategy but able to 'sense and respond' appropriately. Like urban planners who put in place city frameworks that allow for the inhabitants to 'sense and respond' to their evolving needs. These frameworks should allow for detail to be developed and changed in operation. Think: Paris, Rio de Janeiro or Milton Keynes. This is how architects design buildings and Apple designs the iPhone.

You may be asked the question, 'How do I know I need an organization design?' It is easier to recognize some triggers than others, but consider organization design as intervention when:

- defining or redefining the organizational purpose: 'the organization's reason for being';
- establishing or re-establishing the organization's strategy;
- there are significant changes to operations;
- faced with sustained evolution;
- the organization is not performing as expected.

Always consider organization design when the organization's purpose is defined or redefined. An organization's purpose, its intent, defines what the group is there to do and accomplish together. The purpose is always considered at an organization's creation, but it is not an eternal vision. From time to time the purpose may be reviewed and this is always a reason to reflect on the suitability of the organization's design. This is more frequent when you consider organizations within organizations; for instance, a department within a wider enterprise. It is not uncommon for the department's purpose to change even though the enterprise one remains. For example, Vertex was originally created as a business processing shared service organization within United Utilities plc, Vertex's purpose was then extended to the provision of business processing outsourcing for other organizations. In 2007 Vertex was acquired from United Utilities plc by a private equity consortium; it became an enterprise in its own right. United Utilities' own purpose did not change throughout this transformation. All organizations go through this type of thinking, not just commercial ones. Government departments in the UK separated policy-setting units (the retained 'Departments') from the executing arms ('the Agencies'). The National Trust, like other charities has had to separate its commercial, profit-making arm from its charitable foundation. A shared purpose provides the discipline to help a group 'pull together'. Communities of Practice also have to consider their drivers in terms of their purpose, strategy, operation, and health. Changes to organization's purpose often drive changes to strategic intent, but the organization's purpose may outlive many incarnations of strategy and exist in organizations where there is no formal strategic thinking. (There is a section on defining your organization's purpose in the chapter on 'Outlining your brief'.)

Always consider organization design when the organization's strategy and strategic intent has been established or re-established. Strategy is derived from an understanding of the external factors at work on the organization as well as the strengths of the organization itself. The forces of change may come from many directions: political, technological, social, or competitive; they may be seen as challenges, problems, or opportunities. Common examples are: entering a new business, subsidiary or venture; restructuring; outsourcing; a merger or acquisition; spin-off or divestiture of a product or operation; changes to sustain planned growth or contraction; changing geographic presence – onshoring, offshoring; changing markets; significant changes to product lines; or significant changes or pressures from the external environment; pressures to reduce cost or improve performance; a change in legal structure or a change in leadership. If some of these are repeated patterns, ensure you have an organization designed to cope with that. (There is a section on defining your strategic intent in the chapter on 'Outlining your brief'.)

> When organizational strategy changes, structures, roles, and functions should be realigned with the new objectives. This doesn't always happen, with the result that responsibilities can be overlooked, staffing can be inappropriate, and people – and even functions – can work against each other.
>
> (Corkindale, 2011)

Reorganization has supported a decade of expansion for dunnhumby Ltd. Today dunnhumby is the world's leading customer science company. But back in 2004 it was growing from a very successful partnership with Tesco plc in the UK (providing its Clubcard) to expand into new markets. Apart from in the United States with Kroger it had struggled to enter overseas markets. The global strategy needed a new organizational design to support it. This started small but the design has continued to support the strategy. Three different strands were involved; a team of two people (one commercial, one technical) on the ground in each new market to 'discover' client needs, a core team of experts located centrally to support groups of 'market-focused' teams, and a switch to providing a products base to a matrix of markets and solutions/services for clients. This design has enabled dunnhumby to reach 26 markets in 2013.

Microsoft is currently moving from strategy to design to change. In July 2013 Steve Ballmer announced changes for Microsoft: 'As the times change, so must our company'. The vision that had lasted since Microsoft's inception in 1975 to have 'a computer on every desktop and in every home' seemed long surpassed in many parts of the world. The new vision is 'on creating a family of devices and services for individuals and businesses that empower people around the globe at home, at work and on the go, for the activities they value most' (Microsoft News Centre, 2013). Microsoft 2.0 is how the new organization is phrased by some IT commentators. This will be a huge reorganization with changes far beyond its own organization.

Always consider organization design if you want to change the culture of an organization. Culture is an outcome of changing the tangible things about what the service does for customers and how people do their work (Salz, 2013). Culture is an outcome of organization design and change (see Figure 1.1, organization design in context).

Always consider organization design when faced with significant operational changes, for instance; moving to shared services, outsourcing, significant reductions to costs, introducing new technologies; changing the role of the corporate centre, changing the supply chain, insourcing, merging departments and through significant growth or contraction of work, changing the role of a function, as happened with HR as it has moved from an operational focus to a more strategic one.

During their lifetime organizations evolve. They grow, they change, they adapt, and they flex in response to their environment and pressures they face. New leaders join and bring experiences from elsewhere. Technology evolves. People turn over. A myriad of subtle changes to the organization can sometimes accumulate and lead to an organization getting out of alignment or balance. Other parts of the organization can change around you, requiring your organization to realign. A well-designed organization should cope with degrees of change. Changes may appear small at first with latitude within the organization to absorb them, but when faced with sustained evolution consider whether it is time to review the organization design. Don't be like the 'frog in boiling water' analogy! Respond early to the increases in temperature in the environment and take the needed actions.

Many productivity and performance issues can be attributed to poor organizational design. A company can have a clear mission, talented people, and great leaders, and still not perform well because of poor design.

> Poor organizational design and structure results in a bewildering morass of contradictions: confusion within roles, a lack of coordination among functions, failure to share ideas, and slow decision-making bring managers unnecessary complexity, stress, and conflict. Often those at the top of an organization are oblivious to these problems or, worse, pass them off as challenges to overcome or opportunities to develop.
>
> (Corkindale, 2011)

The risks of doing nothing when faced with change are substantial. If leaders don't adjust the design of their organization with changing circumstances then underperformance ensues. Consider redesigning if an organization is not performing; not delivering the outcomes expected, not thriving, or showing symptoms of organizational stress. Is it now expected to do things that it was not designed for? Changes may have been unconscious or unrecognized; perhaps they have crept up or were a surprise: increases and decreases in workload can do that. Toyota's problems with car faults coming to a head in 2009 and 2010 stem from a global expansion of an organization design that did not stretch with the volumes of sales it reached and a different geographical presence. Sometimes the reorganization of functions within organizations is driven by a dissatisfaction with their contribution to whole. This is perhaps the most challenging area to consider whether organization design is the right intervention, because unlike changes to purpose, strategy or operations where it is clear that an organization design is needed at a particular time (even if not done) it is less clear when an organization is not delivering the performance expected. You can use some of the tools and techniques in Part Two to support further analysis and highlight whether organization design will help put in place a more effective organization.

McKinsey carried out an online survey asking executives why they carried out organization design. They received responses from 2,525 executives, of whom 1,890 had been through an organizational redesign in the past five years. 'They represent the full range of regions, industries, functional specialties, tenures, and company sizes' (McKinsey & Company, 2010). Table 1.1 shows the percentages citing different reasons.

There are some 'watch outs' for design too. In particular: cutting costs, restructuring when a new leader arrives and moving to 'best practice'. 'The highest share saying the redesign had a negative business impact on the area being reorganized – 14 per cent, are respondents who also say their redesigns were driven by a new leader's desire to make changes, suggesting that redesigns do better when driven by a clear business rationale. Less surprisingly, those who were seeking to cut costs came in at a close second, at 12 per cent, reinforcing how difficult it can be to balance immediate cost savings with long-term sustainability and competitiveness.' (McKinsey & Company, 2010)

TABLE 1.1 Reasons cited for organization redesign

Reason cited	Per cent
Responding to growth	18
Cutting costs	12
Moving to a best practice model	12
Introducing change	10
Reducing complexity	8
Increasing revenues	8
Fulfilling a new leader's desire to make changes	7
Responding to a crisis	7
Integrating previous acquisitions	6
Facilitating a merger	6
Responding to regulatory pressure	2
Improving risk management	1
Preparing for a divestiture	1
Other	3

NOTE: Figures sum to more than 100 per cent because of rounding

Thinking like a designer – design should start with needs, purpose and strategy. Oftentimes cutting costs has to be carried out operationally rather than strategically. New leaders may have many motivations for making changes that may or may not relate to redesign. 'Best practice' is useful for lessons and insight, but design should be bespoke. As Capozzi, Kellen and Smit (2012) state, 'Observers and management theorists alike, blinded by star power, eventually assume that everything these companies do should be regarded as best practice – often without examining the context in which they derive their success or without parsing the true nature of their accomplishments.'

Conclusion

In our many different roles in private, public and not-for-profit organizations whether as leaders, as customers, as shareholders, as employees or as recipients of services, there are many reasons why we should care that organizations are designed well and redesigned appropriately to reflect change. 'A great wind is blowing, and that gives you either imagination or a headache' – Catherine the Great. Organization design can ease the headache and stimulate the imagination to build a more effective organization for the future.

Organization design is driven by defining or redefining the organization's purpose; establishing or re-establishing the organization's strategic intent; significant changes to operations; sustained evolution; and sometimes is an appropriate response when organizations are not performing as expected. Whatever the drivers: the considerations from an organization design perspective are the same.

Organization design is about the process of designing an organization and the resulting configuration, using a design discipline, framework and mindset. To design an organization is to think like a designer and act like a designer.

Organization design uses models, processes, tools and techniques that allow the creation of the design in enough detail to deliver the design blueprint and future state organization. Organization design matters because it delivers results by creating a culture of accountability, translating strategy into action that helps organizations fulfil their strategic intent and helps organizations deal with change. You should now have the strategic context for organization design. Now we will take a look at the model and process for organization design that will be used throughout this book.

Familiarize yourself with the Organization Design Compass and the OPTIMAL Way

02

> *Organization design and structure requires thinking, analysis and a systematic approach.*
>
> **(PETER F DRUCKER)**

KEY POINTS

Organization Design Models:

- A model is a way of representing a complex reality so that it is easier to understand.

- A variety of organization design models have been developed with varying strengths and weaknesses at different stages of design and for different audiences.

▶

◀

- The Organization Design Compass introduced provides a means of analysing, designing and changing the components of an organization while seeing the whole picture.

- 'The Compass' covers: Norms and behaviours, Structure, Enablers and Work.

Design Process:

- Organization design requires participants to think like a designer.

- As well as using different models, design processes vary in terms of their:
  - principles;
  - number of steps;
  - design filters;
  - tools and techniques applied;
  - scale of engagement and methodologies.

- The OPTIMAL Way is the organization design process we show you. It will help you think like a designer step-by-step.

So far you have learned that organization design comprises: models; tools and techniques; and a process to carry out design that results in the definition of the future organization. We have also promised you a map and compass to help you navigate to your destination. The aim of this chapter is to familiarize you with the model and process that will be used in this book. This chapter looks at what organization design models are and why they are useful; a brief view of evolving thinking on organization design models and introduces you to the authors' model: the Organization Design Compass. It also familiarizes you with our map (the OPTIMAL Way); the process to help you on your journey and also help you define your end point. There is insight into how to use the process. Using organization design models is important because they help people understand how organizations work today and how they could work in future. They make the complex easier to grasp: providing a basis for dialogues with people at all organizational levels throughout the design process. Using a good process is important because having control in design work comes from the confidence that the process will deliver the best outcomes for the organization rather than locking into pre-determined outcomes. You need to be confident that you are using a solid approach. This chapter gives you an understanding of a robust organization design model and process that have been designed to work together.

Organization design models

A model is a way of representing a complex reality so that it is easier to understand. Models are used extensively in all design-based professions, including architecture, engineering, and landscape design. These professions have a wide variety of models with associated styles and languages that designers adopt across their professions, spanning various practices, for different purposes and at different stages in their design work. Organization designers do the same.

Using models helps the designer and the group they are working with, to think things through, generate new possibilities and ideas, and manipulate these as they develop their thoughts. They help with understanding, diagnosis and analysis, because they allow users to make connections, join up thinking and make links with what is already known. As Christopher Alexander said, 'drawings help people to work out intricate relationships between parts'. They are powerful communication tools: allowing people to synthesize their ideas and express their thoughts so that information can be exchanged with or presented to others. This allows feedback and helps others to embrace new challenges and ideas. Working with models in a group allows the creation of shared understanding of what is required. They have benefits beyond the design stage as they allow you to predict outcomes from your design choices, translate ideas into action and put them into effect and ultimately deliver benefits that exceed the sum of their parts.

For organization designers, models help identify meaning and share understanding of the current organization, how the organization needs to be in future, and what needs to change. They capture more than thoughts, ideas, and facts; they also help capture feelings, experiences, and sensations. A good model can make the invisible, visible and the tacit, tangible. It pulls together all the key dimensions of the organization to make them accessible and usable. It can be used at various stages in the design process.

How organization design models have evolved

Since Fredrick Taylor in the early 1920s, people working in the organization design field have been developing models to help them think about how organizations work. Of the many organization design models available, those that we see most widely applied in practice are Leavitt's Diamond, Galbraith's Star Model, McKinsey's 7-S, and the Burke–Litwin model. These four also show how thinking on organization design models has evolved over time with later forms extending the range of elements described. Key strengths in all of them are their ability to represent some of the complexity found in organizations and their acknowledgement that the elements are all interdependent with important interactions between elements.

In 1964 Harold J Leavitt produced a model for analysing the management of change (Leavitt, 1964). This is generally referred to as Leavitt's Diamond.

It is based on the idea that it is rare for any change to occur in isolation. There are four elements of the diamond that are interdependent: technology, tasks, people, and structure. Leavitt argued that change at any one point of the diamond would impact some or all of the other elements and that any failure to manage their interdependencies at critical times of change could create problems. For example, a change in tasks in a core production process affects the people involved, the structure in which they work, and the technology that they use; and needs adjustments throughout.

Later the American academic and consultant Jay Galbraith advocated that the starting point of design is strategy and that the factors in his model must be internally consistent to enable effective behaviour, which in turn drives performance (Galbraith, 1973). Galbraith's Star Model contains five factors: strategy, structure, processes, rewards, and people. It provides a useful tool that helps designers avoid overlooking these factors and their linkages in design work. Later work documented a process to apply this model in practice (Galbraith, Downey and Kates, 2001). The Star Model remains one of the most-used models in practical organization design work.

In the late 1970s, consultants working at McKinsey & Company developed the 7-S model. The model appeared in two hugely successful and popular management books in the early 1980s when Richard Pascale and Antony Athos used it in their examination of why Japanese industry was so successful (Pascale and Athos, 1981) and the following year Tom Peters and Robert Waterman used it as they were exploring what made a company excellent (Peters and Waterman, 1982). In developing the model, they built on models like Leavitt's. Their significant breakthrough was the recognition that balancing hard and soft elements was vital. The model has seven internal variables of an organization: the hard elements are strategy, structure, and systems; and the soft elements are shared values, skills, style, and staff. Like Galbraith and Leavitt they also stress the interconnection of the variables and the need for alignment for an organization to be successful.

The Burke–Litwin model, developed in 1992, incorporates the elements of the McKinsey 7-S model and adds external environment and performance variables and shows how the variables interact (Burke and Litwin, 1992). A change in any one of them can eventually impact on the others. The model is useful in explaining both how organizations perform and how they can be changed to improve performance. The Burke–Litwin model describes how:

- transformational change happens in response to the external environment and how this directly affects mission, strategy, leadership and culture;
- in turn, the transactional elements are affected: structure, systems, management practices and work climate;
- both the transformational and transactional elements together affect motivation, which in turn affects performance;
- feedback from the organization's performance can affect the external environment.

Other similar models include Marvin Weisbord's (1976) Six-Box Model and the Congruence Model developed by Columbia University professors David A Nadler and Michael L Tushman (1980). None of these models implies any particular kind of organization (hierarchical or flat; centralized or decentralized; closed or networked); rather they look at the organization as a whole system.

Using organization design models in practice

Different people use different models in practice and this is partly due to where both the people and models are taught, as well as where the models strengths and limitations are. Some of the models are at very high level: which can be useful with the most senior executives, at early stages of exploring possibilities, to tease out thinking, and throughout a design process to explore understanding and for two-way communication. Other models have a lot more elements and interconnections, which are useful for capturing more detail; they have been designed for diagnosis and analysis, which needs deeper thinking. However, while this is attractive to some people it can appear overwhelming to others. So, in practice, what tends to happen is that:

- People use what they know.
- One model is picked for use across an organization.
- The model chosen is linked and biased towards the needs of the section that is responsible for organization design in a particular organization whether or not the model is appropriate to help other parts of the organization: McKinsey 7-S is often used by strategy groups while Burke–Litwin can be favoured by Human Resources.
- Different design practices and consultancies may favour differ models (including their own proprietary ones). More experienced organization designers tend to use different models at different stages in design work and for different purposes; as well as avoiding particular models in other circumstances.

More experienced organization designers also adapt the models so that they are appropriate for the circumstances of the design they are working on and to make them more generically applicable. All of this can be very confusing and even disruptive to the wider organization.

The Organization Design Compass

The Organization Design Compass shown in Figure 2.1 and which is introduced here is the authors' model. It has been developed over many years of practice, drawing on thinking from a wide range of academics, consultants,

FIGURE 2.1   The Organization Design Compass

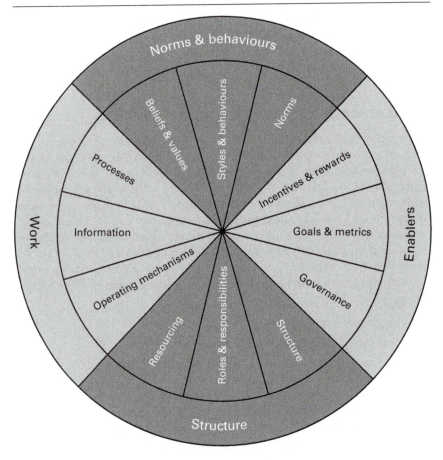

practitioners, and both their and the authors' experiences to encapsulate the benefits of other models. It is built on the best features of many other models. It has a high-level view: simple enough for understanding and communication and a more detailed view for diagnosis and analysis. The breakdown into segments has enabled the model to be flexed for specific situations in different organizations and sectors at different times. In use and to aid reading, it is sometimes abbreviated to 'the Compass'.

The earlier definition of organization design (as a noun) showed that it was composed of a number of different components. Any of the organization design models above satisfies some of these; as they are a means of deliberately thinking through an idea for a group; and a means of conveying information about it in covering the whole and/or parts of it and showing details and features of it. However, when it comes to a means of constructing the group in an ordered form so that its parts are arranged and coordinated into a systematic whole; both a model and a process are needed. Generally models have been designed, in isolation from practice, which is where process is developed, tried, and tested. So they can have limitations when used with an organization design process and associated toolsets. The Organization Design Compass, the OPTIMAL Way, and the toolset used in this book are specifically designed to work together.

At the highest level the Compass is divided into quadrants: Norms and behaviours, Enablers, Structure, and Work. Each quadrant is sub-divided into three segments. All 12 segments are interdependent and for the design to work the quadrants and segments have to be aligned. The quadrants with their segments are described below:

- Work (or Work to be done): Processes; Information; and Operating mechanisms.
- Structure: Structure, Roles and responsibilities; and Resourcing.
- Enablers: Incentives and rewards; Goals and metrics; and Governance.
- Norms and behaviours: Beliefs and values; Styles and behaviours; and Norms.

The 'Work' or 'Work to be done' quadrant

The 'Work' quadrant covers the operation of the organization: what it needs to do to deliver the business strategy and how it produces and delivers products and services to its customers, clients and users. This quadrant is also of relevance beyond 'operations'. It covers the work to be done in any organization. It is as relevant for an internal or oversight function as it is for a front line operation and as relevant for loosely connected organizations such as a community of practice or network-based organization as it is for a vertically integrated one. These organizations also produce and deliver products or services, and have customers, clients and users. The segments of the quadrant are:

Processes

The work processes that the organization carries out to produce the deliverables for the customer. It includes their input and outputs. Processes include activity within and beyond the organization's boundaries, by third-party suppliers or other parts of a broader organization.

Information

The customer and operational data, information and knowledge that is needed for the work processes to be completed. It includes flows of information within, into, and out of the organization to reach relevant people.

Operating mechanisms

The mechanisms that describe how operational work is done: together with their support systems and the tools needed. It includes property, machinery,

tools, equipment and how the supporting processes are articulated and dis-
seminated, eg through standard operating procedures, instruction manuals,
practices, methods.

The 'Structure' quadrant

The 'Structure' quadrant covers the organization's own internal structure
and any external arrangements in organizations outside their own boundaries
whether in other parts of a broader organization or through third-party arrangements that are critical to the delivery of services. For example, decisions
to use an outsourcing arrangement rather than in-house capability are a
structural decision where specific roles and responsibilities will be required
for the management of the third parties to be defined. The segments of the
quadrant are:

Structure

Structure refers to the way the organization is formally structured internally
and within its wider territory. It includes the hierarchy of authority and
accountability; groupings of people for reporting purposes and the formal
mechanisms necessary to link parts of the structure together, eg cross-unit
teams, meetings, and communities of practice and processes to make the
structure work. It includes temporary structures like project groups and task
forces that are assembled for a specific project or problem and disbanded
when no longer needed. It can cover multiple dimensions, for instance,
a practice-based structure with a project overlay. For design purposes,
it does not include informal or 'hidden' structures that so often make
organizations work.

Structure is typically documented in organization charts and is easily
recognisable, but this segment is more than this; it includes the associated
information and annotated details that support these charts.

Roles and responsibilities

This is the formal specification of roles and responsibilities for groups and
individuals in the organization. It covers the actual capabilities, skills, and
competencies of the group or individual. At lower levels of design it includes
role profiles or job descriptions. It can also be helpful to cover any defined
rules of engagement: what the group or individual is responsible for versus
what others are.

Resourcing

Resourcing covers the group of people that make up the organization
whether within its internal boundaries (however they are supplied) or beyond them to fulfil the organization's purpose, eg partnerships, suppliers,
associates and third parties. The level of detail can vary significantly across
these. Resourcing is about having the right number of people with the right
capabilities who are skilled and trained for the roles identified, available

at the right time and place. It covers having the right processes in place to manage resourcing, eg resource planning; talent planning; learning and development; recruiting and exiting.

The 'Enablers' quadrant

The 'Enablers' quadrant is all about the steerage of an organization and its people. It is akin to the bridge on a ship: the control room's helm that adjusts the rudders. It is concerned with performance and conformance; direction and control; running the organization 'as a business'. Its nature is strategic rather than operational, focused on the future direction; risk appetite and oversight rather than management. 'Enablers' is about providing the organization with the resources, authority, or the opportunity to do what it needs to do. This quadrant is the domain of the senior executives or directors and their specialized support teams in an organization. The segments of the quadrant are:

Incentives and rewards

The way incentives and rewards operate at organizational level and cascade to individual levels. The financial and non-financial incentives and reward processes, mechanisms and content needed to reinforce the achievement of the defined accountabilities, responsibilities, and capabilities, and the demonstration of the defined behaviours. It includes performance management systems, performance appraisal, reward, and bonus schemes. It also covers any disincentives, penalties, and consequence management processes used to dissuade inappropriate actions or behaviour.

Goals and metrics

The enabling processes, mechanisms, and content needed to set, track, and assess organizational and individual goals and objectives towards the organization's strategic intent; both short and long term. These should be 'balanced', so that they cover both soft and hard characteristics. It includes the cascade of accountability, responsibility, capability and behavioural goals and objectives across the organization to people and teams. It incorporates historical patterns, trend analysis, learning from the past as well as leaning towards the future; and feedback mechanisms for both the internal organizational processes and external outcomes in order to continuously improve strategic performance and results. At organization and team levels this is often associated with dashboards, scorecards, targets and portfolio management.

Governance

This covers governance frameworks, structures, processes, and mechanisms that enable the organization to manage performance and conformance. It enables the leaders of the organization to direct and control the delivery of the strategy and manage the inherent risks and opportunities. It covers what is governed by whom and how it is governed. It includes, for instance:

- temporary governance as well as permanent;
- boards, committees, councils and other meetings;
- standards, policies, manuals and other practice guidelines;
- key processes, eg investment management;
- mechanisms for defining governance and keeping it up to date;
- the cascade of authority, decision-making, and controls.

The 'Norms and behaviours' quadrant

The beliefs, values and assumptions have a strong influence on how the organization operates and progresses. Organizational beliefs and values are powerful levers for design and effectiveness of an organization when they are pervasively communicated, shared and have buy-in. It is what is absorbed and assimilated rather than just written down that is powerful. The segments of the quadrant are:

Beliefs and values

This segment covers what the organization believes in; the set of assumptions and mindsets held in common and taken for granted by the organization – 'What we stand for'. Beliefs and values play an important role that goes beyond their information content; they shape how an organization behaves.

Organizational values define the acceptable standards that govern the behaviour of individuals within the organization. Without such values, individuals will pursue behaviours that are in line with their own individual value systems, which may lead to behaviours that the organization does not wish to encourage. An organization's values are sometimes stated, sometimes just desired. Cultural ones may include, for instance, professionalism, attitude to training and commerciality. The strategic ones are typically written down and include an organization's purpose, an organization's values and strategic intent. Assumptions and mindsets are typically so well ingrained that they are hard to recognize from within.

Styles and behaviours

These are the leadership and management styles and behaviours that significantly impact the way the organization works. The kind of styles the organization favours eg autocratic, paternalistic or democratic which impacts for instance, control and decision-making and whether the organization favours councils or boards or individual decision-making. It plays out for instance, in group dynamics, group and interpersonal processes, power and politics and employee participation. Desired styles and behaviours can be specified and rewarded or disincentives put in place for undesired ones.

Norms

Norms indicate the established and approved ways of doing things; they are the customary rules of behaviour. These rules may be explicit or implicit. Failure to follow the rules can result in severe punishments, including exclusion from the group. Artefacts such as how 'we' dress, how 'we' speak, how 'we' interact with each other as well as rights and rituals, myths, metaphors, humour, trophies, celebrations, community support and what goes on the walls; can reveal organizational norms. They may be very easy to sense when you walk into an organization for the first time. Norms are often hard to recognize from within.

Designing the OPTIMAL Way

In this section, we'll introduce you to the OPTIMAL Way – the organization design approach used throughout the book. This is a participative process intended to provide a systematic, step-by-step method for the high-level design of organizations. It is the process the authors have refined and developed to work with the Organization Design Compass and the toolset in this book. Organization design requires participants to think like a designer. The approach we use will lead you through that way of thinking step-by-step. As well as using different models, design processes vary in terms of their:

- principles;
- number of steps;
- design filters;
- tools and techniques applied;
- scale of engagement and methodologies.

The OPTIMAL Design Principles

Our organization design approach follows these design principles:

- Start with needs.
- Understand the context.
- Understand the problem before seeking solutions.
- Challenge your thinking: look widely for inspiration and insight.
- Develop designs based on evidence and with attention to every detail.
- Think holistically: design addressing multiple aspects at once.
- Iterate. Then iterate again.
- Evaluate designs systematically.
- Focus on outcomes (for the people who touch the organization and the value it generates).
- Learn from the journey.

We believe the best way is to:

- Design ethically.
- Follow a structured approach, consciously completing all the steps (even if it's light touch).
- Use project management disciplines and lock in decisions as you go.
- Ensure projects are 'business' owned.
- Manage your own and the organization's anxiety with an emergent approach.
- Ensure wide engagement and dialogue.
- Balance hard and soft skills.
- Mitigate against risk.
- Do the hard work to make it simple.

The OPTIMAL Steps and Design Filters

Designers (of all kinds) break their thinking processes into a number of steps with different activities in each. The number and description of the steps varies (generally between 4 and 10) but the thinking is broadly the same. In our case, we use seven. OPTIMAL is a mnemonic where each letter is a clue to the first letter of the activity for that step. We use OPTIMAL because not only does it help you to recall the steps in the order you need to carry them out; but also it describes the desired outcome: the optimal design for your organization. 'A good plan is like a road map: it shows the final destination and usually the best way to get there' – H Stanley Judd. If you follow this book we hope OPTIMAL will become as familiar to you as other mnemonics you may be more accustomed to; say to remember the order of the planets or the colours of a rainbow. Figure 2.2 shows the main flow through the OPTIMAL Way, mapping OPTIMAL to each of the steps.

Table 2.1 provides an overview of each of the steps in the OPTIMAL Way. Each chapter in Part Two of this book covers a step in the high-level design process. The OPTIMAL Way and the layout of the chapters appear to be largely linear towards a final destination: however, while there is progression through the steps, organization design will out of necessity require some repetition and some overlap in steps. Although the design process is structured and methodical it is not a mechanical process. Mechanical processes have predetermined outcomes. Good leaders of design programmes feel comfortable shepherding people through a process that is genuinely creative. The control is not in forcing the outcome towards predetermined views but in confidence that the process will deliver the best outcomes for your organization. We use the Organization Design Compass throughout the OPTIMAL Way to ensure all aspects of the organization are considered, making them clear and obvious. This enables you to keep checking for completeness, coherence, synthesis, alignment, and balance.

FIGURE 2.2   The OPTIMAL Way

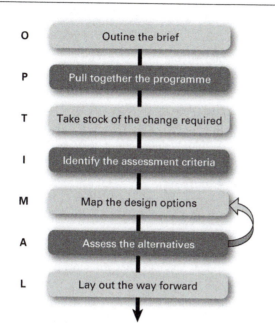

O — Outine the brief

P — Pull together the programme

T — Take stock of the change required

I — Identify the assessment criteria

M — Map the design options

A — Assess the alternatives

L — Lay out the way forward

Vitally, the OPTIMAL Way is used to prompt engagement and dialogues between the design programme team and others. Designing is a creative process: stimulating ideas and conversations that enrich the quality of the outcomes. Ideas will move from an embryonic concept in the early steps to take shape as the design helps the organization learn and reflect. Feedback gathered from the emerging outputs prompts further thoughts and refinement. Designing is a process of going through trial and error, testing and verification of the model until you get to the point where you have a number of alternative designs and insights into the routes for reaching them. The OPTIMAL Way allows for this: it is designed so that ideas can be explored, repeated, refined, practised, worked over, discarded, combined, where alternatives are sought and alternative possibilities explored. A true design process can be messy: with conflict, failure, emotions, and looping circularity that is part of its nature. Leaders need to expect and accept the mess along with the process. Design filters allow you to take many ideas; explore, test and select some concepts; explore, test and narrow down options; iterating and learning until you can select an optimal one. 'MA' does the design filtering in the OPTIMAL Way. When you use it you will be able to produce the unique combination of elements to deliver your strategic intent.

It may be tempting if you are short of time to miss steps: however, we caution against this. In our experience, this is unlikely to result in the best outcomes or even satisfactory ones. It can lead to confusion and poor

TABLE 2.1   Overview of the steps in the OPTIMAL Way

OPTIMAL steps	The Organization Design Approach
Outline the brief	Confirm the sponsorship for the design work, the context for change, the strategic intent, and the capabilities required to deliver the change. Seek inspiration from other organizations. Set out the common understanding of this so there is a clear brief for the programme team who will carry out the organization design work to follow. Confirm the go-ahead for a design programme. Together these provide a firm foundation: the anticipation is energizing.
Pull together the programme	Assemble the leadership and team. Confirm the design model, approach, and the tools and techniques to be used; tailor them if necessary. Establish the programme infrastructure and other workstreams eg governance, management systems, environment, plans, change workstream. Ensure these are agreed and understood by the programme team and key stakeholders. Get formal approval for your chosen route. The programme team is ready to go: shared enthusiasm now can become infectious.
Take stock of the change required	Gather a body of evidence for use in design and implementation to understand more deeply the organization's history, context, and current state. Seek further insight. Establish what the future state organization needs to look like to deliver its strategic intent and associated capabilities. What must be kept? What needs to change? Decide on the most important aspects of change required so that design effort can be focused on these. Get formal agreement to the direction and extent of the changes that are needed. The programme team now knows where to target their efforts and how big a challenge there is; a clearer idea of the destination helps all concerned.

TABLE 2.1 *continued*

OPTIMAL steps	The Organization Design Approach
Identify the assessment criteria	Put in place an evaluation scheme based on design principles and criteria that is impartial, balanced, and aligned to the organization's strategic direction. There is a basis for assessing the optimal design option for the organization which will reduce the politics and emotion from choices made later on: having the ground rules laid down can be comforting to all.
Map the design options	Seek alternatives and explore possibilities. Develop and refine a number of alternative design options for the organization to choose from. First, at a concept level and then develop selected options into more detailed, design outlines. Explore ideas, work through them, repeat, refine, discard some, and combine some. This produces tangible images, descriptions and feelings to share and it is much less daunting once these are narrowed down to a few crafted choices.
Assess the alternatives	Assess individual design options at design concept and design outline level using the criteria identified earlier. Compare the alternative options. Provide feedback on the results of the assessments and comparisons to improve the development of further iterations or lower levels of design. Get confirmation and buy-in by sharing the results. It should be easy to see how closely the design options that are proposed meet the organization's strategic intent. Sharing these more widely can extend the buy-in.
Lay out the way forward	After the assessment of design outlines is complete, the optimal one is chosen. Finalize the high-level design work: turn the optimal design outline into a blueprint. Prepare for implementation: pass on the design team's knowledge and make a clean transition from design to implementation. Get agreement to take the design forward. With a chosen destination point that has detail across many dimensions, there is transparency on the target and the change required. The organization can move forward into implementation confidently.

buy-in. A semblance of progress built on poor foundations; necessitating extra work in implementation and sub-optimal business results in operation. We strongly advise that you consciously complete all the steps, even if you use only a light touch at some points.

When carrying out an organization design process, it may help you to think of the progression in terms of a journey. At the point you start to look at carrying out an organization design you will have already established some things. You know you are going somewhere, sometime (probably soon). You are going to set out what you need to find out more about and refine your plans before you go. You are designing both for the destination and for the journey itself. This preparation is the design phase for an organization's transformation to its future form. If you are like us, then you will have as much fun preparing for the journey, as you do travelling and being there! This is where the excitement begins.

Using project management disciplines

Whether the design you undertake is small or large, contained or spreading, strategic or operational, we recommend that you use project management disciplines to manage an organization design. In the CIPD report; 'Reorganizing for success: A survey of HR's role in change' (CIPD, 2004), it was found that 'successful reorganizations typically draw on project management disciplines' but that 'project management skills were lacking in almost a half of all reorganizations'. Projects can be various shapes and sizes, from the small and straightforward to extremely large and highly complex. Alongside an understanding of organization design, strong project management skills will be a key factor in reaching successful outcomes.

A word on what we mean by project management skills. Project management is the discipline of planning, organizing, and managing resources to bring about the successful completion of specific goals and objectives. Any task that requires some preparation to achieve a successful outcome will probably be done better by using project management techniques as they can help in planning and managing an activity as complex as designing an organization. Programme management covers a group of related and somehow interdependent projects. Portfolio management covers a group of related and somehow interdependent programmes. All of these use project management skills.

The OPTIMAL Way is built to use with project management skills and disciplines. It:

- Maps to the early stages of most project methodologies and frameworks (see Figure 2.3). You may use an in-house set of tools, methodologies and frameworks or one of the increasingly globally recognized ones, for instance, PRINCE2, PMBOK. Rather than reference a particular methodology that may be alien to you, most have a standard process comprising five stages: initiation; planning;

FIGURE 2.3   OPTIMAL mapped against project stages

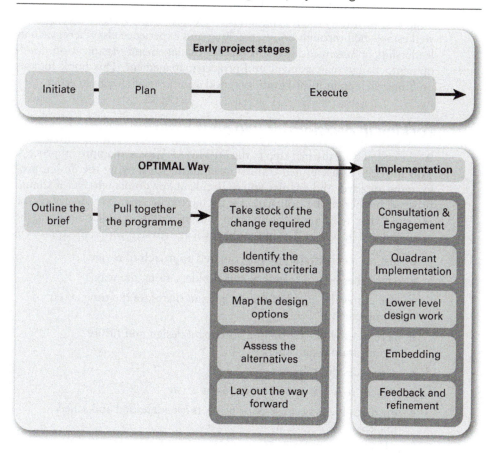

execution or production; monitoring and controlling systems; and completion. 'Outline the brief' maps to initiation. 'Pull together the programme' maps to planning. The balance of the OPTIMAL steps covers the first half of execution or production. Implementation of organization design typically extends beyond the execution phase of programmes.

● Is designed to work with your chosen project, programme, and portfolio disciplines. So you can consider it to be a project in totality or a workstream/project/programme within a wider set of change. The size of the design influences whether your design is part of a project, programme, or portfolio.

For the sake of simplification we look at the OPTIMAL Way as the inception and design phase of a programme within a wider change arena. We will assume there is a wider context which has driven out the need for an organization design and that once the design is complete there will be an implementation and bedding in of the chosen design. Although they are vital to the success of an organization design programme we will not cover areas that are very well established through books, teaching and experience elsewhere: such as leadership, communications, stakeholder management, organization development, change management and project management. This book focuses on filling the gap in information on good organization design practice.

Locking in decisions as you go

At the end of each distinct step in the OPTIMAL Way is an approval process. This provides a disciplined control mechanism for moving the design programme forward, and enables you to decide at key points whether it should proceed further or be adjusted. Each chapter in Part Two describes the activities that need to be completed within that step, what needs to be approved and by whom. The use of approval at each step within the approach:

- ensures a consistent and coordinated approach to reviews;
- establishes buy-in from key stakeholders along the way;
- accelerates the speed of the design and therefore the time taken to implement;
- increases the likelihood of a successful design and future organizational outcomes;
- introduces discipline;
- reduces re-work and other forms of waste;
- improves focus because poor projects are identified and killed quickly;
- achieves efficient and effective allocation of scarce resources;
- ensures a complete process so that no critical steps are omitted;
- maintains momentum through to implementation.

Varying how you deploy the OPTIMAL Way

Designers and architects in other fields have big differences in how they carry out their design work although they go through similar thought processes to get there. In the same way, the OPTIMAL Way is a design process that takes you through the different stages of thinking but allows for different ways to carry it out. How you execute the OPTIMAL Way can vary hugely depending on the needs of any particular programme. So far we've covered the OPTIMAL principles, and given you an overview of the steps and filters (the detail is Part Two). You can also vary the tools and techniques applied, as well as the scale of engagement and methodologies.

The tools and techniques shown throughout the book have been deliberately selected to cover all the individual segments of the Compass and are appropriate for the design process used. They can be supplemented, augmented, or substituted to suit any particular design situation. They are comprehensive, but not the only ones available to you. Please do not think of them as scripts from which you must not deviate – you should respond to the needs of your group. They are designed to give you some ideas and get you started.

Let's now turn to the scale of engagement. Design can be carried out by 'a lone designer' or 'everyone' or more usually, somewhere in between. Some organization design specialists get very heated about the size of the team involved in design work and strongly defend a large group method rather than a smaller scale group of 'experts' or vice versa. Our opinion is, it depends. We are not just sitting on the fence. It is all about the context and the availability of skills. We don't believe that a small team or consultancy should work behind the scenes not talking to anyone and produce the answer out of a hat like a magician! Although, sometimes that is what clients ask for. In our experience, this type of design can easily become shelf-ware. We believe the value is limited in that case. If you don't get wide insight and knowledge, it is difficult to design and almost impossible to create design with any momentum to change the organization. If you want design to lead to change, you need to be more collaborative and engaging. The approach we show in Part Two is carried out by a small/medium expert team involving wider participation, but it can be used with larger groups too. You can use different scales at different stages.

An alternative to the method we show is to use large group interventions (LGIs). LGIs gained prominence and legitimacy through the 1990s in the field of organization development (Bunker and Alban, 1997). LGIs are essentially collaborative inquiries into organizational systems, practices, and processes that are designed to create alignment around strategic direction and system-wide issues. While there are many differences and varieties of LGI methods, they all share in common the values that have informed organization development theory and practice, particularly the imperative for inclusiveness and widespread participation in the change process. LGIs have been used as a component in many organizational change efforts across a range of applications, including organization design and restructuring and parts within them such as defining purpose and values, and process improvement.

A large group intervention is a participative meeting, conference or event where a large number of participants (10 to 2,000) comprising a diverse cross-section of an organization's stakeholders, come together to work on real organizational issues of strategic importance to help bring about fast change. An LGI is more than a mass attendance meeting or conference. It is part of a wider strategic process that includes pre-event work (designing the intervention, often by a design team that is a microcosm of the large group), and post-event activities such as implementing the plans, monitoring progress and modifying the plans if necessary. In some cases a series of events may be called for. Regardless of the method employed, interventions are always customised to meet the particular circumstances.

There are many large group intervention methods including: AmericaSpeaks, Appreciative Inquiry, Conference Model®, Decision Accelerator, Future Search, Open Space Technology, Participative Design, Real Time Strategic Change, Search Conferences, Strategic Change Accelerator/ACT (IBM), and Whole-Scale™ Change. LGIs are not restricted to physically meeting either. Since 2001, IBM has used 'jams' to involve its more than 300,000 employees around the world in far-reaching exploration and problem-solving. In 2003 IBM's ValuesJam brought together its people to redefine the core IBM values for the first time in nearly 100 years. There is information on websites and books on all these. Here are four great books that will give you an overview to their philosophy and methods:

- *Large Group Interventions – Engaging the whole system for rapid change*, by Barbara Bunker and Billie Alban (1997).
- *You Don't Have to Do It Alone: How to involve others to get things done*, by Dick Axelrod *et al* (2004).
- *Terms of Engagement: New ways of leading and changing organizations*, by Dick Axelrod (2010).
- *The Change Handbook: The definitive resource to today's best methods for engaging whole systems*, by Peggy Holman *et al* (2007).

LGIs are often underpinned by common values and assumptions, which you need to understand before selection:

- Organizations are seen as 'whole systems' – this requires the creation of dialogue among all organizational stakeholders.
- Organizations do not exist, but organizing processes and procedures do.
- What we perceive as our collective organizational reality becomes the organization that is created.
- Individuals within organizations have the capacity to self-organize and redefine their reality.
- Humanity shares a set of universal values that are inherently 'good' and these values will ultimately influence voluntary collective action.

Shmulyian *et al* (2010) carried out an analysis of eight LGI methods. They found both 'the art' – excellence in method execution and 'the artist' – the right facilitator(s) are necessary for achieving desired outcomes from LGI methods. They argued that the critical elements of the 'art' include five common elements (or five 'I's):

- having the right *Individuals* in the room;
- aiming the method at resolving the right *Issue*;
- having *Intentional* process (including pre-work, intra-method process, and follow-up);

- having the right *Information* in the meeting;
- using the right *Infrastructure* (such as appropriate physical space, technology, etc).

Shmulyian *et al* (2010) concluded that to achieve the desired outcomes, the execution of large-group methods needs to be both highly premeditated and ingenious and that the future use of these methods will be challenged by the availability of artists who can execute the methods so they lead to desired outcomes.

Another way of varying your design is 'to be the change you want to be' and carry out the design in the way the organization wants to work in future. Looking at the framework below, does it prompt thoughts on how you might want or not want to carry out your design (or as an archetype see next chapter)? Deloitte Consulting use a framework for their 'As One collective leadership' model where they convey eight different ways of working 'as one'. (This is taken from that.) They have a vertical axis which represents the amount of direction-setting and how power is exercised: top-down versus bottom-up while the horizontal axis shows the nature of individuals' tasks and how work is organized – highly scripted to highly creative:

- Architect and builders – a far-sighted architect bringing together a truly diverse group to focus on creative collaboration, which is innovative, ambitious and drives reinvention.
- Conductor and orchestra – a conductor uses a score to bring together orchestra members who understand their role and work together tightly.
- Community organizer and volunteers – there is a compelling purpose and vision that draws together the volunteers to make the change happen.
- Captain and sports team – minimal hierarchy, acts like a single cohesive and dynamic organism, adapting to new strategies and challenges with great agility as they appear. Strong shared identity and extensive and networked communication channels. They carry out the same highly scripted, repeatable tasks. The collective good outweighs the needs of the individual. The captain is part of the team, to motivate and encourage.
- General and soldiers – has a command-and-control-type culture combined with a multilevel hierarchy organized around the general's clear and compelling mission. Soldiers' activities focus on clearly defined and scripted tasks. They are motivated by advancing up the hierarchy through well-defined roles at all levels. Soldiers undergo extensive training to understand the army and its culture, and to learn specific skills. They are committed to the mission, the overall institution, and each other. The general provides strong top-down authoritarian direction to motivate and direct them.
- Landlord and tenants – landlords define the top-down driven strategy and hold power; they control access to highly valuable or scarce

resources; they decide how to generate the most value for themselves and dictate the terms of participation for the tenants. Tenants voluntarily decide to join landlords.

- Senator and citizens – there is a strong sense of responsibility to abide by the values or constitution of the community, which have been outlined by the senators. Sovereignty is held by both senators and citizens, and the citizens thrive on the values of democracy, freedom of expression, and autonomy. Since citizens are autonomous, the community structure is flexible. There is no set framework or direction organizing the citizens. Instead, much of their direction is emergent as they gather ideas and collaborate with other citizens. Senators are the guiding intelligence for the citizens and oversee decision-making for them.

Look, listen, interpret, adapt and deploy

Part Two takes you step-by-step through the OPTIMAL Way, gradually increasing your knowledge, skills, and confidence to carry out an organization design. We provide insight and information so you can customize your own programme. If you follow this approach you will have the knowledge to tailor your design process to meet your organization's needs, so that you can get the best possible results.

Fundamental to our approach is that the designer should work as an interactive consultant. Design is not simply about coming up with solutions or about producing and presenting reports or blueprints. In whichever organization a design is carried out there will be unique dynamics and ways of doing things. You may for instance, decide to orchestrate the design rather than tightly specify it or work through the top level in detail allowing development of subsequent levels to be defined by their leaders within you framework. For the approach to work there needs to be a close relationship between the designer and the people and groups involved so that solutions are created with the active involvement of the clients. You will no doubt want to tailor what we have set out here to achieve your goals: we do. No two organization design programmes are exactly the same because each is to some extent shaped by the clients you and we work with and their ways of working. We have built in opportunities throughout the approach for dialogue with stakeholders, for building fora where information can be shared and where consensus can be reached. How this works in your organization will depend on your organization's culture and way of getting things done. However, to get to solutions that last, it is best to approach workshops and committees with an emphasis on discussion, challenge, openness, and shared decisions.

Organization design and change can be a time for conflict and power plays. But we believe that if the OPTIMAL Way is used with clear rules of behaviour set by your own organization you can minimize the power agendas creating the space for problem-solving and solutions. It is for this reason that organization design is so often seen in partnership with organization development and change management practices.

Conclusion

> He who loves practice without theory is like the sailor who boards ship without a rudder and compass and never knows where he may cast.
>
> (Leonardo da Vinci)

This chapter is fundamental to understanding Part Two of this book. In this chapter, we have covered what organization design models are and why they are useful; briefly looked at their evolution before examining how to complete an organization design. We have introduced you to the design model and process that will be used throughout the book: the Organization Design Compass and the OPTIMAL Way. While these are based in theory they have been tailored by practice. Once you have a grasp of the quadrants of the Compass and the steps that OPTIMAL stands for then you should find it easier to navigate an organization design programme using this book. You will be able to do this whether you are designing an entirely new organization or taking a current organization and realigning it. However, before we can move on to practice there are some essential building blocks from theory to understand and we turn to these next.

Some essential building blocks

"*Ideas are the building blocks of ideas.* (JASON ZEBEHAZY)

KEY POINTS

- There is no universal, best way to organize; effectiveness depends on the situation.

- Think like a designer – deliberately generate options and ideas to create insight.

- There are established ways to think through ideas, create insight, diagnose and learn.

- Archetypes are widely recognized patterns of organizing.

- A range of archetypes is covered – some classic, some newer.

- All organizational theories are based on implicit images or metaphors.

- Metaphors influence how we see, understand, and imagine situations.

- A range of metaphors is explored.

- The environmental complexity and stability framework examines the impact that the environment has on the design.

▶

- The Work standardization framework looks at how the degree of standardization impacts the design.

- Woodward's (1965) classification of operating mechanisms provides insight on successful pairings of the Operating Mechanisms segment with the Structure.

Here we look at some other useful organization design building blocks, to accompany the Organization Design Compass and the OPTIMAL Way. The aim is to show you some ideas (building blocks) to start generating your own organization design ideas. The chapter covers organizational archetypes, metaphors and three frameworks from contingency theory. Archetypes are common forms of organization that are seen repeatedly, that have been well studied and that you can use to help you understand organizations. Metaphors too, create new perspectives and insight. The frameworks provided are useful for examining aspects of organizations and help you understand more about how different organizations work. The archetypes, metaphors and frameworks have been adapted from and built on earlier writers' versions and work with the Compass and the OPTIMAL Way to give you additional insight. Archetypes, metaphors and frameworks are important to the organization designer because all designers need to know some basics about how organizations work before they can design effectively. Just as dress designers need to know about fabrics, as architects need to know about building materials; or as chefs need to know about ingredients: so these are the basic building blocks of knowledge that organization designers need to know. This chapter will give you an understanding of some ideas that you can apply in your design work. You may find it easiest to use this chapter to get an overall understanding of the different ideas and then refer back to the detail as you need to use it in practice.

One of the challenges that can be faced in organization design work is the rush towards 'the solution'. Indeed time shortages can lead to demand for urgent problem-solving and quick solutions, leading to a lack of understanding of the cause of problems or the range of possibilities for solutions. Faced with this it is even more difficult to shift perceptions and move individuals away from their existing mental models to reframe the problem.

Think like a designer. Designers use creative approaches to solving problems. Designers consciously use convergent-divergent thinking. Convergent and divergent thinking represent two different ways of looking at the world. Divergent thinking opens your mind in many different directions and is always looking for more options. This opens up possibilities because it leads you to options that are not necessarily apparent at first. A divergent thinker is looking for options as opposed to choosing among predetermined ones. In contrast, with convergent thinking, you try to solve a discrete challenge quickly and efficiently by selecting the optimal solution from a limited, predetermined number of possible choices. Convergent thinking is good when the challenge is discrete and the solutions are limited to the constraints of a hard reality. However, in the early stages of organization design work, many people get stuck in convergent thinking and as a result they don't see the many possibilities available. The OPTIMAL organization design approach deliberately takes you through iterations of divergent and convergent thinking.

In practice, divergent thinking is more than just brainstorming. All ideas are not always created equal. Some analysis is needed so you don't have too many tools in your Swiss army knife, and don't hamstring yourself with too many constraints, either. Art, myth, archetypes and metaphors can foster divergent thinking and serve as channels for integrating imagination and evocative ambiguity into traditional analysis and problem-solving. They are like lenses, in the sense they change the way we think depending on the perspective used. Here we'll look at archetypes and metaphors that can help in organization design work.

Organizational archetypes to get you started

Organizational archetypes are widely recognized patterns that are associated with particular structural arrangements in organizations. But they are more than structure. Each archetype has a specific successful mix of operating philosophies, work processes, information flows, operating technology, hierarchy, leaders, membership, control systems, decision-making processes, values and behaviours, styles and norms. Organizational archetypes go beyond their objective descriptions of formal power and status relationships between individuals and groups; they also have implications on the informal structures.

Organizational archetypes are very useful models for designers and the groups they work with. They help you understand and learn from other organizations; understand your own current organization; and design your new organization by providing a set of templates to choose from that are quick and easy to apply. We use them in the OPTIMAL Way when mapping the design options for the new organization to give clues as to what the new structures might be. There is evidence to show that some types of structures are more appropriate to some types of organizational situations than others and the descriptions of the archetypes will help you understand what might be appropriate for you. Of course in practice, every organization is unique and you will need to adapt these templates as necessary and your design may be based on a hybrid mix of archetypes. They do though, let you quickly narrow down the number of options for your design. Archetypes are shorthand to ideas, not shorthand to 'the solution' for your design. The design that is optimal for a particular situation needs to fit the organization's purpose, strategy and understand the implications on capabilities.

There are many archetypes that you can use for inspiration. However, space limits us to a selection here. We've included some of the classic ones that are still frequently used and some to perhaps to inspire and challenge you. Most of the classic types reflect what might be described as a structuralist view of organization design, offering a clear chain of command and a hierarchical organization, but that isn't the only way to organize.

Functional archetype

The functional archetype is based on separation of groups in terms of their specialties, skills, and knowledge (see Figure 3.1). The functions themselves will depend on the organization types. Retailers may have buying, marketing/sales, customer care, and finance. Hospitals may have medical services, housekeeping, ancillary services, human resources, finance and research and development. The functional archetype is best suited for organizations:

- that need to maximize margins through economies of scale and functional expertise;
- at early stages of their development or that are relatively small;
- in stable conditions: markets, work environment, products;
- with well-understood customer requirements;
- with narrow product lines;
- with long product development and life cycles;
- where specialists are needed.

The functional archetype is less helpful when organizations:

- are larger and/or more diverse in terms of customers, products, services, operations or geography because managers may become overburdened with everyday operational issues, or rely on their specialist skills rather than taking wider perspectives;
- have to change because problem-solving and coordination across multiple functions is complex;

FIGURE 3.1 Functional archetype

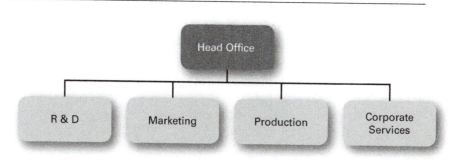

- want to innovate because functionalism can encourage narrow viewpoints;
- have work processes that cut across functions because there can be delays as one function waits for another to complete its work.

The functional archetype is found in:

- divisions of larger organizations;
- traditional organizations with strong command and control;
- processing utility type organizations producing a single product, eg electricity companies where competition is intense and the products offered by different suppliers are all alike and there is a need is to maximize profit margins through economies of scale;
- organizations where technical skills are advantageous, eg hospitals; and in movie-making where the casting team, scriptwriters, editing team, soundtrack team, post-production team and others all have specific clearly defined expertise and functional roles.

Geographical archetype

The geographical archetype is based on the separation of groups in terms of the physical location where activities are carried out: regions, countries, and territories (see Figure 3.2). Customers are geographically dispersed. Products and services are produced and used in the same geographic area, which may or may not have unique needs. This archetype is often adopted as organizations expand either internationally or in their domestic market where they need to recognize local cultures and operating conditions. The geographical archetype is best suited for organizations:

- that have a high degree of variation in operating environment in different locations;
- that need to be close to the customer for delivery and support;
- that need a fast response;
- that need to reduce distribution costs and provide 'just in time' delivery;
- with service delivery on site;
- with a low value-to-transport cost ratio;
- where products, services and/or delivery are tailored for local requirements;
- when growth makes it ineffective to manage from the centre.

FIGURE 3.2 Geographical archetype

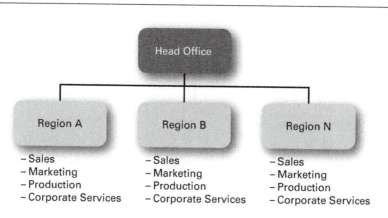

The geographical archetype is less helpful when organizations:

- want consistency across geographies because of the local variations;
- need to co-locate production because of economies of scale or efficiency;
- are operating in an industry sector clustered together with supporting infrastructure.

The geographical archetype is found in:

- service industries, where the service is provided on site, eg supermarkets, railways, car servicing;
- organizations where goods need to be produced close to the customer, eg airline catering;
- manufacturing that is dependent on being near source materials, eg cement.

Customer or market archetype

The customer or market archetype is based on the separation of groups in terms of their market segments: customers, clients, or industries (see Figure 3.3). It is organized around segments that have specific and different requirements. The customer or market archetype is best suited for organizations:

- that need to respond to strong customer power and to respond quickly to customers or markets;
- with well-defined segments;
- with market or customer-focused culture and knowledge;
- where after-sales service and advice are part of the offering;
- where deep knowledge of customer or market are essential to success;
- where relationship management and customer contact are key.

FIGURE 3.3 Customer or market archetype

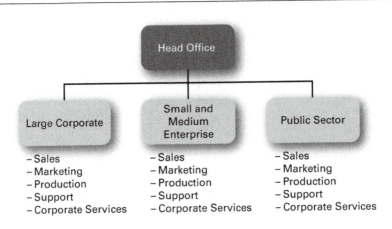

The customer or market archetype is less helpful when organizations:

- operate in a market that does not break naturally into segments;
- cannot respond to the customer or market because product or service innovation is slow;
- deliver products or services that are not differentiated across markets;
- have a customer base that is widely dispersed with different demands across regions because there may be a lack of responsiveness to local conditions.

The customer or market archetype is found in:

- service industries where there are extreme differences in customer or market demands, eg some large financial services organizations, management consultancy, many banks where there are separate divisions for retail customers, offshore customers, small business customers, and large corporate customers;
- organizations that deliver the same product but with different after-sales services to different customers, eg telecoms.

Product archetype

The product archetype is based on the separation of groups in terms of their product or service categories (see Figure 3.4). Typically, each group in this archetype runs as an independent business. Below we use 'product' as the umbrella term. The product archetype is best suited for organizations:

- with different customers, different competitive environments and different operating requirements and with low synergies between product lines;
- focusing on offering multiple products to separate customer groups;
- with high processing costs;
- with multiple distribution channels;
- with relatively distinct technologies, process and markets;
- that can take advantage of efficiencies of scale based on volume;
- whose markets and/or products are rapidly evolving.

FIGURE 3.4 Product archetype

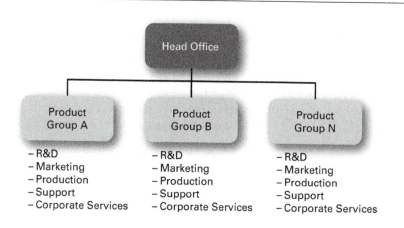

The product archetype is less helpful when organizations:

- serve customers with complex product needs because they cannot tailor or bundle products easily;
- need to respond to different geographical demands because they cannot easily adapt to local requirements.

The product archetype is found in:

- Retail services where different brands are targeted at different customers and distributed through different outlets; eg the Arcadia group, the UK's largest privately owned clothing retailer with more than 2,500 outlets, organizes around seven different brands each with its own distinctive identity and market segment. Their brand position includes Burton (mid-market menswear), Dorothy Perkins (women's fashion aged 25–35 market), Evans (women aged 25–45 who want to celebrate their curves), Topshop (young women's fashion) and Topman (young men's fashion). For them, the need to be close to their customer segments and respond quickly to fashion and demand is key.

- Large business-to-business-based companies, eg BASF (the global chemical company) organizes around products: oil and gas to chemicals, plastics, performance products, agricultural products, and fine chemicals. For many years BASF has followed their 'verbund' strategy. In this they strive to make efficient use of resources. Production plants at large sites are closely interlinked, creating efficient production chains where outputs from one process become the feedstock of another process. This organizational response to their strategy enables BASF to efficiently make a product range from basic chemicals right through to high-value-added products.

Process archetype

The process archetype is based around complete end-to-end core processes within the organization and the strategic focus is on process issues: see Figure 3.5. It has a horizontal design that cuts across traditional functions with key decisions made by process rather than functions. The process archetype is best suited for organizations:

- that have short product lives and need to focus on process innovation, faster times to market, reducing process cycle times, reducing cost and working capital through lower inventory costs;
- where clients and employees are inclined towards process thinking;
- with well-defined processes defined and managed across the whole organization;
- with little interdependency between core processes, eg customer service versus distribution;
- with different cultures and/or workforces between core processes.

The process archetype is less helpful when organizations:

- are changing from an existing structure (because it is very difficult to implement);
- have difficulty identifying their key processes;
- have much of the work being project-based.

FIGURE 3.5   Process archetype

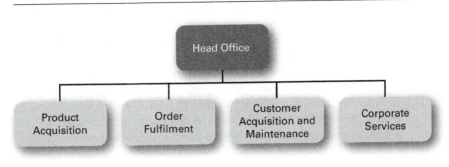

The process archetype is found in:

- manufacturing more commonly than in service industries as it needs an engineering mindset to make it work, eg Japanese car manufacturers in the 1990s such as Toyota and Honda brought this concept to their manufacturing operations across the globe;
- organizations that also have a strong quality management or lean thinking focus;
- organizations seeking to radically reduce their operating costs;
- organizations that have a strong need to exercise and demonstrate compliance with statutory or regulatory requirements.

Matrix archetype

The matrix archetype is based on a combination of any two or more design approaches, eg product with function; or function with market. It balances these approaches to produce mutually beneficial allocation of resources (see Figure 3.6). The matrix archetype aims to provide innovative solutions through effectively using teams of highly skilled individuals from different disciplines. It has a dual authority structure, each equally responsible for the same decisions, hence in Figure 3.6 it is shown as two solid lines for

FIGURE 3.6 Matrix archetype

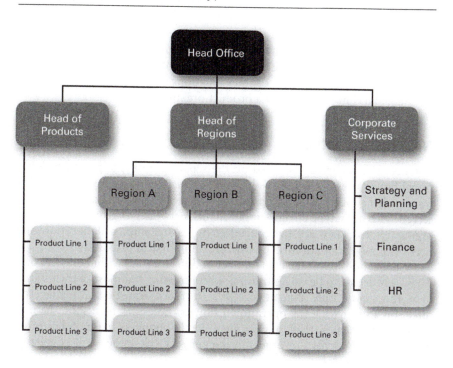

reporting. It is extremely difficult to make matrix organizations work because individuals can suffer from conflicting role clarity and managers may have conflicting priorities, so they need to be highly skilled to make trade-offs.

The matrix archetype is best suited for organizations:

- that have obvious interdependencies between any two organizing dimensions;
- that have many interdependencies in their operations;
- that have people with well-developed interpersonal skills;
- where key skills are in short supply in the market;
- where operating costs are driven by people costs.

The matrix archetype is less helpful when organizations:

- do not have clearly articulated and shared organizational goals because both sides of the matrix are pulled in different directions driven by their own goals.

The matrix archetype is found in:

- medium-sized organizations with multiple products in manufacturing, retail and some service organizations;
- multinationals that need to balance geography with any one other organizing dimension;
- temporary organizations: which are often are based on the matrix archetype;
- many organizations in accessing corporate service/functional specialists, eg it is common to see finance teams located within business units reporting to both the head of the business unit and the central finance function or sales functions with a matrix reporting to a geographic area and to a product organization.

Network archetype

The network archetype is based on the separation of groups across traditional boundaries: see Figure 3.7. 'The organization' is a network of organizations held together by the products or services required and customers served. This archetype covers supply chains, networks of groups and virtual organizations. They are held together by partnership, collaboration and networking rather than formal structure and physical proximity.

Organizations may take on a number of different roles within the network. They may decide to be orchestrators, subcontracting out most of their work. Here they retain only a small core of staff to set strategic and managerial direction and provide the operational support necessary to sustain the network. In other cases, they may decide to be the suppliers to an orchestrator or suppliers of services to others in the network. Here they will be part of

FIGURE 3.7   Network archetype

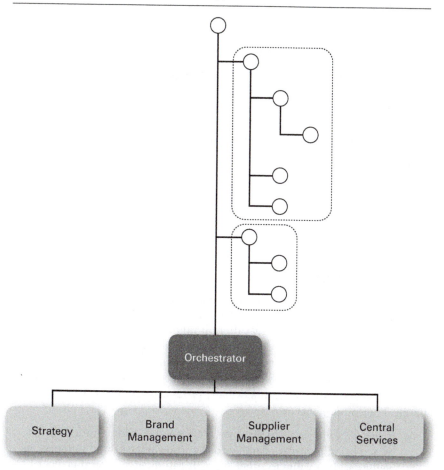

a network archetype and have to consider what archetype(s) are appropriate for their own organization.

The network archetype is best suited for organizations:

- that need greater efficiency in meeting customer needs;
- that need to reduce service costs or lead times;
- that need to integrate supply and demand;
- that want to make best use of it for instance: outsourcing, joint ventures, alliances;
- that are suppliers who want strategic relationships;
- that work in complex, rapidly changing environments;
- with a strong brand and identity so that customers do not see multiple sources;

- where grouping together provides either scale or enhanced product range;
- where specialization is cost-effective.

The network archetype is less helpful when organizations:

- have an advantage through vertical integration;
- already have economies of scale.

The network archetype is found in:

- organizations, where reliable forecasting of customer need is possible;
- professional service firms that partner with others to achieve scale or enhanced products;
- many organizations in the fashion industry where companies like Nike benefit from strong branding but use network structures to access manufacturing suppliers.

Structured network

This is a different type of archetype from Goold and Campbell (2002). The structured network is a really useful adjunct to the other archetypes because the thinking is more about how different units within a whole organization work, individually and in relation to each other. It describes the differing roles and responsibilities they have. It is complimentary to the other archetypes because in terms of thinking you still need to consider, for instance, whether business units are functional-, product-, geographic- or network-based. The components are:

- (Corporate) Parent: should have a clear value-adding rationale for its activities, in terms of obligatory corporate tasks and influence as well as adding value to other units. It can include several layers of management and groups as well as the corporate head office.
- Core resource units: which develop and nurture scarce resources and are key to competitive advantage to several business units, eg R & D.
- Shared service units: which provide services that are needed by several other units in the company, eg operational and IT services.
- Project units: which carry out temporary tasks or projects that cut across other units.
- Overlaying units: which is an umbrella organization used in larger organizations to manage groupings of other units.
- Business units and sub-business units: which are responsible for profits, have relatively high decision-making autonomy and generally adopt one of the archetypes discussed earlier. Sub-business units are subdivisions of business units.

- Corporate services (Functions): eg finance, HR, marketing and IT that may support Parents and/or act as core-resource and shared-service units and whose activities may overlap with overlaying and project units.

HR Business Partner Model

The Business Partner Model has developed from David Ulrich's work, *Human Resource Champions: The next agenda for adding value and delivering results* (1996). This is an archetype for HR within wider organizations. Ulrich defined HR roles shift to four new areas:

- Strategic Partner: relating the HR functions and enterprises with the organization's global business strategy with HR management and HR Business Partners carrying out this role.
- Change Agent: bringing in change and evolution of the business through the organization's human capital. They support the change activities during the change effort, and create capacity for the changes brought about.
- Administrative Expert: ensuring high-quality service delivery at the lowest costs to the organization.
- Employee Champion: taking care of the employees' needs and issues and looking after them during the change process.

The HR Business Partner Model, sometimes referred to as the 'three-legged stool' model envisions three key elements: business partners, shared services and centres of expertise:

- Business Partner: establish relationships with customers – line/business units; contribute to business unit plans; develop organizational capabilities; implement HR practices; represent central HR; log needs and coordinate HR services; front office.
- Shared Services: deliver HR services; manage routine processes effectively and efficiently – often using a single HRIS, intranets to provide basic information and call centres for specific queries, maybe outsourced services; back office.
- Centre of Expertise: create HR frameworks; develop and introduce strategic HR initiatives; specialized areas such as compensation and benefits, employee relations, learning and development, talent management, OD, staffing, diversity, and workforce planning; often depend on the business partners to roll out programmes to the business.

This more than any other archetype has come in for much criticism in recent years. Unfortunately it has too often been lifted and dropped in as a solution, without thinking through the design requirements for the organizations where it has been applied. Design does not start with solutions. Archetypes are shorthand to ideas, not shorthand to 'the solution' for your design. The design that is optimal for a particular situation needs to fit the organization's purpose, strategy and understand the implications on capabilities.

Other useful archetypes

In addition to these, other archetypes you may find useful to explore include:

- Front-back: hybrid structures that often evolve over time rather than being designed deliberately. They include customer facing units at the front of the organization and product line or manufacturing units at the back.

- Customer-centric: complex forms that align their entire structure around delivering the greatest value to the best customer at the best cost base. They go beyond just serving customers to creating complex packages of added-value product for their best customers and delivering these in a cost-efficient way.

- Cellular: network-like structures where strategy, structures and processes are fluid rather than fixed and they work best in innovation-centred knowledge businesses.

- Multi-dimensional: sophisticated, complex forms where the responsibility for a number of dimensions – say, turnover, cost, profit, or market share – is distributed across different cross-sections of the organization; eg product category, geographical area, business unit or any other axis relevant for the organization. Management information on different aspects of performance is reported simultaneously on all dimensions. IBM operates this way.

- Solutions organizations: opportunity-based design bringing together the resources and capabilities to focus on a problem in the environment. They provide strategic flexibility and focus with that focus on the shared purpose. Work tends to be subcontracted and use alliances. Teams work together across lines. The film industry works this way.

- Miles and Snow Organization Types: their theory holds that in order to be superior, there must be a clear and direct match between the organization's mission/values, the organization's strategies and the organization's functional strategies (their characteristics and behaviour). Their types include: Defenders, Prospectors, Analyzers, and Reactors (Miles and Snow, 1978).

- Peer-to-peer leader networks: Mila Baker (2014) argues that in this form of organization, leadership can come from anywhere, the network requirements defines where. These networks have 'peer leaders' with 'equipotent' nodes of power rather than leader-follower networks. Baker exemplifies this highlighting Gore and Herman Miller as users of these principles.

- Adaptive work systems: Stu Winby's work defines networks as production systems, which is quite a different capability than the network organization described above (Winby, 2010a, 2010b).

- *Adaptive Enterprise Design* (Maupin and Ordowich, 2012): This is emerging work on new archetypes that has been developed by the Socio-technical System Round Table – Adaptive Enterprise Team (Doug Austrom, Don DeGuerre, Helen Maupin, Craig McGee, Bernard Mohr, Joe Norton, Carolyn Ordowich). It demonstrates thinking beyond a traditional bounded organization (unusual in archetypes) and picks up the messy complexity we see in organizations. Adaptive enterprises are evolving and an adaptive enterprise may contain all three levels of system they identify, which reflect their context. At the firm context are Vertically integrated, Decentralized Organizations (VIDO). These are controlled within the boundaries of one company with several functions performed by other suppliers. At the network context are Value Realization Networks (VRN). These consist of multiple entities bound by shared customer-driven outcomes. They are bound together by a shared value proposition. At the societal context are Issue-based Social Ecosystems (IBSE). These consist of multiple systems (eg VIDOs and VRNs) and are bounded by a shared issue. Inter-organizational domains (usually societal big problems) are areas of concern for ecosystems. These 'wicked problems' affect every organization and/or person but no one sector (government, corporate, civil society, etc) can resolve them working independently.

- Holacracy®: A social technology or system of organizational governance in which authority and decision-making are distributed throughout self-organizing teams rather than being vested at the top of a hierarchy. This requires a different process for designing than described in this book. Whole Foods Market operates this way.

- Some archetypes focus on roles rather than structure; they may be flat/networked, circles, fluid.

Metaphors to change your perspective

A metaphor is a form of imagery, where one image is used to clarify another. They can originate from association. Frequently they come from a known domain (like architecture, nature or theatre), from which mental schemes are translated into another domain. This creates a new perspective to look at the subject or situation. This is why metaphors are very useful in communication and for analysing problems. Experiences are seen in another 'light'. While thinking of one subject, certain other issues can arise consciously or subconsciously that are related. A metaphor has the same characteristics as a spotlight: it enlightens some aspects and the rest stays in the shade. Gareth Morgan focused the spotlight on metaphors in his classic book, *Images of Organization* first published in 1986. The reason they are important in looking at organizations is wonderfully captured by Morgan (Morgan, 2006):

> All theories of organization and management are based on implicit images or metaphors that persuade us to see, understand, and imagine situations in partial ways. ... Metaphors create insight. But they also distort. They have strengths. But they also have limitations. In creating ways of seeing, they create ways of not seeing. Hence there can be no single theory or metaphor that gives an all-purpose point of view. There can be no 'correct theory' for structuring everything we do.

Metaphors are useful tools to help us shift our perceptions and look at different options as we design. Morgan talked about eight metaphors that are associated with organizations:

- Machines associated with efficiency, waste, maintenance, order, clockwork, cogs in a wheel, programmes, inputs and outputs, standardization, production, measurement and control, design associated with Taylorism; suggests planning, ordering and a high degree of control.

- Organisms associated with living systems, environmental conditions, adaptation, life cycles, recycling, needs, homeostasis, evolution, survival of the fittest, health, illness; suggests ideas like 'organizational health' 'organizational DNA', birth, maturity and death, life processes, evolution.

- Brains associated with learning, parallel information processing, distributed control, mindsets, intelligence, feedback, requisite variety, knowledge, networks; suggests learning, development, how information spreads, what is known and not known.

- Cultures associated with society, values, beliefs, laws, ideology, rituals, diversity, traditions, history, service, shared vision and mission, understanding, qualities, families; suggests groupings and paternalism.

- Political Systems associated with interests and rights, power, hidden agendas and back-room deals, authority, alliances, party-line, censorship, gatekeepers, leaders, conflict management; suggests division, secrecy and competition.

- Psychic Prisons associated with conscious and unconscious processes, repression and regression, ego, denial, projection, coping and defence mechanisms, pain and pleasure principle, dysfunction, workaholism; suggests resistance and limitations to growth.

- Flux and Transformation associated with constant change, dynamic equilibrium, flow, self-organization, systemic wisdom, attractors, chaos, complexity, butterfly effect, emergent properties, dialectics, paradox; suggests water flowing – eddies and whirlpools, streams coming back to calm waters, stability, currents of energy oscillating; and trying to establish a natural balance.

- Instruments of Domination associated with alienation, repression, imposing values, compliance, charisma, maintenance of power, force, exploitation, divide-and-rule, discrimination, corporate interest; suggests oppression, sweat-shops and military rule.

The main reason *Images of Organization* is so valuable is that most organizational conversations stay exclusively within one metaphor. Worse, most people are permanently stuck in their favourite metaphor and simply cannot understand things said within other metaphors. Morgan asserted that 'one of the most basic problems of modern management is that the mechanical way of thinking is so ingrained in our everyday conception of organizations that it is often difficult to organize in any other way'. He suggested that we could explore a number of alternative metaphors to create new ways of thinking about organization and use metaphors to analyse and diagnose problems and to improve the management and design of organizations.

In *Imaginization* Morgan (1997) looked at the practical art of using metaphor for organizational analysis and creative management. The underlying principle is: 'it is impossible to develop new styles of organization and management while continuing to think in old ways'. In this book, Morgan recognizes that people within organizations can describe their own metaphors and create new ones. He concludes, 'the challenge facing the modern manager is to become accomplished in the art of using metaphor: To find appropriate ways of seeing, understanding, and shaping the situations with which they have to deal'.

One example of an applied metaphor is *The Starfish and the Spider* by Ori Brafman and Rod Beckstrom (2006). The spider and starfish analogy refers to the contrasting biological nature of the respective organisms. The starfish with their decentralized neural structure permitting regeneration are compared with the recent rise of decentralized organizations such as Wikipedia and YouTube. In contrast the spider represents centralized organizations which find regeneration difficult or impossible, such as *Encyclopaedia Britannica*. They acknowledge, however that many organizations choose to import some of the 'softer' elements of the starfish, for example, knowledge sharing and empowerment, while leaving their original hierarchical structures more or less intact.

- Can looking at metaphors help you diagnose and design?
- What metaphors would you apply to your existing organization?
- What insight does that give you?
- If you used other metaphors, what fresh insight would you have?
- What metaphors would help you create a future organization?

Experience teaches us it often takes more than 'fixes from the past' as we redesign the underlying work structures and processes. Chris Argyris and

Donald Schön (1978) called this single-loop learning – reflecting on our actions and making changes accordingly. They argued that double-loop learning takes us a step further by including reflection on the deep, taken-for-granted assumptions our actions are rooted in, so as to reframe our underlying patterns of thought. Both single- and double-loop responses are driven by past experience. In today's turbulent, complex and rapidly changing global context, reflecting on past experience is necessary but not sufficient. The third and more sophisticated learning loop is sense-making or learning from the future as it emerges. Sense-making is an iterative process that requires prototyping, feedback, evaluation, and further sense-making. Metaphors can help sense-making and reframing.

Three frameworks to help you position an organization

In this section we present three frameworks that are helpful in understanding current organizations and future designs. These can be used to diagnose a current organization, to explore and learn from other organizations, to give clues to future design options, and to help align the segments of a new design. These frameworks draw on contingency theory; this states that there is no one, universal, best way to organize and that what is effective in some situations, may be not be effective in other situations. The best choices for any particular organization depend on various external and internal factors. In the frameworks shown here, the external factors are the environment that the organization operates in and the internal factors cover the nature of the work and the operating mechanisms.

Environmental complexity and stability framework

Here, environment covers all the elements outside the boundary of the organization being designed. All organizations operate within a sector, geography and marketplace or a wider organization. Availability and need for raw materials, human resources and financial resources are elements of the environment. Further key elements include customers and suppliers that the organization interacts with and the types of regulatory frameworks or governmental influences on the organization. Many of these are interdependent and all vary in their significance for different organizations.

Environmental complexity is determined by the number of external influences that the organization has to deal with and the extent to which they are different. In a simple environment, the organization deals with few (three or four) external influences that are all similar in the way they influence it; for example, where the only external influence on the organization is the clients and they all want the same range of products or services. In a complex environment, the organization has to deal with a multitude of external influences which are all different, for example, a pharmaceutical company like AstraZeneca operates in a very complex environment dealing with many groups such as doctors, hospitals, patients, pharmacists, external research establishments, regulators, other government advisory bodies, health insurance providers; labour markets, and many suppliers. AstraZeneca deals with these groups in many countries with varying local economic conditions, health care arrangements, and regulatory regimes.

Environmental stability refers to whether environmental influences are stable or unstable. In recent years there has generally been a decrease in stability. The environment is classified as stable if it remains the same over a period of months or years, for example, HMRC (Her Majesty's Revenue and Customs) in the UK: the regulatory regime for taxation is refined annually; major changes in the structure of UK tax collection are unusual; the client bases have minimal changes; and changes to systems are planned and carefully implemented. Under unstable conditions the environmental influences shift abruptly. Airlines are a good example: they frequently have to deal with unpredictable events such as volatile fuel prices, terrorist threats leading to security changes, vagaries of weather and other natural forces, worldwide health issues, and multiple countries' legal and regulatory controls.

The environmental complexity and stability framework shown in Figure 3.8 allows you to consider the nature of environment the organization operates in and the impact that the environment has on the organization design. The implications in practice are mainly felt by organizations that face high uncertainty. When an organization faces high uncertainty it needs to respond and it can:

FIGURE 3.8 Environmental complexity and stability framework

		Moderate to high uncertainty	High uncertainty
Environmental stability	Unstable	A few similar elements that change frequently and unpredictably	A lot of dissimilar elements that change frequently and unpredictably
	Stable	**Low uncertainty** A few similar elements that change slowly or not at all	**Low to moderate uncertainty** A lot of dissimilar elements that change slowly or not at all
		Simple	Complex
		Environmental complexity	

- increase the ability for information to flow to those that need it ensuring that all parts of the organization have the information they need to operate effectively;
- increase its ability to predict through planning and forecasting functions;
- create more boundary-spanning roles in the structure to sense and respond to the environment;
- create 'buffer' departments that separate its internal organization from the environment;
- formalize and strengthen the Enablers quadrant by specifying the mechanisms for incentives, rewards, goal setting, and the governance rules and frameworks to a greater degree.

For instance in responding to uncertainty two examples of creating buffers: an IT department may create a strong relationship management function to face the businesses it services; a pharmaceutical company may create a department to deal with US health insurance companies and get its products on their approved/funded lists. Another common response to uncertainty is to model the organization on the current 'best practice' of other organizations. That may provide insight but may not be suitable to deliver the required strategy and fulfil the purpose of the 'copying' organization.

Conversely, in more certain and simpler environments the information needed is more straightforward; planning and forecasting is simpler; the structure is less complex with fewer of the boundary-spanning roles and buffer departments; and the Enablers can be less formal.

Work standardization framework

This framework is a way of examining the Work quadrant of the Organization Design Compass. Work standardization is the degree to which work processes within the organization are similar or varied and the degree to which the tasks that people carry out are analysable. There are two dimensions: work variety and work analysability. Work variety is the frequency with which unexpected or novel events occur in the work processes. When day-to-day work requirements are repetitive with few unexpected situations then variety is considered low. When there are a large number of unexpected situations and there a few established rules or procedures developed to deal with these, variety is considered high. Work analysability is the degree to which people can follow a codified procedure to carry out the work. Standard procedures, use of manuals, checklists, and handbooks are all signs of highly analysable work. When there is no store of techniques or procedures and people have to draw on their own experience, wisdom, intuition, or judgement then the analysability is low. By codifying the organization design process in this book, the authors are moving the analysability of organization design work from low (rarely codified today) to

FIGURE 3.9   Work standardization framework

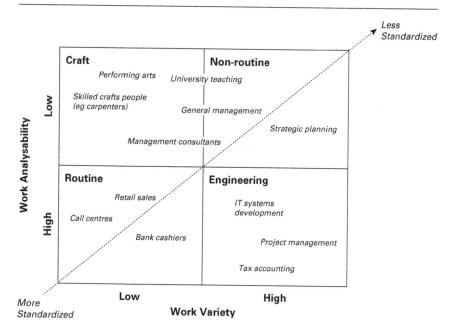

higher. Figure 3.9 shows the work standardization framework where these two dimensions are plotted together giving four types of work (craft, non-routine, routine, and engineering) with some jobs positioned on it for illustration. Understanding the work standardization framework helps design thinking because there are associated organizational characteristics. Where work is more standardized:

- information flows mainly vertically rather than horizontally and is written via communications and standardized reports rather than informally distributed;
- structures are more formally defined;
- organizations can have wider spans of control;
- organizations need lower skill levels among people and reduced costs;
- in Enablers, rules and governance arrangements are clear and highly defined;
- goals emphasize quantity and efficiency.

Conversely, where work is less standardized:

- information flows need to be horizontal across and between teams;
- structures are looser and less defined;
- there can be a lot of ad hoc project teams;

- generally people working in the organization need to have higher skill levels;
- training and experience are both valued;
- training programmes often emphasize communications skills, teamwork and problem-solving;
- in Enablers, reward systems emphasize behaviours and high-level outcomes rather than adherence to processes and procedures.

Classification of operating mechanisms

Research by Woodward (1965), found that organizations are more effective when their 'technology' (the operating mechanisms in the Organization Design Compass), is aligned with the organization's structure. The research classifies three successful ways of pairing operating mechanisms with structure. Although the names attributed to these draw on a manufacturing vocabulary they are applicable to service organizations too as the examples below show:

- Small batch and unit production: these organizations act like 'job shop operations' with single outputs tailored and delivered to specific individual customer orders. Tools, techniques, and actions also tend to be tailored to specific customer orders. Here the organization relies on individual people's skills rather than on programmed machines or systems. Relatively flat organizations work best; usually there are no more than three levels to any hierarchy, with narrow spans of control for managers. Decisions are managed as they occur, through dialogues and mutual adjustments are made. Typically an organic structure fits small-batch technology. Organizational examples in this category include: small manufacturers, customized furniture makers and boutique management consultancies.
- Large batch and mass production: these are organizations that have assembly-line characteristics, where the processes are typically long production runs of standardized outputs. Tools, techniques, and actions tend to be standardized and production is controlled. The structure needs to be taller and wider with four or more levels to any hierarchy. Managerial spans of control increase by about 30 per cent compared to small batch organizations as rules and procedures act to coordinate more work processes. Organizational examples in this category include: car manufacturing, food packaging, call centres, helpdesks, and accounts payable processes.
- Continuous processes: these are organizations where the start and end of processes are not easily identifiable and their processes run continuously. Production is highly automated and work processes are mainly concerned with monitoring the equipment and dealing quickly with irregularities. Managers tend to have narrow spans of

control and teams work closely. Teams are made up of highly trained people and who need to communicate freely about the work processes, any irregularities that are noticed and then problem-solve quickly. This need for quick responses makes an organic structure desirable. Example organizations include: chemical engineering plants, data centre operations.

Conclusion

This chapter has covered some essential building blocks from organization design theory that can help you design organizations. It has described organizational archetypes, metaphors and three frameworks which are associated with particular characteristics that an organization may have, may require, or want to avoid. The archetypes, metaphors and frameworks can help you interpret organizations from various perspectives and give you insight into what might be appropriate for any organization you design or features you can use. These building blocks are ideas, from which you can formulate appropriate ideas for many situations. Now we are going to put all these into practice, using the OPTIMAL Way. As Ludwig Mies van der Rohe said, 'Architecture starts when you carefully put two bricks together. There it begins'.

PART TWO
Designing your organization the OPTIMAL Way

Outlining your brief

> *To whom does design address itself: to the greatest number, to the specialist of an enlightened matter, to a privileged social class? Design addresses itself to the need.*
>
> **(CHARLES EAMES)**

KEY POINTS

Aim:

To establish a clear design brief.

Activities:

- Understanding the context for change.
- Learning from outside your organization.
- Encapsulating the organizational purpose.
- Distilling the strategic intent.
- Defining the capabilities required.
- Establishing a programme brief for design to change.

This is the first step in the OPTIMAL Way. Whether you are investigating if an organization design or redesign is necessary; shaping a programme of design work for others to follow; or leading an organization design programme, you start here. The aim of this step is to crystallize the client's requirements of the design; so that the brief is clearly defined for both the client and the design team that will be put in place in the next step. This chapter covers how to get off to a good start; shaping, understanding and challenging the brief; creating a design brief to determine the design phase of a programme of work (which includes a shared understanding of the design and change context, a distillation of the strategic intent, identified target capabilities required to deliver this, and a programme brief); as well as getting the sponsor's agreement to progressing this. This step is important because the seeds of success for a major programme are sown right at the start, as are the seeds of failure. Attention to the first 10 per cent of any work is crucial, to ensure that everyone knows what they have to do and why: so the team is able to make a good start and because there may be severe limitations to changing later. You should gain an insight into how to commission an organization design programme with a clear design brief and firm foundation that has buy-in from the client(s) and can direct the design work ahead.

There are four parts to the process. First making sure the right people are involved. Then exploring the design and change context and optionally looking beyond the organization being designed for wider lessons and insight. There are tools to help you distil the strategic intent into succinct strategic statements and identify the target capabilities that these imply for your organization. Lastly the focus turns to capturing a brief for a programme of work. The time taken to carry out this step is largely dependent on what previous strategic work and thinking has been done. It can take as little time as a few days for meetings, workshops, and writing up, if strategic thinking is well advanced or you are looking at designing for a small team and their role within the broader organization's strategy is clear. The OPTIMAL Way can be used to fast track and capture any 'strategic insight' that is held. It will take longer if your organization needs or wants to precede this with further strategy work and/or take time at this step to look at alternative organizations for reference and lessons.

Getting off to a good start

There is a Zen saying that, 'a thousand-mile journey begins with one step', and when it comes to design programmes it is best to make it a firm one. The role of design is the translation of the emergent ideas into something more tangible. Irrespective of where the organization is in its thinking, or whether you already think you 'know' some of the answers, it is valid and necessary to ask lots of questions. This is because your focus will be to solicit all the information, concepts, and feelings from a variety of stakeholders needed in order to create a design for the organization. Often any work that will have been done in advance is not carried out with an emphasis on design or a focus on the range and breath of information required for successful organization design and/or implementation. If you come from a programme background then an inception step where you set out the brief may be familiar territory for you and to some extent this will be similar to other programme initiations that you may have carried out. However, there are some important differences that are specific to organization design. This is inception with design in mind. An organization design programme is a complex programme with potential for widespread ramifications across an entire organization or any part of it and across some or all aspects of its activities or in our terms, segments of the Compass. Avoid drifting into execution or feeling/being pressurized into action too quickly. There is a delicate balance between acting quickly and acting wisely and an intensive orientation phase prior to starting will yield benefits later. For many people it is uncomfortable, even unnatural to want to put effort into planning, particularly if there has been time already spent on the strategy but starting well means challenging this natural desire to want to get on and do things.

Who to involve from the start

There are three key leadership roles needed from the start of an organization design programme: a sponsor, a commissioner, and a senior HR leader. Good design starts with the needs of the client (the person or organization commissioning and paying for the work), finding out what they want. As Edwin Lutyens said, 'there will never be great architects or great architecture without great patrons'. The sponsor is a senior individual from the client organization, who acts a single focal point for contact on the day-to-day interests of the client organization. Their role is to actively champion the change that is proposed throughout the duration of the design programme; ensuring the programme is visible, resourced, supported, and well led to enable it to deliver what the client wants. A committed and involved line sponsor is vital to the programme's success. You need to identify a suitable sponsor, if one is not already in place.

If you have been asked to carry out an organization design, look at whether an organization design is necessary, or shape a programme of design work for others to follow, you start here. We refer to this start-up role as the 'commissioner': it is generally an individual or small team. Their role is to establish whether there is a firm basis for the programme to go ahead and if so to shape the design phase of the work and help to set up the programme. They work out what needs to be done and why; articulate and challenge the brief, work with the sponsor to establish the nature of the team required to carry out the design including either specific individuals or areas. The commissioner may or may not subsequently become part of the design team and work on the programme, but they often do. They may be the programme leader, an organization design expert involved throughout the design, an HR business partner, or a senior consultant in a change organization. Whatever their title and experience, this role requires very strong consultancy skills. Consultancy skills are those that allow a person to take a critical view of an organization, to diagnose it, and give advice on how to change it along with the ability to persuade others of the need for action. A good consultant is able to identify and investigate problems and opportunities; to recommend the right action to take and implement those recommendations. Leadership in consultancy comes from experience, expertise, and influence coupled with a passion for communicating the ideas and bringing others along on the journey. Appendix 1 covers consultancy and other skills required in an organization design team. In this step, the sponsor works closely with the commissioner; in subsequent steps with the programme leader when they are appointed.

Because of the nature of the change whenever there is a design or re-design, HR should be involved from the start and throughout the design and implementation phases; a senior HR leader should work with the programme throughout its life cycle. In addition to these three key roles, the key people to involve in this step are the executive or senior team. You may also want to involve people with knowledge of existing work, for instance strategies; people with influence; people with resources and people who care about the outcome.

Clarifying the terms of reference for this step

As 'commissioner', your first discussion should be with the sponsor of the work. Clarify your terms of reference:

- What are your respective roles and responsibilities as sponsor and commissioner?
- What will the commissioner's role be in the programme?
- What is the sponsor's role in dealing with the problem, issue, or opportunity?
- What do you have to deliver and when?
- What are your respective expectations, for instance access to people, information, process, and budget?
- What are the basic ground rules that will frame discussions with executives and the wider organization in this and subsequent steps?
- Who are the key stakeholders that need to be involved?
- How will this programme be presented to the organization?
- How will the commissioner be presented to the organization?

Shaping the brief, understanding it, challenging it

The client that has called you in may have done a lot of preparatory thinking and work already ahead of this point or they may just have an idea at an embryonic stage with emergent thoughts. You need an understanding of the strategic and operational context for this organization as well as the brief for this piece of work. In these early steps you need to think broadly and question, question, question. In asking lots of questions there are many parallels with other similar professions: architects, consultants, event specialists, travel agents. The presenting problem or solution(s) may not hold up to closer scrutiny. Think like a designer. The main purpose is to understand the strategic intent, to see what needs to change and what needs to remain. When you look at the question sets shown in the book you may find they need tailoring to your organization, however they will give you some ideas of areas to look for.

Understanding the context for design and change

Many books on organization design make an assumption that design starts with strategy. In our experience, this assumption does not hold true for large numbers of organizations. It can even be unhelpful because some executives are put off organization design because they think that it cannot be done without substantial time and effort spent upfront developing strategies. Also, even if strategic thinking has taken place it is rarely done or presented with design in mind. Strategies can be emergent with organizations more opportunistic than strictly planned. Work in government organizations may be driven more by policy and legislation rather than an overarching formal strategy. And even if a client arrives with firm ideas of what they want, you should treat these as the starting point for dialogues that will establish the brief clearly for you and the design team and ensure you have a shared understanding with your client. You need to locate the information, intelligence, and insight into the organization's strategy that will provide a thorough foundation for the design work. Some will be written down, but much more will be tacit, residing in the minds of key individuals, and you need to bring out as much as possible of this hidden thinking. Throughout these dialogues you are looking for insight that will inform the client's requirements for the design. As you do this, it will help clarify their thinking too.

Expensive decisions and big impacts will be made on the basis of the design and the organization will have to live with the consequences. For this reason, you should not hesitate to challenge the findings of earlier work: they may be insufficiently detailed and could impose restrictions on the future organization within them that is not being considered. As an example, a global credit card company outsourced its IT to support their strategy of cost containment. It obtained the results it thought it wanted, 'a partner company delivering more for less and faster'. However, when it adjusted its strategy two years later for European expansion it found that its organization design limited it even though it had only just been implemented. Its CEO said, 'We have replaced the stairs with an escalator, only to find that what we actually needed to do was install a lift in a different building'.

At this point, start to gather together information and insight on the broader context for change. Is there any customer or market insight that can help? If the situation is highly uncertain or unpredictable, has scenario planning been carried out? It could help to frame the strategic thinking, and the design work. The scenarios can also be used at the assessment step to judge design options. In Part Three, the chapter on 'How to choose between design options when the environment is very uncertain' looks at this.

'Always design a thing by considering it in its next larger context – a chair in a room, a room in a house, a house in an environment, an environment in a city plan.' This advice from the Finnish architect, Eliel Saarinen is equally valuable for organization designers. It helps to understand the part of the organization you are designing within a wider context or a whole organization in its operating context and where the organization is going in future. This will also help you to scope the programme of work and understand where higher-level context informs the organization that is being designed (see Figure 4.1). In this figure units may be divisions, business units, shared service, or functional units.

FIGURE 4.1   Design in a wider organizational context

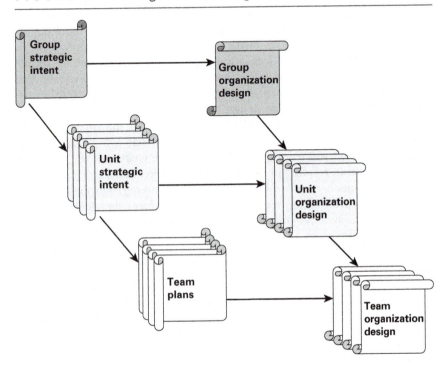

Although at this stage you may not have chosen an organization design model to use throughout the process, if you have one it can be helpful to use it. We find it useful to consider the different aspects of the Organization Design Compass (Work, Norms and behaviours, Enablers, Structure); as a prompt to facilitate discussions; to enquire on a range of perspectives; to understand any preconceptions and conventions in use, that may be tested later; as a means of capturing ideas, 'dreams' and concepts as well as documenting information.

The best way of doing this is to conduct individual interviews initially; then repeat these as a group exercise with key stakeholders (see Tool 4.1). Although you can use just the group exercise, you will get far richer insight by doing both. Repeating questions in the group exercise that have been asked individually often highlights nuances of understanding between people. If you carry out interviews the number you carry out depends on how far knowledge is spread and the time available. Individual interviews allow you to:

- Involve people who may not be involved later on, for example, those who have a solid understanding of prior strategic work or operational problems. They can provide deeper insight into why conclusions were reached rather than just the bare conclusions alone.

- Involve people with specific knowledge/perspectives and a wider range of perspectives.

- Avoid group think.

- Obtain a different sense or quality of information.

- Gain a perception into the hopes and fears of the individuals themselves and their sections.

- Understand the make-up of key individuals.

Group exercises enable the commissioner to reach people quickly and stimulate dialogue between people allowing the group to:

- share real understanding and different perspectives;

- discuss and learn from each other;

- reach shared and agreed points of view resulting in a consistent message;

- plug gaps in preparatory thinking.

For the individual interviews: include some or all of the people who will be involved in the group exercise as well as widening the net for broader wisdom. Consider the context in which the organization is operating today and in future, use the prompts in Table 4.1 to understand the programme and design context. Aim to document the insight at a high level in appropriate forms, for instance, as statements and sketches as well as notes. You should collate an information and evidence base as you go so that it can be referenced in the later steps by the design team. From these individual interviews you will end up with multiple perspectives on the programme and design context. Prepare a 'chorus of voices': anonymous insight, collected from the individual interviews focusing particularly on areas of agreement and where there are different views to help establish a shared understanding. This will lead to a more productive group meeting.

Tool 4.1 Understanding the change context

The objective of this exercise is for the commissioner and the participants to get a shared understanding of the context for change.

Who to involve

Include members of the senior team with knowledge of the context for change: strategy and/or operational problems. If market and customer insight has not already been captured through your strategy, include people with this understanding. Ensure you involve strategic HR; they are a key partner in organization design.

Inputs

The 'chorus of voices' drawn from individual interviews.

Instructions

- Present the 'chorus of voices': use this to start the debate confirming areas of agreement and highlight areas of divergent thinking.
- Consider the context in which the organization is operating today and in future: use the prompts in Table 4.1 to understand the design and change context. Tailor this to draw out a shared understanding based on what has been learned from the 'chorus of voices'.
- Aim to document the findings at a high level in appropriate forms, for instance, as statements and sketches as well as notes.
- After the meeting document the shared view of the design and change context.

Outputs

Shared view of the design and change context.

TABLE 4.1   Prompts to understand the design and change context

Problem statement	Always start with the problem statement • What is the problem that needs to be solved? • What is the operational objective to be met? • What is the vision for improvement? • What has been done already to solve the problem, issue, or improvement? • What has happened as a result of what has been done already? • What are the symptoms of any failure to deliver expected performance?
Organizational history	Understanding this can help identify hidden dynamics that define identity and resistance • How old is the organization? • What is the previous history in the organization of this type of change? • What else has been done in the recent past? • What was the experience of previous changes? • What is the experience of design and change for key stakeholders?
External environment	• What is the environment in which the organization is competing, eg sector, industry? • Are there are significant changes impacting the organization from its external environment, industry sector, market, legislation, regulations, government, technology? • What is the outlook for the organization's sector and why?
Organizational purpose (Mission)	• What is the group there to do and accomplish together? For whom? • What is different for its people, the organization, and the world as a result of the organization's existence? • Is the organization's purpose shared, understood, and followed? • Does the purpose need to fit within a wider organization's purpose? Does the purpose have to be cognizant of any other contexts, eg partners?

TABLE 4.1 *continued*

Vision	• What does the organization want to be (in future)? • How does that look and feel?
Strategy	• What are you trying to achieve? Where? When? • What is the intent behind the strategy? • Can you describe what the strategy means for each operational unit? • Are there supporting strategies, eg people strategy, IT strategy, marketing strategy? • What does the organization want to be when it has changed? • What is the business case for this change?
Organizational goals and objectives	• What are the long-term goals of the organization? • What are the short-term goals of the organization? • What are the group's objectives?
Operational drivers	• What must the organization achieve operationally? • What does the organization want to avoid operationally?
Structure	• How is your organization structured? • Obtain an organization chart • How large is the organization? • How many people does the organization employ? • How many locations does the organization operate in? • What are your latest key financial and other critical measures? • Are there any strategic choices made that have structural implications eg legal basis, philosophy around how units within the organization will work together?
Criteria for success	• When is the organization successful? • Which building blocks does the organization need to realize its goals? • What does the organization want to achieve? • How will success be measured?

TABLE 4.1 *continued*

Scope – Boundaries	• What are the boundaries of the organization being designed? • What organizations bound this organization? • What are the boundaries for change in terms of the 12 segments of the Compass? • What else is going on inside or outside the organization that this design needs to link to?
Scope – Constraints	Establish what can and cannot change and ensure that the programme is able to tell the difference • What are the legal, regulatory and/or policy frameworks the organization has to operate within? • Is anything ring-fenced? • What cannot be changed?
Approach	• How will the organization be aligned and people inspired to achieve superior execution? • Are there any sensitive areas the programme needs to be aware of, eg those involving regulators, union consultation, and legal constraints? (TSB needed an act of Parliament in the 1980s. CO-OP and Britannia needed another in 2009. Competition authorities are often involved in mergers and acquisitions)
Risks	• What are the risks to the business and to customers of making this change?
Timescales	• What timings are required for the design and/or the implementation of the resulting change? • What links are there to other programmes/events in the organization?
Anything else?	• Is there any other information that sheds light on the problem, issue, or opportunity?

Learning from beyond your organization

When you carry out an organization design it is often useful to compare your design thinking against organizations that are similar by sector, markets, geography, technology or that have already moved in a direction that you are considering: eg set up shared services, outsourced that function, set up a business in that territory; or perhaps have had a similar challenge and done something radically different. This is optional; it can be done during this step or later on or not all; but can be very useful. It is about exploring, gaining inspiration, understanding the pitfalls that you may need to avoid as you go through the journey, rather than benchmarking or analysis. It is about learning from other organizations that operate the way you are thinking about; or have undertaken similar transformations. You can learn from written material, visits, and meetings undertaken directly or via intermediaries such as consultancies and research organizations. If it is a major change, encourage your leaders to talk to and see other organizations. A word of caution though, as well as looking at their solutions and successes or otherwise, it is important to make sure you understand the context these organizations are operating in. This will help establish whether their solutions will be more or less suitable for your organization and/or easier or harder to implement. It is not good practice to lift and drop 'best practice', you should understand your requirements first. To echo Charles Eames – design addresses itself to the need. Fashion can masquerade as best practice.

This can be a one-off process of visits but external learning can also provide a basis for support along the journey for senior leaders. One of the authors established and ran an Advisory Board for one group of senior executives as they went through a major outsourcing change, with a range of C-level executives drawn from public and commercial organizations which had designed and implemented similar organization designs, had the scars and 'lived with' the subsequent operations. In October 2010 Sir Gus O'Donnell, the then UK Cabinet Secretary, requested help from the private sector for the Civil Service to learn from the business experiences on how to reduce the number of jobs by thousands, without losing key functions.

Sometimes organization design work can become very internally focused. Designing from the inside-out rather than outside-in. Think like a designer. Look at the situation in the round and make sure you understand it properly and how the people affected think and act. Design with customer in mind. Design with your suppliers in mind. Design with your employees in mind. Make sure you have insight from the people who the organization must work for and with. For instance, there are lots of ways of hearing the voice of the customer. Here are a few suggestions from IDEO Method Cards:

- 'Fly on the wall': observe and record behaviour within its context, without interfering with people's activities – to see what customers actually do and within what timescales.
- 'Role playing': identify the stakeholders involved in delivering the customer product/service and ask researchers/team members to act

out customer processes – to understand the customer's experience of your product/service and empathize with the customer better to identify real needs and wants.

- 'Cognitive maps': ask customers to map an existing or virtual space and show how they navigate it – a useful way of discovering the significant behavioural elements of a customer's experience.

- 'Flow analysis or process mapping': represent the flow of information or activity through all phases of a system or process – to document key processes of a customer's experience, how long they take and where there are repetitions and/or delays.

Encapsulating a resonant organizational purpose

It may seem really obvious, but sometimes the obvious is taken for granted or assumed to be understood. Earlier in the book, we defined an organization as 'a group of people brought together for a purpose and arranged to form a systematic whole with interdependent and coordinated underlying parts'. The purpose is absolutely fundamental to an organization; it defines 'why the work the group does is important'. It is the lifeblood of the organization. Employees should find the purpose inspirational and motivational. It is the cause that defines their contribution to society through work. It serves to attract people, both members and non-members, in a deeply human way. People are attracted to be involved in organizations to make a difference. This applies to all types of organizations, even commercial ones. Although, businesses exist to make a profit, they also exist to make a difference. Through work, individuals can make a difference and be part of a meaningful legacy. The drive to create something that is positive, meaningful, lasting and greater than any one individual is the heart and soul of the organization's purpose.

A statement of the organization's purpose (or mission statement) captures succinctly why the organization exists and what it does. It should be memorable enough so that everyone connected to the organization can remember it and use it. A clearly articulated purpose has many uses. It not only provides members of an organization with a frame for making sense of the world, but also provides the foundation upon which to build an organization that is compassionate and resilient during times of both bounty and uncertainty. It can guide the use of resources. It can be used as a benchmark for decision-making and planning. It can be used to build morale. And it helps to gain support and understanding inside and outside the organization. It allows individuals to focus on the 'true purpose' without distraction from fads and vagueness in direction. It allows people to see what your organization is about, and can encourage them to join you. 'This is what we are about, if that resonates with you, join us and together we can try to accomplish it.'

Where there are multiple parts to an organization, there should be an overarching organizational purpose – any subordinate ones should support the highest-level one (Salz, 2013). A unifying, super-ordinate purpose has been shown to help break down distrust and build trust in organizations (Bijlsma-Frankema and Weibel, 2006). It is particularly important when growing through change as people can lose sight of the bigger picture. It is also important operationally as when there is unclear direction of what has to be done it can provide insight into how to respond and how to behave. Salz (2013) reviewing issues in Barclays reported,

> The research also shows that cultures defined by overly commercial and competitive features, with little regard for other elements, lead to poor outcomes. It is inherent in most people to seek purpose beyond the purely commercial. In many successful organizations, this purpose is expressed around their promise to customers and their role in society at large. In our view, Barclays did not, until recently, have a clear statement of a common purpose across its businesses. It rather emphasised growth and financial success.
>
> (Salz, 2013)

Barclays now has a redefined purpose that reflects its intent to overcome the criticism on how some parts of the business and some individuals working there behaved. Its purpose is now 'Helping people achieve their ambitions – in the right way' (Barclays, 2013). Here are some other good examples:

- Samsung's philosophy is 'to devote our talent and technology to creating superior products and services that contribute to a better global society'.
- Coca-Cola's purpose is 'to refresh the world ... to inspire moments of optimism and happiness ... and to create value and make a difference'.
- Google aims 'to organize the world's information and make it universally accessible and useful'.

Values too are vital to understanding an organization. The values of the organization are 'what we stand for'. Organizational values identify the principles and ethics by which the organization and its people conduct themselves and their activities. An organization's values can be deep-rooted and hard to articulate. Often, they are the product of tradition and the attitudes and actions of founders and/or influential leaders, imitated and passed on until they have become second nature, so it is not easy to change them.

> Values drive everyday behaviour, helping to define what is normal and acceptable, explaining how things ought to be (for example, staff ought to put customers first). Values provide a framework through which the natural and often difficult conflicts that arise in people's day-to-day work can be resolved. But they will not always provide the answers. Organizations need to create an environment where employees feel it is safe to resolve the frequent differences that arise. For example, on a daily basis, retail bank staff can face

the dilemma of determining which deposit product best meets customer needs given the frequency with which interest rates and conditions can change ... Most companies communicate their values; what distinguishes them is not typically the precise words but rather the way in which values become pervasive, reinforced through formal and informal processes, and demonstrably evident in leaders' attitudes, behaviours and decision-making.

(Salz, 2013)

Distilling the strategic intent and framing the brief

So far all the focus and activity has been about understanding the organization and its operating context: data-gathering, analysis, describing and understanding the organization from various views inside and out. It is a process driven and developed around fact-gathering, evaluating, and defining. This is a good time for the sponsor and the commissioner to have a conversation about what has come out from the internal and external work and start to consider any adjustments and plans for the work ahead.

Irrespective of what has been done before, what depth it has been done to, and how it has been articulated, you now need to encapsulate very clearly the strategic intent that will drive the design and identify the distinctive capabilities that align with that intent. The next two activities help you set that out so you can determine what you need to be able to change over time.

Defining strategic statements

The next step is to define clear, distinctive, and differentiated strategic statements. The aim of this is to distil the strategic thinking and all the information and knowledge gained to date to achieve clarity of intent. A strategic statement is a succinct description of the core things an organization needs to exploit its opportunities and avoid threats. People can internalize these and use them to guide them in difficult choices and trade-offs in the design process.

Articulating effective strategic statements focuses on creativity and differentiation. It is developed and written around the intuitive, differentiating elements of the organization discovered in the earlier activities and work done. Your strategic statements should state what will drive the organization's direction. If you are not able to do this it is probably because there is some more preparatory work to do. Tool 4.2 shows you how to formulate strategic statements that are clearly defined. Laying them out the way suggested makes it easier to devise them, because executives know what you are looking for. Using this structure and adding additional information to the statements to explain why makes them more credible and more straightforward for the design team and wider organization because the strategy's essence can be readily communicated; the strategic intent is simpler to understand and internalize.

Crafting these is not straightforward; it can lead to heated discussions around individual words, but it is this dialogue that focuses executives' understanding of the challenge and starts them thinking about the implications. Depending on the scope of your design you may need to do this for a number of different units: the overall organization, each section, and each functional area. Any lower-level strategic statements must be in agreement with the overall organization's strategic statement and aligned with each other. A global pharmaceutical company's strategic statements might include:

- operate a world-class research and development function to maintain a pipeline;
- expand generic products in emerging markets to generate business growth;
- outsource operations and collaborate with strategic partners to develop the target business shape.

Tool 4.2 Defining strategic statements

To define the key strategic themes that focuses the organization on delivering its strategic intent and shape the organization being designed.

Who to involve

Include: the senior team responsible for the design (a subset of people you have had dialogue with, but ensure you include strategic HR); people with knowledge of the context for change: strategy, operational problems; people with influence; people with access to resources; people who care about the outcome; senior leaders from the current organization can also be considered.

Inputs

Inputs are any relevant strategic material as well as insight gathered for understanding the context and the shared view of the design and change context.

Instructions

Look back at the strategic material and insight you have gathered.
Create a set of high-level statements that capture the essence of your

strategic intent (usually four to eight statements are enough to encapsulate the major streams). Well-defined strategic statements will have these elements:

- Activity: what are the key actions that the organization is going to focus on?
- Time period: by when is it going to do it?
- Geographic location: where is it going to carry it out?
- Reason for doing it: why are you going to do this?

Review and refine the set of strategic statements:

- Do they include the big things that you need to continue and/or the new areas you want to concentrate on?
- Do they describe your offerings products/services, market/customers?
- Do they describe what products/services are to be brought to the market and for whom?
- Do they describe the style of organization you are moving toward, eg vertically integrated or highly networked?
- Do they clarify what makes your organization distinctive?
- Do they agree and are they in sync with other levels and parts of the organization's statements?
- Do they fit with this organization's role within its wider organizational setting?
- Do they differentiate this organization from its competitors/'near neighbours'?
- Statements of 'how' need only be included if they provide significant strategic direction.
- Are the elements of the statements unique, actionable and value-adding?
- Are they stated in broad, descriptive, general, non-tactical terms?
- Are they clear enough to guide the managers of the organization, as they make operational decisions?
- Are they specific enough to give clear direction?
- Are they brief and clear for internal and external stakeholders, eg employees, suppliers?
- Is it clear what any boundaries are?

Outputs

Strategic statements.

Defining target capabilities

If strategy is the organization's intent and plan, then capability is the main factor that enables the chosen strategy to be pursued. Amit and Schoemaker (1993) defined capability as the ability of the organization to engage in productive activity to attain a certain objective. Different capabilities are required to deliver different strategic intents. Target capabilities are what an organization will need to do outstandingly well to execute its strategy. Each capability is likely to have an impact on many aspects of the organization. Target capabilities cover what the organization must know how to do to execute its strategy and how people in the organization work together to get things done. They are the fundamental blocks to excel at. For example, a Financial Services business must know how to manage risk and design innovative products. If an organization wants to have a global presence, it will need to be good at international management. Some capabilities are not that obvious, for instance, the Child Support Agency in the UK needs to be good at debt recovery. Other capabilities are more easily recognized after major events; Bob Dudley, CEO of BP speaking in October 2010 after the Deepwater Horizon rig disaster in the Gulf of Mexico said, 'There are lessons for us relating to the way we operate, the way we organize our company and the way we manage risk ... (BP) will, over time, become one of the best companies in our industry at managing risk.'

Capabilities are hard for competitors to match because they can take time to build and can be hard to emulate or acquire. It helps to think about capabilities in terms of:

- Core capabilities: these focus on the strategic aspects of what needs to be done; delivering the products or services that you market.

- Enabling capabilities: these focus on the relational aspects how people work together to get work done; they support the delivery of core products; for instance in talent management, collaboration, organizational planning, strategy, and investment; the organization's ability to integrate, build, and reconfigure internal and external competences to address rapidly changing environments. Of course if you are designing an HR Department, talent management will probably be core to you!

Decisions on capability have implications on the design. Each capability impacts for instance, the work done, the skills and competencies you require, the behaviours required from the organization's people and/or suppliers and how performance is measured and rewarded. A capacity for leveraging resources and competences to support a capability can create a long-term competitive advantage for an organization. Building capabilities involves building and developing skills in a range of areas. In April 2013, the UK Civil Service announced an extended capabilities plan for the whole of the Civil Service. This focuses on four key areas: leading and managing change; commercial skills and behaviours; delivering successful projects and programmes; and redesigning services and delivering them digitally, (UK Civil Service, 2013).

When you define your organization's capabilities make sure you are thinking systematically, touching every aspect of organizational functioning. Tool 4.3 can be used to define your organization's target capabilities. To show you how this works in practice, Table 4.2 shows a draft first pass list of capabilities drawn up from the strategic intent shown on the website of a global pharmaceutical. It is used here to produce a first pass list of target capabilities and to illustrate the thinking process in moving from strategic intent or strategic statements to target capabilities. A list like this can start the dialogues needed; the draft target capabilities would need to be reviewed, confirmed and slimed down to the key 8 to 10 capabilities and then annotated.

Tool 4.3 Defining target capabilities

To define an annotated list of the top 8 to 10 capabilities required to deliver your strategy.

Who to involve

Include the people involved in defining the strategic statements.

Inputs

Strategic statements.

Instructions

- Considering the strategic statements, define what these tell you that you need to be really good at: capture these using the template in Table 4.3.

- Have you considered both core and enabling capabilities?

- Prioritize the top 8 to 10 (often the first pass list is too long).

- Annotate the target capabilities to explain why the capability is required. This cements the group's thinking and provides information for the design team.

Outputs

- Annotated target capabilities.

TABLE 4.2   First pass list of global pharmaceutical's capabilities

Strategic intent	Draft capabilities needed
Pipeline	
Operate a world-class research and development function	• Original research • Applied research • Exploitation of research ideas
Source innovation from outside	• Manage relationships • Industry scanning
Business growth	
Partner with payers to understand needs of customers	• Manage relationships • Consumer/customer/market research
Expand generic products in emerging markets	• Production efficiency • International logistics
Business shape	
Operate an efficient and effective business using Lean Sigma	• Manage using Lean Sigma • Manage programmes • Manage change
Outsource operations and collaborate with strategic partners	• Manage suppliers • Manage services • Manage demand
Culture and behaviours	
Foster creativity and collaboration	• Collaboration • Innovation
Promote a culture of responsibility and accountability	• Responsible and accountable organization

TABLE 4.3 Annotated list of target capabilities template

Target capabilities	Reasons why the capability is required
Capability 1	Include annotation for each capability
Capability 2	
Capability n	

TIP

Build on your existing capabilities if sensible – the change will be faster and easier.

For example when Microsoft changed its strategy in 2013 to 'focus on creating a family of devices and services for individuals and businesses that empower people around the globe at home, at work and on the go, for the activities they value most'. They chose to take advantage of their 'critical assets' (Microsoft News Centre, 2013). Their new capabilities are:

- a business model based on partner and first-party devices with both consumer and enterprise services;

- optimization for activities people value most;

- a family of devices powered by a service-enabled shell;

- design for enterprise extensibility and enterprise needs.

Consider these two organizations – how might their capabilities change as they do?

- Carpigiani is an Italian firm that makes ice-cream machines. Its home market is saturated. Italy has 37,000 artisanal *gelato* makers. Exports make up 80 per cent of Carpigiani's business. But most foreigners have no idea how to make a proper *gelato*. So Carpigiani has gone into education and set up Gelato University to teach them. Most training will be done abroad. (*The Economist*, 2013)

- In 2013 AstraZeneca describes itself as 'a global, biopharmaceutical company with research and development at its core'. It has changed over the years from a pharmaceutical company adding biotechnology to be a biopharmaceutical.

OPTIMAL programme considerations

Setting out the programme brief

Once you have a shared view of the design and change context, the strategic statements and the annotated target capabilities there is only one more component to include in 'a design brief', namely the programme brief. The programme brief sets out the specific change for the design programme (which may be a subset of the information explored); this information needs to be collated and the thinking behind it needs to take place now. This is generally pulled together by the commissioner working with the sponsor. A programme brief checklist with areas to be covered is shown in Table 4.4. The primary use of this is to:

- ensure that the programme has a firm foundation before asking the programme sponsor to make any major commitment to the programme;
- act as a base document against which the programme steering committee and programme leader (both set up in the next step) can assess progress, issues and ongoing viability;
- provide a reference so that people joining the programme can quickly and easily find out what the programme is about.

Does the programme brief:

- Document information captured in this step?
- Address and solve the right problems?
- Form a sound basis on which to initiate a programme?
- Accurately reflect the mandate for the programme and the requirements of the client?
- Indicate how the sponsor will assess the acceptability of the finished product(s)?
- Provide clarity for all stakeholders, not just those working on the programme?

In the next step, the contents of the programme brief are extended and refined to create the programme definition and plan, after which the programme brief is no longer maintained.

TABLE 4.4 Programme brief checklist

Section	Description
Goals	The programme goals (not the organizational goals)
Objectives	The programme objectives (not the organizational objectives)
	• Does the programme cover design only? (common where design is likely to result in many programmes for implementation and covers whole organization change in large-scale organizations)
	• Does the programme cover the whole change? (more likely in smaller or medium-size change)
Programme success criteria	Criteria for measuring success against which you can confirm that the programme has delivered all of its objectives and outcomes
	• Consider any sub-themes or programmes
	• Consider thinking this through in terms of the organization design model that may be used (if that is known at this stage)
Introduction	Brief outline of the background to the programme
	• The context that has been established
	• Outline of rationale for the organization design and the programme
	• Details of sponsor who commissioned the programme, drivers etc
	• Statement of fit within a wider organization
Vision	Brief description of the organization design vision statement (if there is one) – the desired end state. A statement describing the clear and inspirational long-term change, resulting from the design
Business case	High-level statement of the business case with broad brush measures

TABLE 4.4 *continued*

Section	Description
Scope	Scoping statements stating what is in and out of scope for the programme • Include details of boundaries and ring-fenced areas you have found Note: actively resist churn in the programme's scope
Constraints	Details of constraints or difficulties that the programme may encounter, eg legislation, regulation, policies, compliance issues
Interdependencies	Potential overlaps with other programmes (or their parts) where ownership or issues etc need to be clear • What this programme needs from others • What others need from this programme • Include ownership and timescales
External factors	Brief description of any external factors that may impact on the programme Brief statement of how this programme may impact others
Key assumptions	Details of initial key programme-level assumptions made on which the design and programme will be based • State level of confidence
Key risks	Key risks to the programme • With details of likelihood, any countermeasures, contingency plans • Include these in a risk log to be managed
Key issues	Live programme-level issues for the programme

TABLE 4.4 *continued*

Section	Description
Resources	This needs to cover you through until the programme is pulled together when you will look at resources in more depth
	In particular focus on sourcing the programme leader, the design leader and key roles: consider whether suitable expertise is in-house or if you need to go outside the organization. Are there any specific teams or individuals that need to be involved?
	Brief description on how the programme is to be funded: this may cover the design phase only at this step or the whole programme
	Brief description of the people required
	• Who are they?
	• What are they required to do?
	• Are they needed on a full-time or part-time basis?
	Brief description of any other key resources that may be required covering for instance skills, consultants, accommodation, technology
Stakeholders	Record the programme's key stakeholders
	• their location
	• their interest
Communications	• Brief details of how programme-level communications are to be run
	• Record any high-level communications and messages that need to be encapsulated at this point
	• Any sensitivities should also be considered
Quality	Brief description of any quality assurance process

Taking the programme forward

The key person to get approval and sign-off from at the end of this step is the programme sponsor. They will want to see the documented design brief. If the sponsor can answer yes to all of the following questions the design programme should be well positioned to progress:

- Is there sufficient information to make a decision?
- Is change necessary given the context seen?
- Is organization design the right response for the organization?
- Is there enough information to get started or is there more to do?
- Is now the right time to undertake the design and change?

If you answered no to any of the questions, what alternatives can be recommended?

Given that organization design now is the choice, either to the whole or parts of the organization it is time to start to pull together a design programme. The OPTIMAL Way will provide a high-level design and can also be used in implementing and embedding as design is cascaded to lower levels of detail. The design phase covers the overall architecture, not every aspect of design. Work out now with the sponsor how much detail the organization feels comfortable with defining upfront and what can be left until later on to define. For instance, will the design phase only cover defining the overall shape; allowing appointed managers to define the detail they need to at a later step or does it need to be more prescriptive? This will tailor the approach decided as the programme is pulled together. The same organization will take different approaches at different times and in different circumstances: just as the same person has contrasting needs for distinctive holidays, they may plan in detail, 'go with the flow', or have elements of both. Some organizations have a preferential style just as individuals on holiday do. People in organizations can feel uncomfortable being over-planned or under-planned. Allowing a high degree of emergence can be seen as the only way to embed change or conversely result in high degrees of discomfort.

The commissioner's role is fulfilled. The team or individual who has carried out this role may stay on the programme to be set up or may leave. If necessary, ensure a clean handover.

TIP

From research being carried out at the University of Westminster in 2013, the most-frequently mentioned enablers in creating a macro (high-level) organization design – accounting for 73 per cent of all enablers mentioned by respondents – were: a clear vision of the future organization; a complete, clearly articulated strategy; a strong case for change and organizational energy and commitment.

Conclusion

At the beginning of a programme your main focus should be outcomes, not just outputs. The outcomes from this step are that you have shaped the problem, reached a shared understanding of the challenge and what needs to be designed. This has been articulated for the programme and agreed to by the programme sponsor and any wider executive/senior people that have been involved. You will also have produced some key outputs that help you achieve these outcomes and will be required throughout later steps of the organization design programme:

- Programme leadership identified programme sponsor, senior HR leader, and the commissioner; the latter may or may not be involved in later stages of the programme.
- Working papers:
  - from the individual interviews – multiple perspectives on the programme and design context;
  - a 'chorus of voices' collating key areas from the individual interviews.
- Lessons from other organizations.
- Design brief:
  - the shared view of the design and change context;
  - strategic statements;
  - annotated target capabilities;
  - programme brief.

Keep sight of the outcomes and the reason you are doing this work. 'An organization's reason for being, like that of any organism, is to help the parts that are in relationship to each other, to be able to deal with change in the environment' – Kevin Kelly. You should now be in a position to take forward an organization design programme. By the time you complete this step you will have the knowledge to initiate an organization design programme yourself and know how to do this so you can get the go ahead to proceed. You will be able to do this whether you are designing an entirely new organization from scratch or taking a current organization and realigning it. Walt Disney said, 'You don't build it for yourself. You know what the people want and you build it for them.' However, you cannot build it on your own, so now we turn to putting the team together to design and build it.

Pulling together your programme

05

> *The secret of getting ahead is getting started. The secret of getting started is breaking your complex, overwhelming tasks into small manageable tasks, and then starting on the first one.* (MARK TWAIN)

KEY POINTS

Aim:

To establish a programme that delivers the design brief.

Activities:

- establishing the leadership for the change;
- resourcing the design participants;
- choosing the organization design model, process, approach, tools and techniques;
- establishing the wider change programme.

There is a clear, shared brief and the go ahead for an organization design programme. This step of the OPTIMAL Way is about preparing for the journey ahead. The aim of this step is to put in place the programme to deliver a high-level design that meets the brief. This chapter covers the assembly of the design programme leadership and team; setting out the approach that will be used (the design model, process and toolset); and ensuring everyone has sufficient understanding of the requirements and approach to enable fast progress to be made. It includes the skills required for design work and how to identify the people who have them. We then look at setting up your programme on a sound basis and finally document the route you are going to take. This is important because design work should be run using project management disciplines. It is a multidisciplinary activity requiring common ground and knowledge as well as a shared vision of where the programme is heading. People from different disciplines, often different locations, and existing organizations need to be aligned and ready to work together. You should gain an insight into how to establish a fully resourced organization design programme with a team that is kitted out, ready to go and success-fully deliver the programme's design brief.

This chapter explains the tasks for the person or people setting up the programme, generally a programme leader with a design leader. They may be the same person on smaller projects. A number of things are happening in parallel in this step: the broader programme and the design elements are established. At different levels the step covers: resourcing; making choices on how the programme will work and ensuring everyone has sufficient knowledge to commence work. Everything is brought together at the end ready for steering committee sign-off. The key determinant in how long this step takes is access to suitable resources.

Resourcing the programme

Who leads organization design work? This sounds quite a straightforward question, but in practice, there are multiple leadership roles and levels in carrying out an organization design programme. The following case of leader-ship of organization design programmes at Barclays in the early 2000s shows different aspects of leadership required from their business units, HR and organization design.

Background

In the early 2000s, Barclays Bank PLC brought in a new CEO, Mathew Barrett, who with his Executive and Board reviewed the bank's strategy to focus on it becoming a major global financial services provider, delivering a chosen set of products to selected marketplaces. This needed a significant transformation to change it from a series of standalone businesses each operating in their own way and largely UK-dominant, to having a coherent global business model with value added by all parts of the organization: the newly created individual business units, a newly created shared services organization for operations and IT, as well as the group's central functions.

At the time, it was recognized that a significant transformational change was required and this required deep expertise in new skills while the external consultancy fees were not to be increased. One response to contain consultancy expenditure was to create a professional internal management consultancy unit. Within that group, one of the practices established was an organization design practice. Independently and at the same time the HR function was becoming more strategically focused and moving to a business-partner centre of excellence model. It too had recognised the need to establish an organization design centre of excellence capability.

In effect, two organization design competency centres were being built separately; both were small and formative but existing on parallel tracks. Neither was sufficiently resourced for the pending demand given the amount and complexity of the change going on throughout the group. Some business units would go to the HR centre of excellence and some to the internal consultancy for their organization design support. This was because of existing relationships within the Barclays group, and neither offered access to a comprehensive range of organization design skills. This was a waste of scarce resources.

HR's own role was transforming from a more transactional organization to fulfil a more strategic function. Within HR's organization design centre of excellence, relationships with strategic planning were formative and there was limited access to business executives for the HR staff involved in organization design. Those involved in organization design from HR generally were less senior than the internal consultants. In addition, there was a conflict in the central HR's role as policy setters in the organization design space versus their role as designers.

The internal consultancy did not have ready access to the emerging HR strategies and policies or HR information in various data sources. They also lacked vital HR skills, such as resource and talent planning, employee relations and use of employee metrics.

The resolution

The HR centre of excellence developed the overarching Barclays' organization design principles. The internal consultancy and businesses adhered to these. HR also provided relevant input to all aspects within their domain. The internal consultancy supported the business with the provision of other competencies that the businesses did not have themselves (which varied from business to business). Business leadership was provided by the business unit, shared services or functional unit going through the change and by group executives for fit with the overall enterprise direction. In this case the following areas provided different skills, knowledge, capabilities, and leadership:

- Group executives:
  - Business leadership: fit with Barclays Group purpose, strategy, values, business model and other business areas, business objectives.
- Business unit executives:
  - Business leadership: sponsorship and executive direction informing organizational purpose, strategy, values, business objectives, policies. This included HR.

- The HR centre of excellence for organization design:
  - Strategic leadership: development of Group level HR strategies, policies, and principles.
- HR business partners:
  - HR generalist knowledge with an understanding of the business units they worked in and ability to access relevant HR specialists and information sources.
  - Strong links to HR for access to HR data and the ability to change some enabling processes, like rewards, performance appraisal, as well as learning and development.
  - An ability to understand the implications on people and provide solutions; for instance, protecting key people through major transformation and ensuring management of talent.
- The organization design internal consultancy:
  - Access to strategic thinking: to understand what change was required at executive level with the business; with close links to strategy development and a broad understanding of the impact on process and technology as well as people.
  - Good consultancy skills; such as understanding root causes of problems rather than addressing symptoms of perceived business problems.
  - Good organization design skills; developed through experience as well as theory.
- Business units, shared service units, functions:
  - Programme and project management disciplines.

Change management was variously supplied by business units, HR and internal consultants depending on the business unit. This case highlights some of the different capability requirements organization design needs and where these were located at that time in Barclays. It draws out the multiplicity of leadership roles on an organization design programme well. Typically, there are five different leadership roles in an organization design programme; these are leadership from the 'business' or 'client', programme leadership, design leadership, HR leadership and leadership from specialists.

Business leadership

Organization design should always be led by the business. Effective leadership has been consistently found to be a critical success factor and key enabler in delivering effective design and change leading to successful outcomes. Business leadership is needed to shape the nature and the content of the future organization, particularly drawing on the capabilities, attitudes, behaviours, and knowledge of the senior management. Senior management's leadership plays a pivotal role, particularly their experience gained from other organizations that they have worked in and people they have worked with. Business leaders ensure that the design developed is linked to their thinking on the organizational purpose and strategic direction, ensuring sponsorship of the design, obtaining their buy-in and driving the execution of the design.

Programme leadership

Leadership is required from the person who leads the execution of the design work and/or the change. The person who is asked to carry out an organization design programme may or may not have past experience of carrying out an organization design. They may also lead the organization involved or lead other change programmes. A programme sponsor often straddles both business and programme leadership. There are other dimensions to programme leadership too from other programme specialists, eg change management.

Design leadership

Design leadership comes from:

- providing confidence to the organization that the process will deliver optimal results;
- assuring the process is robust and followed;
- facilitating the process;
- assuring the design meets any external design requirements of it;
- assuring the design meets the requirements of the programme;
- leading the design to produce high-quality outputs and outcomes;
- being an expert in organization design.

An additional independent assurance function can be provided by a design authority on large complex programmes.

HR leadership

HR leadership involves:

- aligning organization design work with HR strategy;
- linking organization design to HR policies, standards and frameworks;
- ensuring tight linkage of outcomes with talent management and learning and development;
- connecting with individual performance management processes;
- joining up organization design with culture, norms and behaviours, organization development, resource management.

Specialist representation

Other team members involved in an organization design programme will be leaders in their own area, whether that is in:

- business and operational expertise related to the organization being transforming, eg running part of the process being changed in a contact centre;
- a central services or functional area, eg from Risk, Finance, and IT units;
- HR which may be involved in various detailed ways.

Of course functions and HR may be the area being transformed in which case they may have multiple roles on the programme. Good organization design leaders, like programme leaders, need to know something about everything. They are generalists, not specialists: the conductors of the symphony, not virtuosos who play every instrument perfectly. As a practitioner, an organization design leader coordinates a team of professionals from many disciplines. In James Crupi's words, 'the leader's job is not to cover all the bases – it is to see that all bases are covered'. Typically, the interests of some team members will compete with the interests of others. An organization design leader must know enough about each discipline to negotiate and synthesize competing demands while ordering the needs of the client and integrity of the entire programme. Appendix 1 lists the skills generally required in an organization design team; from medium to expert. This is covered further in establishing the design team below. In addition, both the leaders and team involved on an organization programme need to be highly skilled at working collaboratively: working in partnership across hierarchy, organizations, and functions to deliver the defined objectives.

Participation in the OPTIMAL Way is not just a matter of asking people what they want and then giving it to them. It is a fragile and delicate process of negotiation, a conversation about many different experiences and perspectives, points of view and values to take into account. Designers may take on the role of educator, interpreter, critical friend, negotiator, or advocate. Organization design is both an art and a science. So the design leaders will use both the rational, analytical side of their brains as choices are made based on evidence and the creative side as sparks of inspiration can make any design great. Just think of outstanding architects, their skills, and their legacy; they encapsulate the qualities of an outstanding design leader.

Putting the programme and design leaders in place

The programme sponsor and senior HR leader should have been established in the previous step and already be in place. This will ensure that if someone from HR is not fulfilling either the programme leader or design leader role, that the design work is aligned to HR strategy and vice versa. The commissioning role is complete, now is the time to assign the programme and designer leader roles. In practice, on a small project they may be one and the same person while on larger, complex programmes they are usually different people. In addition, on major programmes with either a large-scale design piece of work or long term and significant implementation implications, it is not uncommon for these leaders to be assisted and strengthened by a design authority. A design authority is a role, that will quality assure the organization design process and outputs. It is typically only found on large or complex design programmes. A design authority is an assurance function not a compliance function. Its role is to advise not to veto. In Part Three we look in more detail at the role of a design authority. The design authority person or team can also act as an advisor to the wider leadership community. If you are going to have a design authority on the programme they are best brought in, upfront with the leadership, before major decisions are made and ahead of the bulk of the team.

Identifying and resourcing the design team

Any team embarking on an organization design will require a number of skills or access to them. Appendix 1 lists the skills generally required in an organization design team. These are the skills required at the design phase; some of these will also be required in implementation but will change in prominence. We have tried to give a sense of the relative skill levels and shown those at medium level and above. The nature of your challenge will also influence the specific skill and the levels required. Smaller, simpler changes obviously do not require the skill levels and experience that larger, complex scale challenges do. To make it easier to digest we have clustered the skills into: consultancy; change management; HR specialist and generalist; and programme/project management. Many of the team will be leaders in their own fields and all will need to be highly skilled at working collaboratively: working in partnership across hierarchy, organizations, and functions to deliver the defined objectives.

These skills do not have to reside in one individual. Depending on how large and/or significant the design to be undertaken is, these are likely to be spread across a number of individuals or teams. People interested in organization design tend to be highly business-orientated and want to be proactive in influencing the future. They are results-focused, as well as goal- and improvement-orientated. They are likely to value progress, change, teamworking, knowledge and expertise. Non-functional skills that are required are very high amounts of critical thinking, planning, problem-solving; high amounts of logical thinking and decision-making. Because organization design is a broad skill set, it attracts people who enjoy using their creative and analytic skills. The creative side often attracts those who are visionary and innovative. The analytical side attracts people who enjoy assessment, seeking multiple perspectives, gathering more information where necessary, and identifying the key issues that need to be addressed.

Organization design teams are often characterized by a small number of full-time team members and a larger number of part-time participants brought in for their specialized expertise. Organizations differ in how they secure resources for programme teams, so here we can only offer you general advice. In resourcing the team, some factors and further guidance we consider are:

- Look for insight in Appendix 2: Organization designers' typical backgrounds.
- Work with your organization's current resourcing processes to find suitable people.
- Look out for the brightest and best in the organization. Quick, agile and open minds are as important as existing organization design skills.
- Select influential people who will have the power to see changes through. Unless your organization is prepared to change, the programme will lead nowhere.
- Aim to resource the extended team from a range of levels, not just the top tiers.
- Involve people that the leaders expect to be part of the future and have credibility with their colleagues (can HR identify some potential people for you?).
- Watch out for change-resistant managers who nominate people who will maintain the status quo. Consider getting the section heads to recommend two to three people from other sections.
- Involve functional people where relevant, typically finance and HR, and sometimes marketing or compliance. Get the balance right between number of functional people and number of line people.
- Ensure you have sufficient technical skills in organization design work on the team, for instance in facilitation and process mapping.

As a cross check and different perspective have you got:

- a good spread of people with different viewpoints and attitudes to generate a healthy dialogue and spark creativity;
- representatives from different locations (if that is relevant);
- a mix of people with different lengths of service with the enterprise organization;
- a mix of people with different experiences of other organizations;
- a cross-section reflecting the diversity of your people?

Ensuring the business leadership is in place to support the programme

Successful programme outcomes are not just dependent on programme management techniques, processes, and good technology. They have much to do with leadership, culture, and inculcating good behaviours, yet these people skills are often given insufficient attention. You also need to set up the programme governance. This will almost certainly include a programme steering committee (or board). A few thoughts on what is different in organization design steering committees:

- Numerical targets often have a very high focus; eg numbers of people, cost per head.
- Control is about influencing what is about to happen.
- There needs to be clarity on how and to whom reports and conversations will be presented and when. Sensitive information will need to be carefully released.
- They need to govern the design process, so that any design reviews assess design maturity rather than using them to release budget for the subsequent step.
- They should include the senior HR leader.

You may also want to consider setting up a business user group to support the design work and resolve questions as you progress. Business user groups are senior managers, heads of departments or senior team leaders who really understand the implications any design will have on the organization within their area of responsibility. They can be very beneficial to resolving thorny issues and making trade-offs that can be implemented. In the OPTIMAL Way, an effective use of a business user group is to review each design level as it is completed.

Programme structures and roles differ from organization to organization, from programme to programme. Figure 5.1 shows Chevron's preferred organization design roles. Chevron, the multinational oil company has an in-house organization design group who assist business units in redesign work. This group maintains a standard design methodology that is deployed across the organization and they have templates of their preferred roles in any design programme, eg problem-owner and change agent.

FIGURE 5.1 Chevron's preferred organization design roles

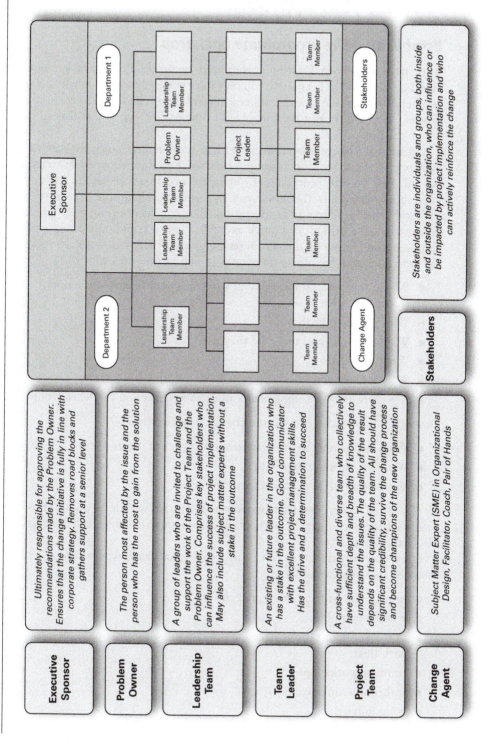

Executive Sponsor

Ultimately responsible for approving the recommendations made by the Problem Owner. Ensures that the change initiative is fully in line with corporate strategy. Removes road blocks and gathers support at a senior level

Problem Owner

The person most affected by the issue and the person who has the most to gain from the solution

Leadership Team

A group of leaders who are invited to challenge and support the work of the Project Team and the Problem Owner. Comprises key stakeholders who can influence the success of project implementation. May also include subject matter experts without a stake in the outcome

Team Leader

An existing or future leader in the organization who has a stake in the outcome. Good communicator with excellent project management skills. Has the drive and a determination to succeed

Project Team

A cross-functional and diverse team who collectively have sufficient depth and breadth of knowledge to understand the issues. The quality of the result depends on the quality of the team. All should have significant credibility, survive the change process and become champions of the new organization

Change Agent

Subject Matter Expert (SME) in Organizational Design, Facilitator, Coach, Pair of Hands

Stakeholders

Stakeholders are individuals and groups, both inside and outside the organization, who can influence or be impacted by project implementation and who can actively reinforce the change

Shaping your approach

Establishing the programme backdrop

If you have not followed 'outlining your brief' because a different programme initiation method has been used, you may have some gaps to fill. In particular you need to define the strategic statements and target capabilities before you proceed. If you have not been involved in the earlier step you will need to get up to speed.

Organization design programmes are often one of many change programmes in an organization. Most organizations have some established ways of carrying out all their change programmes, including organization design. Identify what these are and how they affect you. In particular, where your organization has established practices and expectations then consider reusing these where you can or have to. This is a quick exercise. Plan to spend only a relatively short amount of time on this. From past organization design work, consider the outcomes and the impact on people as well as the process:

- What other organization design work has your organization done recently?
- Who was involved?
- What methods and tools did they use?
- What worked?
- What did not work?
- Are there any post-implementation reviews that you can learn from?

Drawing on the wider portfolio of change programmes:

- What will people in the organization expect to use and see?
- What are they familiar with?
- What established practices can you reuse?

Are there any higher-level frameworks and standards within the organization that you have to conform to, particularly: programme management, financial, HR, risk, change?

Does your organization have any established frameworks, tools, and methods that you can use for:

- project and programme management;
- process mapping;
- drawing organization charts (many HR software systems come with this);
- running workshops;
- stakeholder management;
- communications;
- engagement?

Choosing how you will carry out the design: part 1, models and process

Good leaders of design programmes feel comfortable shepherding people through a process that is genuinely creative. The control is not in forcing the outcome towards predetermined views but in confidence that the process will deliver the best outcomes for the organization. Therefore one of the first steps that the programme and design leaders (with a design authority, if they are in place) need to work together on is ensuring that they have a robust process on which to build their plans and take others with them on the journey (the wider leadership, the team and the wider organization). From here on, we assume you have chosen the OPTIMAL Way and the Compass. You can be confident that this process works well with the accompanying model and toolset.

The decision on the choices of models, processes, tools and techniques rests with the programme leader and designer: they are the ones to give leadership and direction on this. Your own practical experience and expertise, along with the nature of the challenge, will largely guide your choice. The programme leader agrees with the sponsor how decisions will be made throughout the programme. Document these decisions in the programme definition. A checklist of what to include is shown in Table 5.1.

You can vary how you deploy the OPTIMAL Way: choose what suits your particular programme – what tools and techniques to apply; whether to use small expert teams or large group interventions; how you will assess alternative design options; and how the major decisions on your programme will be made. In Part One, Chapter 2 we looked at different ways of carrying out organization design. From here on, we assume you have chosen to use a core design team. It is easier in a book to explain one consistent way and the various large group methods warrant specific techniques to pull off. As Shmulyian *et al* (2010) point out, 'The art' – excellence in method execution – and 'the artist' – the right facilitator – are necessary for achieving desired outcomes of the large group methods. Of course, you can use the Compass and OPTIMAL Way and the tools and techniques that accompany it in this book with large groups and 'everyone in the room'. Think like a designer – same tools but different ways of using them. What all the methods give you is a whole system approach to consider – vital for organization design. There is no right answer in how to carry out design work – you can use different size groups at different stages in the process.

It is less common for someone working in organization design to be given the task of designing a large, enterprise-wide organization. Usually the task is to design a part of an organization: a business unit, a functional unit, a department, a team, a company. Or the task is reorganizing a part of the organization to deliver a set of processes or functions, maybe setting up an operational shared service centre or setting up a new section. The more of the organization that you are designing or redesigning, the more freedom you have about what you can change, how much you can change, and how you can tackle the design process. Conversely, the less of your organization you are designing, unless it is a highly autonomous small specialist unit, then the more you will be constrained by the decisions, policies and practices that you inherit from the larger umbrella organization. Tailor your model, process, tools and techniques to the complexity of the challenge. If your organization already has a model they understand then it can be helpful to use that as it will be easier to communicate.

As an organization design programme can be completed by a small expert team or large participatory groups and there are pros and cons for each method, it is best to look at what is important to your organization and programme. Consider:

- What skills do you have available? Working with small teams and facilitating large groups need different skills sets. Can you supplement your own organization's skills with external ones such as consultants or contractors for part of design work?

- Your organization's norms and behaviours are important. Sometimes you will want to work with the norms of your organization but sometimes you will want to deliberately work in a different way. Look at whether the organization mainly solves problems using small expert groups or is mainly an organization that uses large groups. Then you can ask which you want it to be in future. Is it the same or different? Perhaps you want to signal an intention to change or to force a different perspective. Modelling your future norms and behaviours during the design programme can be a powerful tool in demonstrating how you want things to be in the future. As Mahatma Gandhi said, 'be the change you want to see in the world'.

In later steps, we describe how to set up an evaluation scheme; develop a number of design options at concept level, assess these and iterate through the development of design outlines and assessment of these. As you iterate, you develop more detail for preferred options. The number of options at each level that you want consider as well as how to assess the options are choices are made now. Decide:

- How many design options at concept and outline level will you generate and review?

- How will you assess the design options and compare alternatives and who will do this?

- If the environment is very uncertain or complex, do you want to add scenario testing to your assessment?

Getting the programme team and leadership ready for this programme

With the team in place, they need to work together to deliver the requirements identified in the design brief as well as understand and follow the approach you have chosen for your programme. Depending on the skills and experience of the team, you may also need to provide the team members with some basic education on organization design. Make sure that this is about a real understanding: make this very interactive. Many groups that are new to design use experienced organization designers to provide or support this as they can bring the models, methods, and techniques to life with examples. Senior leaders involved in the previous step can help to bring the strategic thinking to life. Consider covering:

- Organization design theory
  - what organization design is about;
  - information on your design philosophy;
  - some wider perspectives on the background to organization design; what to do; what to expect and what experiences have been seen elsewhere;
  - what works in the current organization or in others you have experience of;
  - draw out existing knowledge and experiences from the team members.
- How organization design will be carried out on this programme
  - an overview of the model to be used;
  - an overview of the process to be used and how you will carry it out;
  - insight from the programme backdrop.
- Design brief focusing on requirements to deliver the OPTIMAL design
  - aspects from the shared view of the design and change context;
  - strategic statements;
  - target capabilities;
  - aspects from the programme brief.

A shortened version of the training provided for the design team is generally more appropriate for the steering committee, business user groups, and any other workstreams that need to get up to speed. You may want a separate steering committee meeting to do this before going through the specifics of the programme definition and plan. An 'intelligent client' who can understand, challenge or accept, and ultimately approve the designs is essential to your success.

Choosing how you will carry out the design: part 2, methods, tools and techniques

The design models and process to use have been chosen, now we choose the design methods, tools, and techniques. The aim here is to establish any workbooks, templates, and software that the design team will use during the programme. This is particularly useful if the programme involves a large geographic spread. This activity is usually carried out by the team with the lead designer having the greatest input. In it draw on the experiences of the team members' past uses of methods, tools and techniques and adapt them to this programme's requirements. There are a range of tools and techniques in later chapters of this book for you to use too. A typical toolkit might include descriptions, documentation and instruction on using the chosen organization design model, process and methods, tools and techniques, as well as how to run the interviews, workshops and discussion groups; consider:

- Contents of a toolkit
- Methodology
  - process mapping methods;
  - activity mapping methods;
  - methods for producing organization charts;
  - document templates;
  - presentation templates;
  - intranet templates (if used).
- Interviews, workshop and discussion group
  - scripts to introduce the programme and the team members;
  - interview checklists for all steps;
  - workshop techniques to be applied;
  - outline workshop templates;
  - how you will document workshops.

You may need additional training events in your chosen methodology and toolkit where these are not familiar to team members. You may also want to consider how to present your toolkit. Birmingham City Council has recently developed a methodology and toolkit for organization design to be used across all the Council's organization design programmes. They are using an Intranet to document the methods and train and guide people in how to use them.

OPTIMAL programme considerations

The design leadership, team, model, processes, methods, tools and techniques are now in place. In parallel, the programme as a whole is being constructed. Change leadership and HR leadership are vital to the success of organization design programmes. Your aim is to deliver hearts, not just charts.

Change leadership and other workstreams

Throughout the design phase the programme needs to prepare the ground for implementation. These may be workstreams or activities within workstreams depending on how you configure each programme. They will run alongside the design workstream which this book focuses on. The areas that need particular consideration on an organization design programme are:

In HR/Talent management/Organization development:

- Start planning for any potentially difficult challenges, eg significant changes in numbers of people; types of people; skills or in employment terms and conditions.
- Identify when there is a need to halt or refocus current, business-as-usual recruitment and training activities.
- Work out when and how to go through formal consultation processes with trade unions, works councils and other staff bodies. Do different geographies have different requirements? Do different legal entities need to be looked at?
- Start identifying the people the organization really wants to keep: keeping talented individuals in place for long enough to make a difference particularly when other jobs are easy to secure.
- Monitor where, when and how the design impacts organization development work.
- Consider changes to culture.

Across change management:

- ensure buy-in as the programme progresses: with strong engagement, stakeholder management, communication management, and continuing leadership support;
- establish which people and groups to involve when; how to coach and support the business leaders;
- align communications messages with other change programmes in the organization.

In finance:

- handling financial complexities and modelling;
- managing the costs and benefits of the programme;
- planning how to manage the release of financial figures that are sensitive both internally within the organization and also to financial markets.

FIGURE 5.2   OPTIMAL steps within a programme

Programme Leadership							
	Management Systems						
Design							
O	P	T	I	M	A	L	
	Change Leadership and other workstreams						
	eg Stakeholder Management, Communication						

You may need others too depending on your programme, eg a commercial workstream for a programme with sourcing. There are so many variants that can be used alongside OPTIMAL that we do not want to be prescriptive on which ones you use, but do want you to see the whole picture of what is involved. Figure 5.2 shows how other programme aspects relate to the OPTIMAL steps. Figure 2.3 shows a broader programme picture with OPTIMAL focused on the high-level design.

If you are going to undertake a cultural assessment now is the best time to do it because it influences how you are going to run the programme. It will inform what you need to change around Norms and behaviours in the next step and how you manage stakeholder engagement.

Establishing management systems and the programme environment

This covers all the usual factors that go with setting up a programme office and environment for a team. The working environment, the systems for sharing files and maintaining documentation and control need to be established at this point. There are a few specific considerations that need particular thought for an organization design programme:

- Desk/hot desk requirements. How many of the design team will be full-time and how many will be part-time while working on other jobs? Do you need to co-locate people or will they continue working at their own desks?

- Often there is confidential and/or sensitive information with restricted access to some data. How will confidentiality be handled?

- All incur direct expenses; eg for workshop venues, for getting specialist help like facilitation; for travel and accommodation for team members. Are budgets and financial control systems clear? Who can incur costs? How are costs authorized and approved?

Control mechanisms that support the programme will also need to be put in place. The best way to do this is through a well-functioning programme office. Programme offices for organization design programmes are little different from those on other programmes. They support the programme leader managing, for instance, the programme costs and budget; the business case; risks, assumptions, issues and dependency logs; milestone and plan tracking.

You need to define the decision-making framework for the programme. This will be mainly the responsibility of the programme leader in dialogue with the sponsor, steering committee members, and the secretariat to any higher-level board if you expect them to be involved in the final decision point. The choices will generally reflect what is usual in your organization for a change programme of similar scale and complexity. Consider:

- Where will the final approval for the design take place?
- What do they want to see, eg is it just your final design recommendation; or do they want to see three alternate designs and a recommendation? This may colour the output you need to produce during the programme and the time it will take.
- How often does this group meet?
- What else will be on the agenda at that time?
- How do they expect it to be presented to them in terms of documentation and style?
- What length of presentation and discussion will it need?
- How far ahead of meetings do papers need to be submitted?
- Do background-briefing papers need to be sent as well as discussion papers for the meeting?

We only focus on outputs connected with the design workstream in this and subsequent steps, eg taking design outputs to Steering Groups: there will of course be updates from change workstream and other activity too. Ensure you retain a consistent design philosophy in the face of programmatic pressures; monitoring real progress (rather than false metrics); and retaining focus on the key programme objectives and stakeholder needs.

Risk inherent in organization design programmes can be higher than some other types of change, but there is no hard and fast rule to this, it really does depend on each programme's characteristics. You may find you need to focus on different areas of risk too, for instance people risk. Could the change that is being made increase your turnover of key people or key talent? As Donald Will Douglas said, 'When you design it, think how you would feel if you had to fly it! Safety first!'

Set out the programme definition and plan

Two key further deliverables from this stage are the programme definition and plan. The programme definition extends and refines the programme brief with the work done and knowledge obtained in this step. How you achieve this will vary depending on the usual practices of your organization and there is a wealth of other literature to guide you. Generally there is no need to maintain the programme brief once the definition is in place. An annotated programme definition to assist your thinking is shown in Table 5.1. The primary uses of these are to:

- Ensure that the programme has a firm foundation and is on sound basis before asking the programme steering committee to make any major commitment to the programme.

- Act as a base document against which the programme steering committee and programme leader can assess progress, issues, and ongoing viability. This forms the 'contract' between them.

- Provide a reference so that people joining the programme can quickly and easily find out what the programme is about, and how it is being managed.

The programme definition and plan should be maintained throughout the programme, reflecting the current status, plans, and controls. It consists of a number of component products. These should be baselined at the end of this step and will need to be updated and re-baselined, as necessary, at the end of each step, to reflect the current status of its constituent parts. This first version can be used at the end of the design phase/programme to assess the programme. The programme leader with the team should also establish a plan for the design phase using whatever planning methods your organization favours.

You just need approval and the newly formed Steering Committee should give you that. Work with your programme sponsor to clarify what and in how much detail they need to see things now and at each step along the way. Remember the funding and business case, if you have a vision and no resources it is just a dream: a programme generally starts when the business case has been approved and the appropriate funding is in place.

TABLE 5.1 Programme planning and definition checklist

Section	Description
Goals and objectives	From the programme brief – the programme goals and objectives
Programme success criteria	From the programme brief, often added to as the programme is pulled together and thinking matures • Criteria for measuring success against which you can confirm that the programme has delivered all of its objectives and outcomes • Consider any sub-themes or programmes • Consider thinking through in terms of the elements of the model you propose to use
Introduction	From the programme brief • Often added to as the programme is pulled together and thinking matures
Scope	From the programme brief • Updated only if necessary
Structure	How the programme will be • Structured including a high-level organization chart • Governed including a governance framework (if appropriate), terms of reference for any committees, details of escalation mechanisms or requirements For each key work strand within the programme • Who owns them • Their priority
Approach	Include • The model and process you are using • The methods, tools and techniques you are applying • Type of involvement (small expert teams or large-group interventions) • Number of design options to be generated and reviewed at each level • How the design options will be assessed and who will make the assessment
Key risks	Latest view of key risks to the programme • With details of their likelihood, any countermeasures and/or contingency plans • Include these in a risk log to be managed

TABLE 5.1   *continued*

Section	Description
Key assumptions	Latest view of key programme-level assumptions on which the design and programme will be based • State level of confidence
Key issues	Current issues for the programme
Interdependencies	Definition as in the programme brief • These are much better understood as a programme progresses and should be updated here
Deliverables	Developed from the programme brief's statements on programme success criteria, drill down to: • The major outcomes, outputs and targets the programme will deliver • Focus on delivery of measurable benefits • Consider thinking through in terms of your chosen model • Include any firm dates that will drive the programme
Resources	The resources needed for the design phase of the programme • Brief description of the people required • Who are they? • What they are required to do? • Are they needed on a full-time or part-time basis? • Brief description of any other key resources that may be required, eg skills, consultants, accommodation, technology
Plan and milestones	• Key milestone dates that need to be tracked • Detailed programme plan to be managed (in whatever format your organization prefers)
Business case	A first view of the business case that will be maintained throughout the programme
Other workstreams	For instance deliverables from change leadership workstream • Stakeholder management • Communications management

Conclusion

You have leaders on board, governance, team, and systems in place. You have chosen and modified the model, processes, methods, tools and techniques you will use. All should be trained and ready to go. Relevant workstreams should be in place to support the design through the next steps making sure that what you do engages and carries others with you. There is a lot now in place:

- Design programme leadership and team:
  - programme leader, design leader, specialist representatives and steering committee;
  - optionally design authority and business user group.
- Programme management systems and environment.
- Other programme workstreams (as required):
  - cultural assessment (optional).
- Design workstream:
  - knowledge from past organization design work and programmes;
  - organization design model: the Compass and how it will be used;
  - design process: the OPTIMAL Way and how it will be used;
  - toolkit: including methods, tools and techniques;
  - training materials on organization design, models, process and design brief;
  - training materials for methods, tool and techniques.
- Programme definition and plan.
- Steering committee pack.

By the time you complete this step you will have the knowledge to set up an organization design programme yourself and know how to do this so that you can get the go ahead to proceed. You will be able to do this whether you are designing an entirely new organization from scratch or taking a current organization and realigning it. The programme team is ready to go: shared enthusiasm now can become infectious. In David Mahoney's words 'There comes a time when you have to stop revving up the car and shove it into gear.'

Taking stock of the change required

06

Before attempting to create something new, it is vital to have a good appreciation of everything that already exists in this field. **(MIKHAIL KALASHNIKOV)**

KEY POINTS

Aim:

To identify the most critical aspects of the organization to change.

Key activities:

- Gathering evidence from within the organization.

- Gaining further insight – internally and externally.

- Reflecting on the organization's current state.

- Envisioning the future state.

- Establishing and then prioritizing the key changes required.

Now the design team is in place and you have the agreement to go ahead, you start to look at the changes needed. The aim of this step is to identify the most critical aspects of the organization to change so that the strategic intent can be delivered with the target capabilities embedded; to get an understanding of the implications of this so that the subsequent design effort and programme can be tightly focused; and to provide the programme with information to support the design and implementation. This chapter covers a detailed understanding of the current state and a view of the future state organization. You look for further insight that might be helpful – in and beyond the organization. There is some diagnostic work. Like any physician or designer in other fields, you have to diagnose before you can prescribe! The information you gather will help you determine what needs to be done and where the priorities lie. It also helps identify potential resistance and starts stakeholder engagement. It uses the Organization Design Compass and various frameworks to explore what the gap between the current and future state organizations is. Lastly the specific change areas that the programme should look at in the design work are selected and any implications on the programme factored in. This is important because the change is based on evidence and a multi-dimensional point of view which allows the exercise of sound judgement and results in informed choices about the new design and how to implement it. You should gain the knowledge of how to build an evidence base for an organization, how to establish a future state organization; how to draw out the direction and extent of change that a design programme will follow and that has buy-in.

Building an evidence base takes the most time in this step. The work is led by the design leader and carried out by the design team. How deeply you delve into evidence depends on the nature of the challenge you face, so it is difficult to generalize on how long producing it will take or how many people are needed to pull an evidence base together. If you are designing a small team, then it may only take you a day or two. If you are designing a new organization or a new section within an existing organization there may be little or no evidence base to collect. If you are involved in a merger of organizations then it may take many weeks, perhaps months. In addition, there is a fine line between being comfortable dealing with ambiguity and making decisions based on good evidence. Judgement on what outcomes must be achieved is paramount to establish the time and effort needed. Assessing the future state and taking stock of the change required is relatively fast once the evidence base is complete: a few days should be sufficient. Allow time at the end for ensuring a good understanding across the programme team, business user groups and to factor in programme changes. The steering committee will also need time to approve the way forward.

Building an evidence base

An evidence base is an information resource with a purpose: to understand the organization's history, the current position and the trends to inform the organization design. It is made up of hard and soft evidence; both are equally important. The formal and the informal are both vital in how an organization works. An evidence base gathers together insight from different perspectives, for instance: the chart and the heart; the planned and the emergent; the expressed and the tacit. Here you will be looking for facts and figures and analysis of these as well as opinions and feelings.

The trend for using rich evidence bases for management decisions is not unique to organization design. Leading organizations, such as Tesco, Google, Coca-Cola, and Capital One use evidence-based techniques in their strategic decision-making to drive their competitiveness. The authors have applied the same rationale for many years in their organization design work. Evidence-based management can change how every manager thinks and acts. It is a way of seeing the world and thinking about the craft of management. The main idea is that using better, deeper logic and employing facts enables leaders to do their jobs better. Evidence-based management entails facing the hard facts about what works and what doesn't. A great book on the subject is Pfeiffer and Sutton's (2006) *Hard Facts, Dangerous Half-Truths and Total Nonsense: Profiting from evidence-based management.* Using an evidence base allows the exercise of sound judgement and results in informed choices about the new design and how to implement it. The evidence base allows you to address questions with an evaluative and qualitative approach. As in all management, informed decision-making correlates very closely with better outcomes than decisions based on assumptions, anecdotal experience, and the occasional hunch. Implementing an organization design is a serious step for any organization. It will impact how the organization performs in future and it will impact the lives of the people that make up the organization as well as its customers. The outcomes can be positive or negative. With so much at stake, it is important to make the best judgements available: a good evidence base is the first significant step to achieving that in organization design. Some uses of an evidence base are to:

- assess the gap between where the organization is currently and where it needs to be in the future;
- inform judgements about possibilities and potential as the future design options are mapped out;
- assist in preparing financial models, employee models and cost-benefit cases to help see the impact of design choices;
- support consultation processes with unions, regulators, and third-party suppliers that have a stake in the design outcomes;
- inform the programme planning and scheduling of the implementation.

You are looking for a level of detail in an evidence base that is appropriate for the design decisions to be made. Watch out for getting bogged down in pursuing spurious accuracy in constructing an evidence base. Usually you collect data at three levels. Start at the organizational level above the one you are designing; then cover the organization you are designing; then its immediate reporting level. Only consider going down another level if the situation is very complex or large. You may find that you need to vary your questions for different levels being reviewed and you may need more precise information at lower levels. As you drill down more levels and into more information, it may be unnecessary to cover every unit or it may be irrelevant to repeat all the questions, eg if incentives and rewards are the same throughout all the levels then you will not need to repeat the research.

There is skill and judgement to apply, in seeking out and sensing the best available evidence. Possible sources of data to draw out knowledge on the organization include:

For hard evidence:

- formally published documentation, eg annual reports to shareholders;
- internal reports, eg business plans;
- HR for employee databases and information;
- finance for management accounts and budget information;
- management information systems.

For the soft evidence:

- company intranets: to see what is promoted, celebrated and held as examples;
- new joiner induction materials: what newcomers are told about in terms of the values, styles, and behaviours required;
- press releases that show how the organization wants to be seen;
- employee surveys;
- physical evidence; eg how are visitors greeted; what is on people's desks; what is in the company newsletter?

Programme information already gathered:

- working papers from the individual interviews on the programme and design context;
- the design brief?

And include:

- questionnaire surveys;
- interviews (face-to-face and telephone-based) as well as discussion groups.

Tool 6.1 helps you establish an evidence base for the organization you are designing. Here the Organization Design Compass is used to ensure that evidence is collected across all areas of the organization. Often the Work quadrant is very tangible and well understood in organizations and a simple, short question set is sufficient to get to the core answers. But if your organization has intangible products or services then you may need to expand on these questions to get a clear understanding of the current position.

Tool 6.1 Establishing the evidence base

Who to involve

This step is carried out by members of the design team who can draw on executives and managers with knowledge of the organization as well as functions such as Finance and HR; all of whom can provide relevant and useful information. For soft evidence: HR including talent management is essential. Although people in an organization are often best placed to articulate the current state, experience shows that they can take a 'rose-tinted' view when assessing their current organization. Consider approaching the organization's customers or suppliers to challenge any self-assessments undertaken.

Instructions

As you do this respect any confidential or 'off the record' statements from interviewees. Establish what you need information on:

- Establish what levels of the organization to consider.

- Formulate a set of questions and topics that you need evidence on. Table 6.1 has a prompt list to get you started. They can be used to help you tailor your own question sets to suit your situation.

Identify appropriate sources to answer your questions:

- Identify people and areas that can help, eg executives, managers and representatives of functions.

- Identify reports, systems and other information sources.

Draw out the relevant information, collate, and document the evidence base as you go:

- Carry out desk research from the information sources.

- Hold interviews and discussions with individuals and groups identified. You may want to tailor prompt lists for different interviews, workshops or discussion groups.

- Keep sketches that people draw of the organization charts. How individual people see the structure may vary from official organization charts and both are evidence.

- Sometimes the stated values differ from those observed. (ie espoused values and the theories in use – Argyris and Schön, 1974). Be alert and note differences.

- People in the organization may hold different opinions; the variations are part of the evidence.

For all the significant data include:

- Sources for the evidence and the date that it applies to.

- Whether the facts presented are exact or estimates.

- If estimates are included, document any assumptions made.

- Dates, times and names of participants at meetings.

- Original outputs from workshops recorded digitally.

Observe and note soft evidence as you do this, add this to your evidence base:

- Listen out for the kinds of language people use in the organization.

- Observe how people treat each other within the organization and how they interact.

- Note characteristics of how people behave: are they professional, friendly, formal, social, open, or directive?

- Observe how meetings are run; are they focused on goals, for socializing ideas or both?

Review the evidence base once all the information is collated:

- Review and critically appraise it, assess its validity and separate personal opinions from hard facts.

- Analyse and summarize the evidence base so the salient points are presented for the design team and other stakeholders that will use it.

- Some evidence you uncover will be contradictory. For example, in establishing how many people work in part of an organization, you may get a range of answers from different sources. 'People' may be counted differently and it may be hard to tease out exactly what any particular figure includes: is it full-time permanent, full-time equivalents, excluding those on maternity leave (or including them), counting contractors or agency people or not? There is lots of scope for variation. You will need to apply judgement on the significance of the differences for your purposes and whether you need to resolve them or not. Soft evidence can be contradictory too.

Outputs

- Working papers:
  - Master prompt list for establishing the evidence base.
  - Tailored prompt lists for establishing the evidence base.
  - Meeting, workshop, and discussion group notes.

- A summary of the key evidence: to share with the steering committee, sponsor, and other stakeholders. This generally contains: a high-level picture of the organization; a one-page overview; and one page per Compass quadrant with key hard and soft evidence.

- A detailed evidence base: that will be the ongoing resource for the design team. There is no set way of documenting the evidence base. The aim is to ensure that it can be read and understood by anyone who may use it subsequently. The evidence base often has a longevity that goes way beyond its original programme and can become part of the knowledge base of the organization. We have seen instances where a detailed evidence base collated for one programme has been used for many years in a multitude of subsequent change programmes. A badly documented evidence base can be misinterpreted down the line, leading to misunderstandings and poor decisions.

The reality of building an evidence base

Although, building an evidence base is vital it is time-consuming. It is frustrating how often organization design interventions start with a team of consultants locked in the basement for months. As excel sheets emerge with requests for data and yet more data, the business speculates over what is intended. In almost every case it becomes painfully clear that the data available is messy, fragmented and incomplete. Exceptions are the rule. The traditional tools for resolving this are excel spreadsheets, supplementary excel spreadsheets, an occasional access database and lots of late hours by sleepless team members. Although an organization design intervention will need to have a clear baseline, the effort to put one together can be a killer, causing disputes and wasted management time. Even what may seem basic information can be missing. On occasions, the Group HR Director does not know how many people work in HR across the whole organization and the Group Finance

TABLE 6.1 Prompt list for establishing an evidence base

Evidence base prompt list

Organization
- What is the purpose of the organization?
- What are its key outputs?
- Who does it provide these for?
- How old is this organization?
- What are the significant milestones in its history?
- What is the organization's current budget?
- How have budgets changed over time?
- Why have they changed?
- Are there any relevant external guidelines, eg current and future regulations and legislation?
- Future projections, eg industry and organization projections of workload.
- Are there any higher-level design principles preferred or mandated for the organization?
- What other change programmes or projects are progressing in the organization that will impact the future design?
- How will these change programmes impact the future design?
- What is the timescale for these change programmes?

Work
- What are the most significant work processes in the current organization?
- What are the key operating mechanisms and information flows that support these?
- What is the core information required?
- How well does the organization work?
- How smoothly do the processes operate?

Structure
Current formal structure:
- How is the organization structured?
- How well defined is the structure?
- Is it followed?
- How well defined are the boundaries between areas?
- Is the structure static or changing frequently?
- What is the business reason for this?
- What percentage of the organization do these make up?

Roles and Responsibilities: How clearly defined are they?

TABLE 6.1 *continued*

Evidence base prompt list

Current resourcing:

- What are current employee numbers?
- What are current employee profiles, eg by grade, service length, age, skills?
- What characterizes the employee, eg full-time versus part-time, agency versus direct employee?
- What are the key competencies in the organization?

History:

- How has this changed over time?
- Why?

Information on the informal structure:

- Who is really key to making the current organization work?
- What makes the current organization work?
- What ad hoc working groups exist beyond the formal structure?
- Who is involved in them?
- What do these groups achieve?

Enablers

Incentives and rewards

- How are units incentivized and rewarded?
- How does the organization disincentivize and penalize unwanted results and activity?
- Who sets both of these?
- How closely are unit rewards linked with business performance?
- How are units managed when they do not perform as expected?
- What are salary increases and bonuses based on?

Goals and metrics

- How are organization goals and metrics established?
- What are the key performance indicators?
- How does the organization perform against expectation?
- How does the organization perform against competition?
- Who sets broad business goals?
- How are they communicated to stakeholders, eg customers, employees, suppliers/partners?

TABLE 6.1 *continued*

Evidence base prompt list

Governance

- What types of governance structures exist and why, eg boards, committees, councils?
- How do they relate to each other and the structure described above?
- What external mechanisms govern the organization, eg regulations, service or supply contracts, audits?
- What external standards are in place, eg quality standards, accreditation, industry bodies?
- What are the key control mechanisms and processes?
- What is the balance between formal and informal control?
- How are approvals granted?
- How are major decisions made and who is involved?
- Are vetoes common or unusual?
- Is single point accountability or group decision-making favoured?
- Who really makes the decisions?
- How effective, integrated and understood are the governance structures, processes and mechanisms?
- How well do they function?

Norms and behaviours

- What are the organization's values?
- What are its key beliefs?
- What styles and behaviours are recognized?
- How would you describe the style of the leaders and managers?
- What behaviours are exhibited?
- How do people treat each other?
- What gets rewarded and celebrated?
- Who are held up as role models and why?

Input from HR including talent management

- What is included in new joiner induction?
- How are managers trained?
- How is employee engagement done?
- What language is used, eg when referring to colleagues, customers, timescales?

Director does not know how much cost is attributable to finance in the Finance function.

And after the data has been collected at great cost and used once, how does the business keep the value of this asset? Unless the data and information are maintained the knowledge is lost and not available as the organization design is embedded and the organization evolves. How do you use this valuable starting point for subsequent design interventions without having to reinvent the wheel? Research shows that organization design reoccurs with increasing frequency – averaging five to six times per year for HR professionals interviewed. Later on in the book, we propose using a design authority to maintain design integrity. But design authorities and HR professionals need a toolkit that is maintainable to make this work easier.

Let's take the people data. To keep the data fresh, it is great if, for instance, HR can make the data operationally useful, day-in, day-out. And to get more value out of the data, link datasets across from one aspect of the business to another: people–roles–clients – competencies–products. This is enormously powerful. Each linkage adds insight, answers key questions and helps to reinforce the value of the people data. An example of such a tool that is really helpful is OrgVue, made by London-based technologists and organization design advisors Concentra. OrgVue is a cloud-based software system focused on people data. It captures data on multiple aspects of the organization, and lets users analyse, visualize and ask questions 'through' the organizational system. It finally addresses the long-held wish for a holistic approach – a system-view. The Dean of Westminster Business School, Barbara Allen, described it as, 'a radical and welcome step forward in organization design and development ... It's the whole approach to thinking more clearly about people, their roles, the skills they need and what they do.'

RS Components, an international logistics firm headquartered in the UK, and with 6,500 people in 29 countries around the world uses OrgVue. An old-style full HR MIS overhaul would have taken one to two years and several millions of pounds. Instead, it used OrgVue to consolidate data quickly from more than 50 separate HR datasets. It set up automatic data uploads each month. As a result it has been able to move from a fragmented view of staff across the business to a single global view of its workforce, diversity, costs and headcount. As a result, it has an evidence base that it can build on and use as the organization evolves.

Getting further insight

An evidence base not only gives you facts and figures, and soft data, importantly it can also lead to new insight. 'Insight is one of the chief sources of design thinking' says Tim Brown (2009) and he suggests we observe how people improvise their way through their daily lives. Not everything is at it appears to be in your own organization. If you look closely at what is happening you may find 'positive deviants'. Positive deviants are those who are succeeding even as others struggle. Somehow, the positive deviants have found a better way to do things, even with access to the same assets.

The term 'Positive Deviance' originated in 1990 in a book by Marian Zeitlin, a Tufts University nutrition professor, *Positive Deviance in Child Nutrition*. She compiled a dozen surveys that documented the existence of 'positive deviant' children in poor communities who were better nourished than others. The positive deviance concept was operationalized as a tool to promote behaviour and social change interventions around the world (see Pascale and Sternin, 2005; and Pascale, Sternin and Sternin, 2010). In the UK, the work of Jane Lewis at Woodward Lewis LLP has taken this a step further by developing a methodology and tools to ensure you can unearth positive deviance within organizations. This is Hidden Insights®.

This is important for organization design because major interventions in organizations tend to focus on the current state, the desired outcome, the process to get there and the management of fear and resistance. And often when interventions start with an assessment of where the organization is today, there is a tendency to focus the discussion unproductively on the negative experiences that have led to the current situation. Ironically strengthening the link from the 'old organization' to the 'new form' can increase the barriers to change unless both the negative management of fear and resistance and the positive aspects of energy and achievement are managed.

Organization design has now evolved to recognize the importance of keeping what people are proud of, focusing on the positive. As Zig Ziglar says, 'positive thinking will let you do everything better than negative thinking will'. Positive deviance has been shown to go beyond understanding what is good but also can provide strategic insight in terms of options for where the organization could move to (Lewis, 2007). Hidden Insights® is well named. A recommended addition to the designers' toolset.

An alternative method to start with the positive is Appreciative Inquiry.

> This is a method for studying and changing social systems (groups, organizations, communities) that advocates collective inquiry into the best of what is in order to imagine what could be, followed by collective design of a desired future state that is compelling and thus, does not require the use of incentives, coercion or persuasion for planned change to occur.
>
> (Bushe, 2013)

There are many good resources on Appreciative Inquiry, for instance the *Appreciative Inquiry Handbook* by Cooperrider, Whitney and Stavros (2008).

In outlining your brief, you may have learned lessons from other organizations. This time go beyond high-level observations, to explore external organizations at a deeper level, to understand aspects of how they are organized. The aim of this activity is to learn from external organizations; obtaining information to help shape your future organization's design. There is probably already a lot of knowledge and experience to hand. The various leaders involved in the programme will bring their previous experiences of organization design and change. You may also be able to call on the knowledge of others within your organization with relevant experience.

Optionally you can augment in-house knowledge with specific primary or secondary research into other organizations; it can be helpful particularly where there is a radical change from the current situation. For example, in early 2010 the UK Civil Service Operational Efficiency Programme investigated the ratio of HR employees to total employees. The Civil Service average ratio was 1:44 compared with UK medium-large companies' average ratio of 1:127. The Operational Efficiency Programme set a target of 1:77 for the Civil Service: based on analysing the detail behind the headline numbers and using that analysis to produce an appropriate ratio for their needs. This is a good example of comparing organizations and applied learning.

Primary research involves visiting other organizations to observe them and interview their people to learn about how they are organized and understand why they are organized that way. Study tours of several different organizations can be used if you need a range of different views. Senior executive networks can give access to other organizations, so can local business groups, and trade associations. Customers and suppliers can be useful cooperative sources. However, primary research is an expensive option. Before embarking on it, set out clearly the questions that you want answers to; identify the organizations you want to study; and decide how you want to collect data. Simple data can be exchanged by using a questionnaire either by post or email or through a phone survey. A site visit will give you a much better feel for how an organization operates. If you use primary research, be prepared to reciprocate and share information about your organization with those organizations that you are getting information from.

Secondary research is where you use published material and carry out desk-based research to interpret that information. Secondary research is cheaper than primary research but it is also less easy to find answers to specific questions. Be conscious of the trade-offs. There are many possible sources including:

- professional benchmarking companies;
- business schools;
- published reports; for instance Corporate Executive Board publications;
- external consultancies;
- specialist research groups in the organization's area; for instance, Gartner or Forester for IT, and Merchants, a Dimension Data company for call centre benchmarking;
- asking questions through professional networking groups; for instance, the Organization Design Forum, LinkedIn.

Whichever route you adopt in your data collection, it is best to document the 'internal and external insight' in terms of the Organization Design Compass. This will help you when you use it. Include a description of the insight you have found, which organization it works for as well as why, and what and who your information source(s) are.

Assessing the direction and extent of change

The summary of the key evidence provides a view of the current state. Next you envision the organization's future state and carry out a gap analysis to assess the direction and extent that it needs to change. The focus of the gap analysis is on what and how much of the organization needs to change to deliver the future strategy. It is about looking at the organization's fitness for where it is going and what it needs to do to get there, rather than assessing its current fitness. In the same way that if you decide to run a marathon, you need to take stock of your current fitness and establish how much training you need to do to be fit enough for the endurance needed.

A workshop approach is the best way to define the future state and assess the gap between the current state and future state organizations. The gap analysis can either be run in the same workshop as identifying the future state or it can be run a few days later. It's best to involve the same people. Running it a few days later allows the design team time to review the earlier workshop and synthesize the outputs. There may be gaps or inconsistencies that the design team will have the chance to review and resolve. Conversely running just one workshop maintains momentum and those involved will get a strong sense of progress. Tool 6.2 describes how to do this; here it is shown as one continuous workshop. A few additional things to consider:

- In facilitating these workshops taking a broad brush view is more important than low-level accuracy and the facilitator should keep the discussions pitched at the high level.
- In the gap analysis, the participants are trying to show direction of movement and extent of travel rather than pinpointing an exact destination.
- The workshop focus is on what will be different, not how that will be achieved, and facilitators need to keep the focus right.
- Getting at future Norms and behaviours can be tricky. It may be useful to ask: what will it look and feel like to customers and employees?

Tool 6.2 Assessing the direction and extent of change

Who to involve

The design team should facilitate the workshop and it is also helpful to involve other members of the design team who need to hear the debate, energy, passion and get a depth of understanding behind the thinking in the output. Involve people drawn from the senior team that have responsibility for the organization being designed; people with knowledge of the context for change including the strategy and operational problems that are triggering the change and people who care about the outcome. We recommend involving a range of people as this helps get understanding and buy-in to subsequent implementation of new organization designs. The more inclusive you can make this step the better.

Inputs

- Environmental complexity and stability framework.

- Work standardization framework.

- Classification of operating mechanisms framework.

- The design brief.

- The summary of the key evidence.

- Internal or external insight.

Instructions

Set up

- Orientation for participants on the design brief using presentations and debate to ensure understanding and to focus the workshop.

Understand the current state.

- Presentation of the summary of the key evidence.

- Review the environmental complexity and stability framework covered in Part One.

- Consider the current organization and plot where it appears on the framework.

- Review the work standardization framework covered in Part One.

- Consider the nature of the work processes in the current organization and plot where the current organization appears on the framework. Would you classify the work as 'craft', 'non-routine', 'routine' or 'engineering'? Does this apply to the whole organization or most of it or are there significant variations across the organization?

- Review the classification of operating mechanisms framework covered in Part One.

- Consider the current organization, plot where it appears on the framework. What is the nature of the operating mechanisms in the organization? Is the classification consistent across the organization or do operating mechanisms vary?

- Discuss what this information is telling you about the current state of the organization.

- Consider the characteristics of the current organization using the Compass to look at each segment in turn; a mind map is a useful tool for capturing your thinking on this (see Figure 6.1).

- Capture the 'current state characteristics': the main 5 to 10 characteristics of the current organization by Compass segment.

- Note any updates to the evidence base at detail and/or summary level that may arise.

Internal and external insight:

- Presentation on insight discovered.

- Discuss what makes them successful and why it is relevant.

- How could this be useful for the organization being designed?

Envision the future state:

- What does the organization need to be like for the future strategy to be fulfilled?

- Review the three frameworks covered in assessing the current organization.

- Consider and plot where the organization needs to be on these.

- Consider the future organization's characteristics by Compass segment.

- What will each segment need to be like to deliver the target capabilities?

- Capture the 'future state characteristics': the main 5 to 10 characteristics by segment.

- A mind map is a useful tool for capturing your thinking on this (see Figure 6.1).

Take stock of the change the organization requires:

- Are there significant changes to your business model in the future; eg consider what and where you source products, services, and resources and distribute them?

- Is the future state different from the current state on the three frameworks used above?

- Identify the changes needed by working around the Compass, taking each segment in turn comparing the current state with the future state. Table 6.2 gives a gap analysis template to use to complete the analysis: for each segment consider:
  - What needs to be kept/retained/protected?
  - What needs to change?
  - How much change is needed?
  - How little change can accomplish the goal?
  - The overall assessment of the amount of change required.
  - How difficult is the change to make?

- A radar chart of change required can be used to show the direction and the extent of change (see Figure 6.2). Assign subjective scores to the Compass segments for the current state and the future state. Plot these on the radar chart.

- It can be very difficult and/or not effective to make changes in all 12 segments at once.

- Consider the Compass: what areas are the most important to the organization to make progress on to deliver its target capabilities and which will have the biggest impact?

- The gap analysis will help this thinking. Establish priorities and preferences for these.

- A heat map of the change required can also be used to show this, focusing on where the programme should focus efforts in design and change. An example of a completed heat map of change required is shown in Figure 6.3.

- Prepare a change specification to accompany the heat map. This should draw on the information from the gap analysis and the priorities and preferences thinking and cover:
  - What needs to be kept/retained/protected?
  - What needs to change?

Outputs

Working papers:

- The current and future organization plotted on:
  - the environmental complexity and stability framework;
  - the work standardization framework;
  - the classification of operating mechanisms framework.
- Other workshop outputs should be captured but do not need writing up formally.

Current and future state:

- The current state characteristics: showing the main 5 to 10 characteristics of the current organization by Compass segment.
- The future state characteristics: showing the main 5 to 10 characteristics of the future organization by Compass segment.

Design and change requirements:

- Gap analysis: showing the characteristics of the change required by Compass segment.
- Radar chart of change required: showing the direction and extent of change required.
- Heat map of change required: showing the priorities for work.
- Change specification: showing what the programme should change and what should remain.

Evidence base updates at detail and/or summary level (if required).

FIGURE 6.1 Organization characteristics template

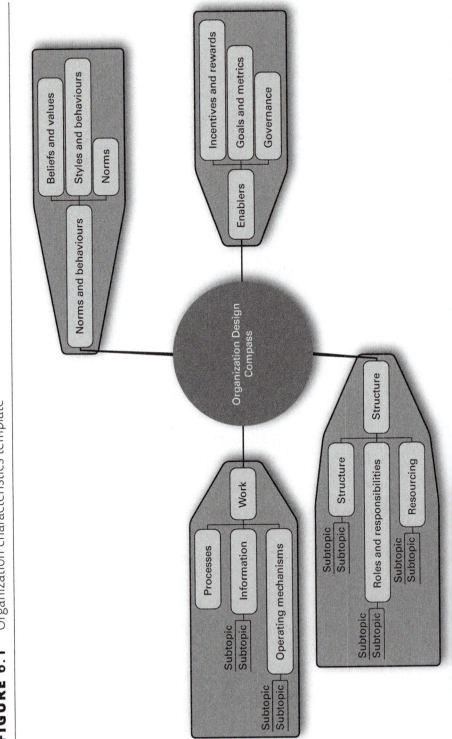

FIGURE 6.2   Example of a radar chart of change required

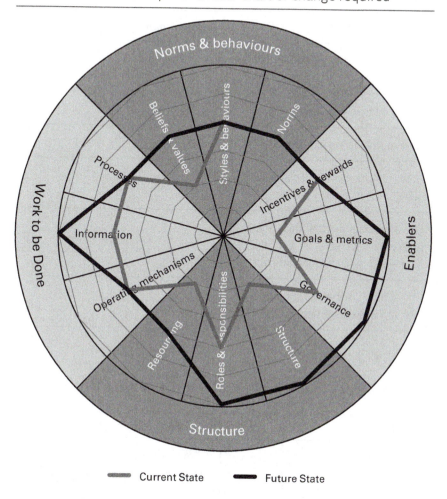

The example shown in Figure 6.3 is based on a Scandinavian learning organization. They started as a small, entrepreneurial company, but at the time of this assessment, the organization had become very successful globally and reached a level of maturity that demanded a step change in their organization. The growth of new business areas resulted in a need to further codify and exploit the skills and assets of the organization and its partner network. The organization had a very strong set of Norms and behaviours that were strongly based on a close knit community at its head office; these needed changing to support the reality of a dynamic global organization.

TABLE 6.2   Gap analysis template

Questions	Segment name
What needs to be kept/retained/protected?	
What needs to change?	
How much change is needed?	
How little change can accomplish the goal?	
Overall assessment of the amount of change required (none/low/medium/high/complete)	
How difficult is the change to make? (not applicable/low/medium/high)	

FIGURE 6.3   Example of a heat map of change required

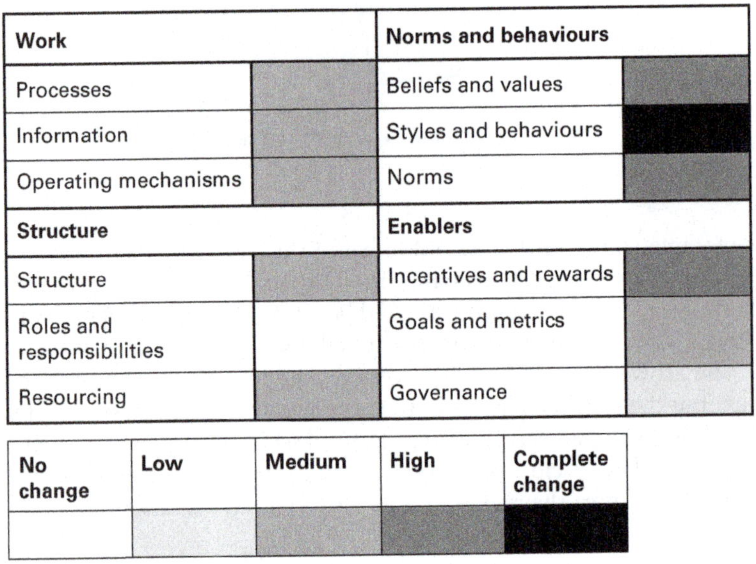

Work		Norms and behaviours	
Processes		Beliefs and values	
Information		Styles and behaviours	
Operating mechanisms		Norms	
Structure		**Enablers**	
Structure		Incentives and rewards	
Roles and responsibilities		Goals and metrics	
Resourcing		Governance	

No change	Low	Medium	High	Complete change

> ### TIP
>
> If your organization is really locked into its current way of thinking or feeling negative about change – try looking at the future first. Give yourselves permission to start with a pristine slate. In this positive environment, articulate your goals in a more optimistic and aspirational context. Focusing clearly on the higher intent of the organization can lead to a greater success in obtaining commitment to a common purpose.

OPTIMAL programme considerations

After this step you have a much clearer picture of the nature of the change required and what the organization wants to pursue across all the segments of the Compass to deliver its strategic intent. You have an assessment of what needs to be done to effectively deliver the target capabilities and move from the current state to the future state organization; which segments will be addressed, and you have a better view of the amount of design and change work that the organization wants to pursue. Make sure all the design team and the wider programme including business user groups are up to date with the latest information. It is important to revisit all aspects of the programme definition and plan because now you have much more detail. It is a good time for a planning day with the whole programme bringing everyone up to date and looking programme-wide at the consequences.

It is vital that this latest view of the design and programme is approved by the sponsor and steering committee; what they want to see differs widely from organization to organization. The important thing to bear in mind is that you are looking for approval to proceed and that the areas you are going to focus your design work on are aligned with your sponsor and steering committee. Tailor a steering committee pack/presentation to meet this need. The contents of this will depend on your organization: it will be highly tailored to the nature of the problem and the steering committee preferences. You will need to judge how much information to take to them for approval. As a guide the pack is likely to include:

- summary of key evidence and the current state characteristics;
- relevant highlights from internal and external insight;
- future state characteristics;
- heat map of change required: showing the priorities for work;
- summary of the change specification: showing what the programme should change and what should remain with commentary on the underlying rationale.

With this further detail on the design programme, the steering committee may wish to review the organization's risk appetite and change appetite so it is advisable to be prepared to discuss:

- options: do it all/do some of it/do none of it;
- analysis of what and who else might be impacted by this programme;
- cost implications (for change and operation of the new design);
- timing estimates for the design and implementation.

The information you take to your steering committee at this stage often becomes an important communication source for circulating and engaging the wider organization. It expresses the changes needed more tangibly than earlier high-level work so the future state organization may now start to become more real for many people. The nebulous is starting to take shape: people can start to see glimpses of how the change may affect their part of the organization and sense what it could mean for them. The HR and change leadership involved in the programme will have an important role in assessing how best to get this across, as well as the work they will need to do throughout the design and implementation phases.

Conclusion

The step really marks a change from strategic thinking and preparation to defining activities. The outcomes from this step are agreement from the sponsor and steering committee to a clearly defined set of changes required by the organization design programme. This will focus the design team's efforts in the next steps of the programme. There will also be a solid knowledge base of evidence and understanding about current organization that can be used throughout the rest of the design phase and into implementation. The outputs produced cover:

Working papers from capturing the evidence base:

- master prompt list for establishing the evidence base;
- tailored prompt lists for establishing the evidence base;
- meeting, workshop and discussion group notes.

Internal and external insight. Current and future state:

- an evidence base: of the current state:
  - a summary of key evidence;
  - a detailed evidence base;
- the current state characteristics: showing the main 5 to 10 characteristics of the current organization by Compass segment;
- the future state characteristics: showing the main 5 to 10 characteristics of the future organization by Compass segment;

- analysis of change required:
  - Gap analysis: characteristics of the gap for each Compass segment;
  - Radar chart of change required;
- direction for the design programme:
  - heat map of change required: showing the priorities for work;
  - change specification: showing what the programme should change and what should remain;
  - updated programme definition and plan (and supporting documents);
- steering committee pack for this step.

Working papers from assessing the direction and extent of change:

- the current and future organization plotted on:
  - the environmental complexity and stability framework;
  - the work standardization framework;
  - the classification of operating mechanisms framework;
- workshop outputs.

On completion of this step you will have the knowledge to lead a design programme in assessing and focusing the design work to deliver the required target capabilities for an organization. Now with a clear view of what is needed: let the design commence. We will move from thinking about what the design must do to thinking about how things must be done. In Steve Jobs's words, 'Design is not just what it looks like and feels like. Design is how it works.'

Identifying assessment criteria

07

In my opinion, no single design is apt to be optimal for everyone. (DONALD NORMAN)

KEY POINTS

Aim:

To establish an evaluation scheme so you can learn from the design options in development. This will help you move from 'reform with rancour' to 'design and concur'.

Activities:

- Defining design principles and criteria.
- Defining a marking scheme.

In this book we have set out to show you how to define the optimal design for your organization to deliver its strategic intent. No single design is likely to be optimal for everyone or from every perspective; there will be many opinions on what the optimal design is for any particular situation. This chapter aims to show you how to identify assessment criteria so that you can ensure you choose the most advantageous design option for your organization and judge the relative strengths and weakness of different design options in meeting your organization's requirements. This is one of the best kept secrets in organization design. This chapter covers what an evaluation scheme is and why you should use one; the evaluation scheme used in the OPTIMAL Way: one based on identifying design principles and criteria; design principles associated with some organization types; and how you can develop design principles and criteria-based evaluation schemes. Using an evaluation scheme is important to an organization because it reduces the impact of preconceptions of outcome and delivers the best-suited design ensuring alignment and trade-offs. It makes the design process better because it is faster, has focus, and has a measure of success. Communication is facilitated increasing the chances of more rational discussions and decision-making, and stakeholder buy-in. Done well, this is one step that pays big dividends and is especially important on larger and/or more complex programmes. You gain an insight into how you can define a suitable evaluation scheme to enable you to assess organization design options.

This step is very straightforward; simply define design principles and criteria and ensure there is a marking scheme you can use with them. It is a very small step in terms of the time and effort. Typically taking only one to two days, with only a couple of people involved whatever the size and complexity of your programme.

Evaluating using design principles and criteria

An evaluation scheme is a means of assessing the extent to which a design meets its objectives. This will help you and others improve the design. There are many reasons why it is helpful to use an evaluation scheme; using one:

Provides focus:

- On strategic issues – because the design criteria are based on design principles it ensures strategic focus is maintained.
- Concentrates design choices on what is most important.

Delivers best-suited design:

- Ensures capabilities required are delivered in the most effective and efficient way by enabling you to select the best-suited design option for your organization.

Ensures alignment and trade-offs:

- It provides another opportunity to ensure all elements of the model you use are covered in the design; that you are aware of the interactions between elements; and that you make conscious trade-offs for the best overall outcome.

Reduces the impact of preconceptions of outcome:

- One of the thorniest challenges faced by designers is when a senior player just 'knows the solution' and cannot be swayed. However, they may be thinking short term rather than strategically and not seeing 'the whole picture'.

Allows more rational discussions and decision-making:

- The problem of preconceptions is compounded when different people have different designs in mind. They are rarely the same but this provides a framework for making trade-offs.
- The results from a design generally have major implications on people, their jobs, their teams, and their lives. There will be political and emotional standpoints. Almost everyone believes they and their people are doing good and worthwhile work for their organization. Any sense of removing or redesigning that is felt personally.
- Design criteria helps people focus on the business issues and gives them a chance to test their opinions but reduces the negative aspects of power politics.

Facilitates communication:

- Facilitates documentation of the rationale for choices made.
- Facilitates the communication of the rationale for the choices made. There is a lot to be said, in the interests of transparency, for publishing the criteria to key stakeholders. It provides a valuable asset to understanding the thinking behind choices made for the implementation team once design is completed.

Increases chances of stakeholder buy-in:

- It greatly increases your chance of getting stakeholder buy-in both logically and emotionally and so eases the implementation path.

Speeds up the design process:

- Later stages of the design process are quicker as design options that fall short of the criteria can be discarded and only those that pass and are selected are iterated.

Provides measures of success:

- It enables testing and marking by different people.
- It provides relative measures between different options.

The evaluation scheme built into the OPTIMAL Way assesses the design as it is being developed. This is in order to improve the learning and understanding about any particular design and improve design decisions. This evaluation scheme is based on design principles and their related design criteria. The design principles are the guiding set of requirements you design around and which prescribe what your design must (or must not) include laid out as a list of succinct, clear statements. Some of these may be set out in advance of the design programme because they are enterprise-wide. Design criteria are the standards against which to judge the design options you have against your design principles. They include what indicators to look for; and any values that are to be applied. For example, if a design principle is 'the organization must be run at the lowest cost' then design criteria could be based on 'lowest operating cost'. Table 7.1 shows how this works in practice looking at the design principles and criteria for an IT and operations shared service organization.

TABLE 7.1 Shared Service organization design principles and criteria

Design principles	Design criteria
Demonstrably delivers the CIO Strategy including the shared service strategy, outsourcing and follow enterprise 'rules'	• Will deliver our shared service strategy • Supports outsourcing of services • Will not duplicate the demand management function embedded in our client business units • Is credible to our clients and to our people • Enables us to not exceed our financial and headcount targets • Can grow, shrink, change flexibly and rapidly as we outsource services
Embeds capabilities required within three years	• Embeds planning • Embeds sourcing services and components from third parties • Embeds packaging services to achieve economies of scale • Embeds end-to-end service management • Embeds supplier management • Preserves required build-and-run competencies
Simplifies current structure	• Clear single points of accountability: no use of 'joint' in role descriptions • Reduced use of matrix organization structures

TABLE 7.1 *continued*

Design principles	Design criteria
Broadens spans of control	• There will be no long-term 1:1 or 1:2 reporting lines • A minimum ratio of 1:6 to 1:8 will be the target for management roles
Simplifies business process	• One process for one purpose – ie consistent and pervasive use of common processes • Minimizes boundaries between our organization and our clients • Minimizes internal hand-offs • Embeds specific process ownership
Embeds an ethos that is professional, commercial and values shareholder return focused on service and supplier management	• Has a commercial outlook in setting up, pricing and invoicing services • Exercises rigorous financial control on all services provided • Has a strong service management culture • Has a rigorous supplier management culture to ensure they deliver quality services in a timely and cost-effective way
Makes best use of enterprise's resources	• Will use enterprise shared services as far as possible – no duplication • Makes the best use of hard-to-find skills • Reduces costs
Minimizes implementation impact	• Minimizes the number of moves of both job and locations that our people experience (once if possible)

Sometimes the design principles and the related criteria appear the same or almost the same. Consider the situation that a bank on Jersey was facing a few years ago. The island of Jersey has an advantageous tax position that makes it attractive for offshore banking for UK citizens living elsewhere and non-UK citizens working in the UK. But the island is small, has a limited population and strictly controlled immigration. There is virtually 100 per cent employment and new or expanding businesses are stretched to recruit new staff. So when this bank was completing an organization design to manage an increase in its work volume from new services and an expanding customer base, one of its requirements was that any new design should not increase staffing. Here, the design principle was 'the new design should not need more staff than the old design' and the criteria was 'number of future staff relative to current staff'.

Marking is an important part of the evaluation scheme. It provides a judgement of how well a design meets the criteria set. The resulting scores and assessment assist learning and can be used for feedback, for decisions on progression, modification or whether not to pursue further.

The example in Table 7.1 is based on a large multinational whose aim was to create an umbrella IT and operations shared service centre for their business units and head office functions. Their three-year strategy included: migrating services which could be shared from these units, achieving internal efficiencies and consolidation, and subsequently outsourcing components to third parties where effective.

Design principles for selected organization types

Different types of organization are generally associated with different characteristics and this leads to different design principles: some generic to the type and some unique to the organization. Looking at some generic principles for these may help you get a better idea about what design principles are and provide a starting point if the organization you are designing is one these types. Table 7.2 shows example design principles for four types of organization. Product leaders and organizational effectiveness types are self-evident but the other two may be less familiar. 'High-reliability organizations' are those where safety is central to what they do. Nuclear and petrochemical industries are examples. In December 2005 at the Buncefield Oil Storage Depot in Hemel Hempstead vapour was ignited, triggering the largest explosion in Britain since the Second World War. In 2009, the official report from the UK Government's inspectors was published. Included in this was the recommendation calling for operators to build and operate 'high-reliability organizations'. The key characteristics they listed inform the design principles below. 'Decision-driven organizations' tune their whole organization to identify and make the most important decisions well, at speed and then act on them. They have a clear process for doing this which impacts their organization's design and everything their people do.

TABLE 7.2   Example design principles for four types of organization

Organization type	Example design principles
Product leadership	• Organization must deliver the best products to customers • Organization must constantly encourage product innovation • Organization supports new ventures that exploit innovations • Product marketing is a key to us • Teamworking and information-sharing across groups is easy • Efficient investment appraisal and allocation of resources to new ideas and ventures
Operational effectiveness	• Organization must deliver high volumes of products or service at lowest total cost to customers • Transactions are easy, pleasant, quick and accurate • Standardization of processes, tools and methods • Minimize waste • Minimize overhead costs
High reliability	• Safety is the primary organizational objective • Reliability takes precedence over efficiency • When systems and processes fail, they must 'fail safe' • Organization must constantly evaluate itself for unexpected problems • Embed appropriate target capabilities • Embed risk management and assessment • Seeks the advice and counsel of experts • We learn from mistakes: all accidents are reported and their root causes examined
Decision-driven	• Organization must improve its decision-making – prioritized on value • Organization must clear the bottlenecks in its decision-making • Organization must have clear roles and accountabilities • Organization must involve the right people at the right level in the right part of the organization at the right time • The goal is to act on the decisions made • Speed and adaptability are crucial • People need to clearly understand their roles in decision-making (if any) • When there is a conflict of hierarchy, decision roles outrank structural roles

Defining design principles and criteria

In defining design principles and criteria it is helpful to have a framework to ensure you consider every area. We find it easiest to reflect on strategic intent; operational efficiency and effectiveness; resource information gathered in earlier steps; ease of implementation and wider organizational level design principles (see Table 7.3). The principles and the criteria are then reviewed for completeness. Design criteria should be measureable wherever possible and:

- may not always stem from principles;
- may measure absolute values;
- may measure relative differences between options;
- may require a yes or no response;
- may have threshold levels;
- may be the same as a design principle, eg supports shared services;
- may be set out as questions or statements.

Tool 7.1 Defining design principles and criteria

Who to involve

Only a couple of senior people from the design team that have worked on developing the target capabilities and/or diagnosing the capability gaps need to be involved. HR Directors are often well placed to be included as they are generally aware of existing principles, both explicit and tacit. Optionally add a design authority, if you have one, or you may choose to use them as a reviewer of your output prior to approval. Those involved will require access to the wider organization so they can clarify requirements as they develop criteria.

Inputs

Insight and information gathered when you outlined the brief and took stock of the changes required including, the design brief, the analysis of change required and the direction for the design programme.

In addition, some organizations have organization design principles that they have already decided will apply to all new designs within the organization. For instance, a business unit within a large corporation might need to be cognizant of the enterprise design principle that 'all Corporate

Services, eg HR, Finance, are to be delivered to business units through shared service centres and centres of expertise'. Another that we have seen is 'any new organization must have no more than five layers'.

Instructions

- Use the prompts in Table 7.3 to help you consider and work out what to include on your list of design principles and criteria. Aim for approximately 12 design principles based on the big things and one to five design criteria per principle.
- Once you have a first-pass set of design principles and criteria, review and refine them.
- Confirm the marking scheme and if required, relative weighting.

Review and refine the principles and criteria

You will have covered most of the Compass in doing this. As a final check for completeness:

- Do your principles and criteria cover every quadrant?
- Are they aligned and not contradictory?
- Is the balance right?
- Are any limits and boundaries that need to be reflected, covered?
- Is it clear what is different in the future organization from the current one and what it means?
- Do they differentiate your organization from others?
- Do they consider all aspects of the organization?

Confirm the marking scheme

- Are the criteria measurable wherever possible?
- Are the criteria consistently written so that a high score for each criterion represents a favourable result and a low score represents an unfavourable result?
- Use a four-point rating scale 1 = poor, 2 = fair, 3 = good and 4 = excellent.
- For a no/yes response: rate no = 1, yes = 4.
- Where a benchmark must be met, eg must operate with a budget of £x million: rate fail = 1, pass = 4.

- Where a score cannot be made in an early pass; leave these blank or score them zero.

- Are some criteria more important than others either, because they are more tightly aligned to delivering the strategy or because of limits and constraints?

- Do you need to weight at criteria or principle level? Say: low, medium or high or on a numerical scale or just mark some as critical.

Outputs

A completed design principles and criteria marking scheme. Table 7.4 shows the template for this. Table 7.1 shows design principles and criteria for an IT and operations shared service organization.

OPTIMAL programme considerations

It is good practice to get the design principles agreed by the steering committee and the design criteria agreed by the programme manager and sponsor. It can help with buy-in and feedback if these are discussed with other stakeholders.

Conclusion

Having the basis agreed to choose an optimal design option for your organization that reduces the politics and emotion later on in the programme may sound like the Holy Grail. However that is the outcome from this step. You can move from 'reform with rancour' to 'design and concur'. Having the ground rules laid down can be comforting. You have clarification and agreement of how you will assess your design options. This is clearly set out in your design principles and criteria marking scheme. They can be tailored to the needs of your organization design programme; it is immaterial if other programmes and organizations choose differently. As David Gill former CEO of Manchester United Ltd said, 'All I can do is assess the value from a Manchester United perspective. Whatever Chelsea do, they may have a different criteria, and different financial assets.' By the time you complete this step you will have the knowledge to put in place an evaluation scheme based on design principles and criteria that is impartial, balanced, and aligned to the organization's strategic direction. Now we start designing the organization.

TABLE 7.3   Prompts for design principles and criteria

Consider the organization's strategic requirements and capabilities

- Are some of your requirements more or less important?
- What trade-offs are demanded by the strategy?
- What products, markets and services are emphasized?
- Have earlier discussions steered you towards one or more archetypes or metaphors?
- Do these archetypes or metaphors suggest principles or criteria to you?
- Does any phrase constantly recur that implies characteristics, eg customer-focused, lean?
- Does the design need to be flexible enough to adapt to future changes?
- Are particular norms, values or behaviours desired?

Consider whether designs will operate efficiently and effectively

- Are the unit's boundaries sensible?
- Are accountabilities effective and in line with strategic intent?
- Will it motivate the talent you want to keep and attract?
- Can you clearly identify the critical deliverables for each unit?
- Can you clearly identify the performance measures for each unit?
- Will the performance measures make sense to stakeholders too?
- Are there specific expensive specialists that you need to highlight?
- Do you need to consider nurturing and grouping any talent pools?
- Do you have specialist cultures or talent pools to consider?
- Do any groups need to operate outside the prevailing corporate culture?
- Do you need to consider the number of layers in a hierarchy?
- Or spans of control/accountability/influence/support?

Consider the resource information gathered in earlier OPTIMAL steps

- As well as evidence what clues did you pick up about resources?
- What are the financial constraints?
- Are there any people constraints, eg headcount, recruitment policies?
- Have you considered the hidden constraints?
- How easy is it to recruit to fill gaps?

TABLE 7.3 *continued*

Consider ease of implementation

- Are leadership and talent accessible to deliver this?
- Are there key players you need to keep through implementation?
- Where are the required skills for the future?
- Does your design help get and keep commitment of key stakeholders?
- Consider barriers to success due to any constraints.
- Consider the availability of people and funding to implement the design.

Consider design principles from your wider organization

- Are there any higher-level design principles that you must adhere to?

TABLE 7.4 Design principles and criteria marking scheme

Design Principles	Design Criteria	Marking	Weight

Mapping the design options

Robert McNamara taught me never make a major decision without having a choice of at least vanilla or chocolate. And if more than a hundred million dollars were at stake, it is a good idea to have strawberry too. **(LEE IACOCCA)**

KEY POINTS

Aim:

To develop alternative design concepts for assessment. Post-assessment, to refine selected design options and develop more detailed design outlines.

Activities:

- Generating design concepts:
  - Understanding the Work to be done.
  - Sketching out the Structure.
  - Bringing Norms and behaviours alive.
  - Compiling and aligning the design concept.
- Developing design outlines:
  - Exploring Work in more detail.
  - Developing the Structure in more detail.
  - Shaping the Enablers.
- Compiling and aligning the design outline.

After getting agreement on the direction and scale of the change required and identifying the evaluation scheme, you move on to generating options for the new organization's design. The aim of this chapter is to develop and refine alternative design options for the organization to choose from. The chapter sets out how to develop a number of options, at a concept level first, then how to develop selected options into more detailed, design outlines. It is important not to settle on 'a solution' too early, or to waste time and effort pursuing too many options too far. The process of developing and refining ideas is neither straightforward nor linear. We urge you to deliberately set out to create several design options and not to rush headlong into the first feasible one that springs to mind. More flavours are better when the scale is large, novel, or complex. In organization design, as in any design process, you are trying to open up possibilities and break down incorrect assumptions about the limits of the challenge. The role of the design leader is to stimulate and encourage lateral thinking and unlock the imagination, ingenuity, and inspiration in their team. Use ideas to spark more ideas. Following this chapter you will gain the skills to generate designs that meet your design brief, moving from the concept level to outline level.

This is a highly creative step. This design process is evolutionary and deliberately involves many dialogues and conversations to see different perspectives, both from the people involved and in terms of how the future organization might work. This allows ideas to be explored, repeated, refined, practised, worked over, discarded, and combined. To quote Seth Godin, 'You win by trying. And failing. Test, try, fail, measure, evolve, repeat, persist.' As you look at your future organization from different perspectives you sketch out one part, look at another; reflect, if necessary adjust the ones you already have done as you go. The process is akin to spinning plates moving back and forward as you define elements: the objective is to define options so that all the parts balance and work together.

In the OPTIMAL organization design approach, organizations are designed in three stages (see Figure 8.1). This is a staged approach based on practice and experience; many other design practices follow a similar pattern. In this approach you consider more options at earlier stages, and then increase the level of detail and areas developed as you progress through the stages. The first two stages are covered in this chapter. To start with, you produce a few, very high-level concepts, then you assess these. The feedback from assessing the alternatives allows you to eliminate some, adjust some, and perhaps generate more ideas that you want to look at. Then, at outline level you develop selected ones further, adding more detail to produce the design outlines, which are in turn assessed. Assessment for both of these stages is covered in the next chapter.

The final stage of the high-level design is to take a chosen design outline – the optimal one to deliver the organization's strategic intent and target capabilities – and produce a design blueprint. This stage is covered in the final step of the OPTIMAL Way. The aim at the end of that stage is akin to an architect getting to the point where they can provide sufficient specification for a builder to pick up and complete their work. Laying out the way forward

FIGURE 8.1 The OPTIMAL design and assessment process

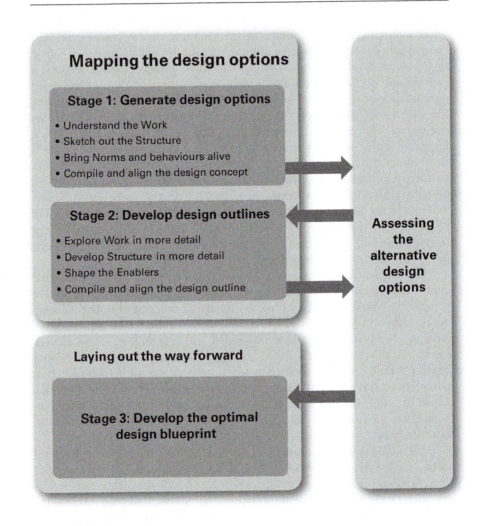

establishes how to take that high-level design down to the 'builder's specification' and in organizational terms into implementation. Beyond that, there is more low-level design work for the line manager who will design and adjust within the frameworks specified to meet their developing needs over time.

As you move through design levels, outputs from the previous stage are subsumed and updated where appropriate, becoming part of the definition for the next level. So a design concept may contain elements retained from the current organization as detailed in the change specification plus outputs from elements generated in the design concept stage. Similarly, a design outline contains elements carried forward from the design concept stage plus the outputs from the design outline stage and so on. Appendix 4 lists the design outputs produced by level and Compass segment.

This is the most complex step in the OPTIMAL Way and it takes the most time in the design phase of the programme. It is difficult to generalize how long this step takes to carry out. It largely depends on the size and complexity of the organization you are designing. Designing options for a team of 50 people is much quicker than an organization with many sub-units, complex supply chains and 10,000 people.

Generating design concepts

Practise safe design: Use a concept.

(Petrula Vrontikis)

Generating design concepts takes the inspiration and ideas from the work you have done in outlining the brief and taking stock of the change required. It draws on the formal outputs, insight, and information produced and documented in those steps. It also draws on all the intangible learning gained so far. You start by taking these ideas and generating embryonic design concepts which have some 'shape' to help the team and organization learn and reflect. Explore pieces of the design that trigger your thinking. Here you are looking at aspects that are essential to how the organization might work and which will drive the design, eg how social networking could change the operation. These ideas may be from the original inspiration that drove the programme to be initiated or themes that have emerged during conversations and dialogues in earlier OPTIMAL steps. You are looking for a range of ideas to galvanize the development of different concepts.

The Compass is used to frame debates throughout design. It does not matter which quadrant you start in, because you will need to explore all the quadrants and revisit earlier ones again as your thinking evolves. The process is not linear and you will circle round developing ideas as you go. The change specification highlights which elements of the current organization are fixed and also the quadrant with greatest impact on the future design – often Work or Structure. The quadrant with the greatest change is generally the best place to start. If you have no preconceived ideas of where to start, begin with the Work quadrant, this is where we start below.

The process below shows how to generate one concept. Repeat the process to generate and explore further concepts. Even if you are designing a small team try to conceive several concepts. The precise number of concepts you generate will depend on the nature of the challenge you have and the decision-making approach agreed with the sponsor and steering committee. If you have no steer we recommend you aim to generate three to five design options at concept level. In the different high-level design concepts:

- Often the key work processes are the same in different design concepts but the work processes use different operating mechanisms; for example automated versus manual.

- There are usually many different ways of structuring and different concepts generally have different structures.

- Different structures can influence the key work process. For example outsourcing is a structural option and in an outsourced structure service, management processes are the key processes rather than production processes.

- Norms and behaviours are usually similar between design concepts and the set you define for your first design concept may well need little, if any, adjustment for subsequent concepts.

Think like a designer. This stage is about divergent thinking. At this stage in other professions they may roughly sketch out dozens of different ideas and quickly narrow them down. Even if these first sketches seem strange they may provoke insights and ideas that are important.

TIP

To generate new ideas, try listing the assumptions you have behind a concept and then challenge the assumptions to diverge ideas.

Understanding the Work to be done

The first thing to look at is what the organization that you are designing has to do to fulfil its role and deliver its outputs. All organizations have work processes whether they are small or large: vertically integrated or networks of loosely connected individuals or groups. Levels of formality in defining work processes differ between organizations. A bank lending to personal customers has very formal, rigidly defined processes which ensure fairness and impartiality in lending decisions. AstraZeneca has formal knowledge harvesting processes in its research groups. In contrast, a master carpenter creating a bespoke piece of furniture has very informal processes; the craftsman's skills are more important; and knowledge sharing via informal internet-based interest groups is also often based on informal processes within the groups.

Tool 8.1 shows you how to identify and document your key future work processes at a high level. Apply this at a level of formality that suits the organization being designed. Focus on the major work processes that are customer- or market-facing or central to production, there is no need to cover internal supporting or enabling work processes.

Tool 8.1 Defining key future work processes

Who to involve

Include the design team, particularly those members with process mapping skills, logical thinking, and experience of the work of the organization under design and include senior leaders to provide business input.

Inputs

The inputs for this are the insight and information gathered during the early steps: the design brief, the current and future state, and the change specification.

Instructions

Identify what the key processes are likely to be. Concentrate just on the work processes (customer- or market-facing) not on any supporting or enabling work processes. Examples might be:

- All manufacturing and production processes.
- Servicing customers: including order taking, materials purchase.
- Business development.
- Product or service development.
- Winning new business or new customers.
- Providing after-sales service.

Prompts to help the discussion:

- What products or services will this unit deliver?
- What will the unit manage: eg customers, products, services, channels?
- What will the unit develop, produce, plan, implement, approve, maintain, operate, monitor, provide, find, solve, diagnose?
- Why does the unit do the things identified above?
- Who does the unit do the things identified above for, remembering that customers can be internal or external?

Include any key processes that straddle the boundary of the organization or that can be executed outside of it, eg in an outsourced arrangement or in adjacent organizations within an enterprise organization. However, keep in mind that you are looking at the processes within the organization you are designing and not the wider organization.

Keep the draft list of processes and the notes from the discussion as a working paper. They can sometimes be reused when generating other concepts or later in the design.

Refine the list to focus on the top 7 to 10 only and list these. At the required level of detail you typically focus on no more than this. If there are more, then think about whether they are actually steps in the same process. If there are fewer, fine!

For each key process produce a high-level process map: record on these the inputs, outputs, operational controls, and operating mechanisms. You can use your organization's preferred high-level process mapping approach or use one like the example in Figure 8.2.

Outputs

- List of top 7 to 10 key work processes.

- High-level process maps of key work processes (Figure 8.2 shows a completed example).

- As working papers: list of work processes identified and the notes from the discussion.

You should have a clear view of the most important future work processes that your organization has to carry out.

In the UK National Health Service, Bevan *et al* (2007) reported using a similar approach to produce a list of '10 high impact changes' that they later developed into 10 key service designs with service owners that they were planning to implement consistently well across the country.

Figure 8.2 shows a completed high-level process, 'envelope stuffing', for a print and mail utility company. They mail about 200,000 statements per day. The process takes printed statements on continuous paper rolls, separates them into A4 sheets, selects the right number of sheets to go to each customer, then folds, and stuffs the sheets into envelopes along with appropriate marketing inserts ready for mailing to customers.

When you have completed the process maps, examine the information captured on all of them about the operating mechanisms. Apply a sense check to see if the operating mechanisms are described at the appropriate

FIGURE 8.2   Example of a completed high-level process map

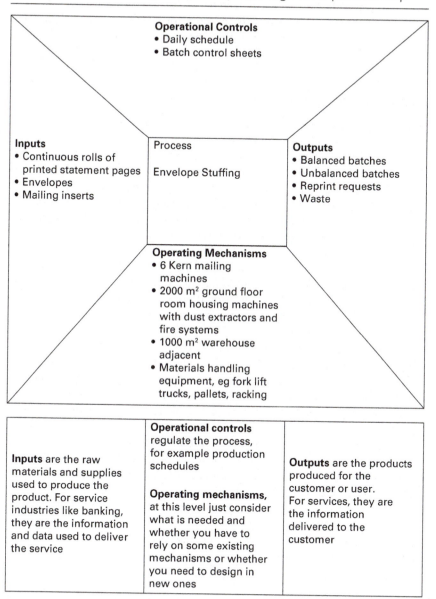

Operational Controls
- Daily schedule
- Batch control sheets

Inputs
- Continuous rolls of printed statement pages
- Envelopes
- Mailing inserts

Process

Envelope Stuffing

Outputs
- Balanced batches
- Unbalanced batches
- Reprint requests
- Waste

Operating Mechanisms
- 6 Kern mailing machines
- 2000 m² ground floor room housing machines with dust extractors and fire systems
- 1000 m² warehouse adjacent
- Materials handling equipment, eg fork lift trucks, pallets, racking

Inputs are the raw materials and supplies used to produce the product. For service industries like banking, they are the information and data used to deliver the service

Operational controls regulate the process, for example production schedules

Operating mechanisms, at this level just consider what is needed and whether you have to rely on some existing mechanisms or whether you need to design in new ones

Outputs are the products produced for the customer or user. For services, they are the information delivered to the customer

level for all the processes. Where processes are assumed to share operating mechanisms, are the descriptions used across the documentation consistent? Revise the key work processes, if necessary. Collate all the information on operating mechanisms and consider the overall picture. If there are significant changes from the current state involve appropriate operations or IT experts, such as business or IT architects, designers, or planners for their insight and comments. They will need to be involved in future operations or technology design work if this design concept is taken forward and their early input is beneficial. As an output, produce a list of operating mechanisms for the top 7 to 10 key work processes.

Sketching out Structure

Next you turn to the Structure quadrant to define the units that will deliver the work. Making choices on the units in the organization separates some activities, functions, and disciplines while combining others. In doing so it shapes the core organization to focus on delivery while de-emphasising less critical work. At the concept stage you identify the main building blocks of the new organization, their responsibilities, and the high-level structure that links them to together. Thinking about structure is not just about considering hierarchical structure: it is also about thinking through how tightly or loosely coupled the structure needs to be and how much structure plays a role in the organization that you are designing. In some organizations, formal structure plays a large part in their design. Other organizations are held together more by a shared organizational purpose and values and they have minimal formal structure, or structures that can be assembled as needed to deliver particular outcomes.

Use Tool 8.2 to create a view of the organization's high-level structure. This is a highly creative exercise rather than an analytic one. Draft and redraft sketches as ideas are explored and thinking developed. There is no sequential process for this, sketch out different thoughts and explore various configurations, iterate this until you have a structure that looks broadly workable.

In deciding on an organization structure, different parts of a large organization may need to work in different ways and a mix of structure types and characteristics may be required. In reality many organizations are hybrids and the skill is in blending structure to the organization's circumstances. If you are considering a hybrid, matrix or multi-dimensional structure, be aware that these can be very easy to sketch on paper but it is much more difficult to get the right mix of skills, norms and behaviour and enablers to make them work in practice.

Tool 8.2 Sketching the structure

To identify the organization's main building blocks, their main responsibilities and linkages.

Aim for simplicity.

Who to involve

Include the design team and representatives from the business user group.

The ideal group size for this is about seven people.

Inputs

- Annotated target capabilities.
- Future state characteristics.
- Analysis of the change required.
- Change specification.
- Working papers from taking stock on the future organization plotted on the three frameworks form 'the essential building blocks'.
- List of top 7 to 10 key work processes.
- High-level process maps of key work processes.
- Organizational Models (archetypes, metaphors, industry/business models).

Instructions

Identifying a concept:

- Review the inputs to focus on the future state required.
- Get any design concepts that individuals already have in mind out on the table early.
- Consider various organizational models for inspiration even the seemingly unpromising.
- A mismatch or disconnect between the model and your situation may spark an idea.
- Do you recognize something in a model that sparks an idea for the future organization?

- Are the group drawn to any particular one that might be the basis of a design concept?

- What are the strengths and weaknesses of the model for your situation?

- What does that tell you about suitable design concepts?

As the design concept emerges, identify the units within the future organization:

- Look at the work documented in the process maps.

- Imagine what main units in the organization could deliver that work.

- What are the units one and two levels below top level responsible for delivering?

- Give a meaningful name to each of these units and list their main responsibilities.

- The organization models may guide and inspire you in naming units.

- At concept stage focus on the units' key responsibilities.

Sketch the organization chart:

- With the units identified, consider what their reporting lines might be.

- Sketch how the units might link together.

- Review relevant organizational models and the frameworks from 'the essential building blocks'.

- Is there additional insight for the structure sketched?

Iterate between the organizational sketch and the draft units:

- Are all key work processes covered within a structure that meets future requirements?

- Is it broadly workable and viable in the organization's context and environment?

Outputs

- Named units drilled down two levels from the top of the organization

- List of the major responsibilities for identified units

- Organization sketch of how units link together.

A structure does not have to be like the pyramids we are so familiar with. In a fascinating article, Caitlin Rosenthal describes Daniel McCallum's 1854 organizational design for the New York and Erie Railroad (regarded as the first organization chart) which resembles a tree rather than a pyramid. It empowered frontline managers by clarifying data flows. It was created in response to the information problem crippling one of the longest railroads in the world. 'In McCallum's chart the hierarchy was reversed: authority over day-to-day scheduling and operations went to the divisional super-intendents down the line, who oversaw the five branch lines of the railroad. The reasoning: they possessed the best operating data, were closer to the action, and thus were best placed to manage the line's persistent inefficiencies' (Rosenthal, 2013). What might you learn if you drew your structure in a different way?

Bringing Norms and behaviours alive

'Norms and behaviours' differs from the other three quadrants in a number of ways; the underlying segments:

- cover the way things get done;
- can awaken people's senses as to where they are going and what it will feel like to be there, connecting people emotionally with an organization;
- are often pervasive across a complete enterprise organization with limited scope to change them further down an organization;
- are the most difficult segments to change, often taking a long time to transform and their implementation can be a big deal because they help make the other segments work together. It is often easier to induct and immerse new recruits than it is to change the practices of years.

Norms and behaviours were examined in taking stock of the change required: in the change specification, what the programme should change and what should remain were captured. In many redesign programmes there will be few changes to be made to these segments. However, there are situations when Norms and behaviours do need to be designed or redesigned. One example is if a new unit is set up that aims to do things radically differently from the rest of the organization. This was very evident in the early incarnations of many e-initiatives, which were often set up heavily ring-fenced from their main organization. Norms and behaviours are also crucial in mergers. In 2006 when Nokia and Siemens announced the merger of their mobile and fixed-line phone network equipment businesses, the newly formed joint Board recognized that creating a unified culture was essential to the success of the new organization. The integration focused on the importance of joint values and behaviours; the aim was for these to shape the design of work processes.

An organization's beliefs and values are vital to all organizations; they can be more important than structure in making an organization work. Salz (2013) repeatedly emphasized this in reviewing Barclays' business practices. This is especially so in organizations that are loosely coupled and with less formally defined structures. Organizational values define the acceptable standards which govern the behaviour of all individuals within the organization. Without such values, individuals (or units within organizations) will pursue behaviours that are in line with their own individual value systems, which may lead to behaviours that the wider organization does not wish to encourage. Strategic beliefs and values are so fundamental to an organization's design that the required ones should have been captured when you outlined the brief for the programme: they will probably include organizational purpose, organization values and strategic intent. The current state beliefs and values should have been ascertained in taking stock of the change required.

At concept level, you need a set of statements that capture the values and looks at the changes from the current state. These are short phrases or words that distil the ethos for the organization and that will have widespread understanding. The aim is to paint a picture of what is required; fleshing out the details will be done in implementation. If there are existing organization values documented you need to annotate them with comments on fitness, highlighting any changes that may be required. We often see this articulated with comments such as: 'more of this' and 'less of that'. In terms of who to involve in producing or reviewing values it really is situational. They can be captured using a top-down approach with strategic leaders or by engaging more widely across the organization. With a smaller team or start-up organization as many people as possible can be involved. The output should be an annotated statement of organizational values.

Styles and behaviours, such as leadership and management styles and behaviours, can be specified and there may be differences between the concepts that you develop. Specifying styles and behaviours can be a leverage point for making lasting changes to organizations. The Work and Structure quadrants specified can inform the way things get done and vice versa. Taking the change specification as a starting point; set out two lists: one for styles and one for behaviours. Capture short statements or phrases that describe the key characteristics needed to make the design work: the styles and behaviours. They may echo some of the sentiments you have already highlighted in beliefs and values. You may want to consider some of the established models of leadership styles, for instance MBTI which is based on the Myers Briggs/Jung typology, to prompt your thinking. You are looking here for major indicators that guide the way, such as the approach to risk. Existing statements may be annotated. The outputs should be two lists of annotated statements: one of leadership and management styles; another of behaviours.

Norms are the established and approved way of doing things: the customary rules of behaviour. You can be very inventive using group exercises to capture norms: some of the emotional feel of the future organization. Although norms may be explicit or implicit in a 'real organization', at concept level your aim should be 'create a sense' of the future organization. Use creative techniques of casting 'the group' forward to the future organization: bring the organization alive and help people 'be there'. There are many great graphic tools for this and lots of ways of doing this: storytelling, coats of arms, painting. Make it fun. The energy will help generate thoughts that may not have come through in the more analytical sessions. Ask open questions like: What does it feel like to work there? What does it feel like to be a customer or supplier? What is rewarded? How is success measured and celebrated? Is there a metaphor for the organization? How do people dress? How do people interrelate with other groups and people? The outputs for this are 'defined norms' in whatever format the technique that you have applied produces them.

Other design professionals sometimes make their purpose and values tangible in their products. The architecture of Oracle Corporation's headquarters on the San Francisco peninsula is shaped like databases. St Ambrose College in Altrincham, Cheshire has been rebuilt shaped as a Celtic cross reflecting its Christian Brothers' heritage. In 1943, Walt Disney Studios issued an organization chart to explain how the company functioned. It was based on their process, from the story idea through direction to the final release of the film. From a distance it looks like a painted clown. How do you bring your values alive?

Compiling and aligning the design concept

Now you bring together all the elements of the design option that you are working on. Design options have outputs from the previous stage subsumed. So a design concept may contain elements retained from the current organization as detailed in the change specification (updated where appropriate) plus outputs from elements generated in the design concept stage. Consider these now and assemble them. Give the option a meaningful, descriptive name to capture the essence of the concept. The work done in reviewing Norms and behaviours can often inspire names for design options.

To unify the design concept, review the latest information on the elements and segments you have information on so far, align the segments, and adjust as necessary to create a coherent whole. There will be some segments that you have no information on at this stage, this is fine. Tool 8.3 will help you to align the design concept.

Tool 8.3 Aligning the design options

The objective is to pull together a coherent overall design option.

Inputs

As input you need information on all the design segments you know about so far, for this option. Include information on the elements produced at this stage and information subsumed from earlier work.

Who to involve

Include senior, experienced members of the design team: people who have worked on previous organization design programmes, who understand organization theories and can judge the interactions and interplays between design segments. If you are using a design authority, their expertise and wisdom is very useful here. We also recommend involving your business unit group for their practical expertise in resolving thorny issues and making trade-offs.

Instructions

A round-table debate involving about seven people is the most effective way to do this. Split groups larger than this up; replicate the exercise and bring the outputs together in a plenary group at the end. Make sure participants understand how the design option grid should be used.
In this exercise you are looking for a broad fit between the segments; an 80 per cent fit is sufficient.

Provide an overview of the design option, summarizing the information known so far about each segment.

Complete a design option alignment grid using the template shown in Figure 8.3. At each intersection consider and mark the grid appropriately:

- Whether there is a relationship between the segments.

- If there is; whether more design work is needed to judge the segments' alignment.

- If there is; whether they are aligned and congruent or misaligned.

If you find any major gaps or serious misalignment, you may need to revisit the thinking already done on one or more segments, and then realign.

As you complete the grid capture insight on what needs to be built into any of the Compass segments and thoughts on what is required in more detailed design work; for instance:

- Implications of following this design option.

- Dependencies, eg a merger and acquisition may have constraints on when some structural changes can be implemented.

- Where the design option makes assumptions about other segments, eg the structure segment often makes assumptions about resourcing.

This is also the design team's chance to consider whether there is anything in the emerging design that may be a major barrier to implementation. This is not a formal assessment but a sense check on how 'doable' the design option is.

Outputs

- Design option (revised if necessary)

- Competed design option alignment grid

- Insight for more detailed design work – some specific to the option and some generic.

You now have a completed design concept ready for assessment. Repeat this until you have three to five design concepts. At that point, you can assess the alternative design concepts (shown in the next chapter), before returning to develop the selected designs and creating design outlines.

FIGURE 8.3 Design option alignment grid

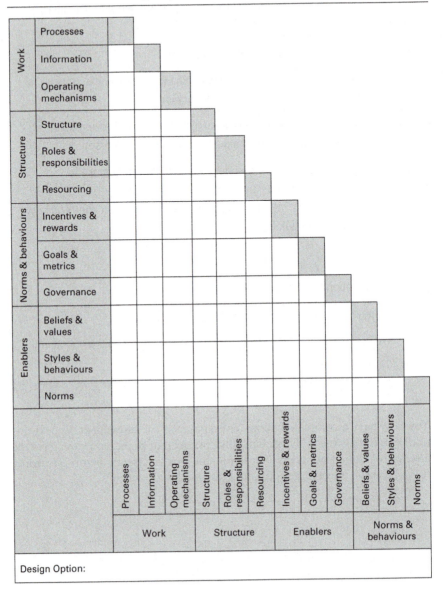

Marking

✓ Segments are aligned and congruent

✗ Segments are misaligned

O No strong connection between segments

- Design work is incomplete; no assessment made

Developing design outlines

> Starting off, all options are always open, but as soon as you choose something, you inevitably limit yourself. If you go for B, A is out.
>
> (Alva Noto)

The alternative design concepts are passed back to the design team, once they have been assessed. All the design concept level assessments including the design option evaluation score sheets and the design option evaluation summary with commentary should be available to the design team. Sometimes the assessors may suggest a hybrid of a couple of the options. If the assessment has suggested a hybrid, the design team will need to cycle back to generate the revised design concept and make sure they have all the concept level outputs from that completed. The assessments from hybrid concept's 'parents' will suffice for this stage rather than reassessing the hybrid itself. Now you take all the inputs and learning to date, the most promising two or three design concepts and the assessment feedback and develop these concepts further to create design outlines. Design options are more tangible and people in the organization will start to understand better what the future organization will feel and look like. The process described below takes one design concept at a time and develops it into design outline. The process is then repeated taking another design concept to produce another design outline and so on. In practice though, particularly where design concepts are similar, you are likely to progress these in parallel.

At this stage, you may want to start involving top talent who are potential candidates for the new organization in some of the design activities as soon as possible (if they are not already involved). Their input will be useful and they will get engaged in the design they are helping to create. Senior HR and talent management should review the emerging structures to help identify possible candidates. Possible clues include: who in the organization do you keep talking to; whose advice does the design team keep seeking; and who is frequently volunteering to give their (useful) input?

Exploring Work in more detail

In the Work quadrant break down each key work process into its component activities, identify the information needed for each process, and understand who or what each process interfaces with (say an organization, another process, or stakeholders). Use Tool 8.4 to identify the activities for the key work processes.

Tool 8.4 Identifying key work process activities

The objective is to get a more detailed view of the key work processes by breaking them down into their component activities.

Who to involve

Include the design team, particularly those members with process mapping skills, logical thinking, and experience of the work of the organization under design and ensure you have input from operations and IT.

Inputs

Inputs are the design concept and the design concept level assessment.

Instructions

Decompose each high-level process into its component activities:

- Identify what are the main things that need to be done in order to fulfil the higher-level process.

- Illustrate how each of these activities relates to each other by mapping the logic between them. Typically activity maps are drawn as a simple flowchart (see Figure 8.4).

- Identify who or what the process will interface with and add these to the activity maps:
  - Who or what supplies inputs to the process?
  - Who or what does the process supply?
  - Who influences the operations of the process?
  - Who is influenced by the process?

- Check that the inputs come from somewhere: either from external sources, or are the output of another process of this unit or another unit.

- Check that the outputs are going somewhere: either to the customer, or are the inputs to another process of this unit or another unit.

Improve the activity maps:

- Apply the questions in Table 8.1 with a view to eliminating unnecessary activities, combining closely related activities, and simplifying the process. This will also test the assumptions made around operating mechanisms and challenge whether these can be improved too.

- Revise the activity maps as needed.

Review all of the activity maps as a package:

- Use the work standardization framework and consider how standardized the activities are. As a general guide, more standardization is associated with increased efficiency and simpler structures. Is there anything you can design in at this stage to help this?

- Revise the activity maps as needed.

Outputs

- One activity map for each key work processes.

- Optionally, you may record working papers on:
  - draft versions of activity maps;
  - reasons for changes to activity maps;
  - any assumptions surfaced in challenging and refining the activity maps;
  - any viable alternatives to the activity maps and the reasons for choices made.

FIGURE 8.4   Activity map template

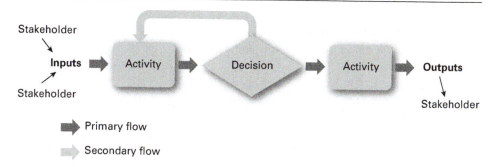

Once the activity mapping is complete, review the maps as a package. Examine the information flows with your IT and operations experts. The organization design team are not usually responsible for specifying information systems; however, the design outline does need a view on the information system requirements. Look at any current information systems

TABLE 8.1   Questions to improve activity maps

Examine the activity	Generate alternatives	Select alternatives
Purpose		
• What is achieved in the activity?	What could be done:	What should be done?
• Is the activity's purpose clear?	• Eliminate	
• Is the activity necessary?	• Modify	
	• Substitute	
	• Simplify	
Sequence		
• When is each activity in the process done?	When else could the activities be done?	When should it be done?
• Need they be done in that sequence?	• Earlier or later?	
• Is there any duplication of activities in the sequence?	• Combine with other steps?	
Place		
• Where is the activity carried out?	Where else could it be done?	Where should it be done?
• Need it be done there?	• Combine work areas?	
	• Centralize or distribute?	
Operating mechanisms		
• How is the activity done?	How else could it be done?	How should it be done?
• What assumptions are made about tools, equipment, and methods?	• Invest in equipment or new technology?	

to see how suitable they are; whether they need to change; and what new system requirements may be. Together with your IT and operations experts, produce a description of the information systems needed to support the key work processes noting if these are current systems, amended systems or new systems.

Developing Structure in more detail

In developing the design outline, you draw an organization chart of the future organization; describe the roles and responsibilities for its units and sub-units and draw the reporting lines between these. In most cases the structure only needs to be developed to two or three levels below the 'head of' unit role but for some complex units go as far as you need to go to make sense and help understanding. This is often where hybrid forms of organization start to make sense. Even if the concept level is, say, a geographic structure then at the lower levels there may be some functional sub-units. Automated charting tools are useful for drafting at this stage as the organization chart gets more detailed.

As you firm up the structure, you start to flesh out the responsibilities at the unit and sub-unit level and develop role definition for key roles in the new structure. As you develop the structure, the resourcing model becomes clearer as you get a picture of what skills, numbers and types of people are needed in that future structure. Make sure the right people from your HR function are involved and consulted at this stage and together start to engage with people who need to get up to speed to understand potential implications. Work on structure and roles and responsibilities in tandem as the thinking on one informs the other, using Tool 8.5.

Tool 8.5 Outlining the organization chart

Who to involve

Include the design team and HR.

Inputs

The change specification, design concept-level assessment, and the design outline so far.

Instructions

The design concept produced a sketch of the structure and listed the main responsibilities for each of the units identified, use this. Starting at the top of the organization, work down the levels and across the units.
  Define each unit's role:

- List the key responsibilities and accountabilities for the unit in the top two boxes of the role definition template in Table 8.2. Responsibilities are what the unit is tasked with doing: the activities, processes, or tasks assigned to the unit. Accountabilities are what the unit will be judged on; for example contribution to profit; quality standards.

Turn the sketch of the structure into an organization chart for these units:

- The units identified in the concept become the boxes on the chart.

- Add reporting lines to join the units.

- Include any important dotted lines.

Identify sub-units for each of the units:

- Examine the major responsibilities for each unit and the relevant activity maps.

- Consider how the unit might break down into sub-units; say based on activity types, roles, markets, skills.

- Assign each sub-unit a meaningful name.

- List the key responsibilities and accountabilities for each sub-unit in the top two boxes of the role definition template in Table 8.2.

When all units have been considered, review whether all the high-level processes and activities have been assigned to units or sub-units. Adjust and amend any unit and sub-unit responsibilities where needed.

Add the sub-units to the organization chart:

- Add reporting lines to join the sub-unit and units.

- Include any important dotted lines.

Review the organization chart:

- Sense-check the chart to see whether the reporting lines are broadly workable, eg too narrow, too wide, unbalanced, inconsistent levels or have overlaps.

- Does the chart fit with your operating environment?

- Refine the organization chart and role definitions for units and sub-units (where necessary).

Complete the role definitions for the units and sub-units:

- Add any important behaviours required if these differ from the organization or level above.

- Add key competencies and skills required.

Hints and tips

RACI charts can be a very useful aid to get clarity on responsibilities; to avoid duplication of responsibilities and to make sure that all responsibilities are covered. Consider the size of the units and sub-units as you draw organization charts. Some units are purposefully kept small, eg when a few experts or specialists are grouped together, or the unit size can be very large with little need for direct supervision, either as a result of training or formalization of processes, outputs, and behaviours. Bear in mind that increases in size of units and sub-units usually leads to a requirement for more formal management roles, more formal processes and more procedures in the Enablers quadrant.

Outputs

- An outline organization chart containing unit and sub-unit names, reporting lines, significant dotted lines, any commentary needed for clarity

- Role definitions for the units and sub-units drawn on the organization chart.

TABLE 8.2   Role definition template

Role definition for unit, sub-unit, work group or role name:	
Activities and responsibilities	Accountability: For what and to whom
Behaviours required	Competencies / Skills Required

There will be some key roles in the new organization that need defining now. Typically these will be the 'head of' positions in the most important units of the organization. Other roles may also be essential for the organization to work. For example, when Barclays set up an internal management consultancy, the role of 'client relationship manager' to connect the business units (their clients) to the consultancy was vital. This role needed to be considered at this stage of design.

The design team should work with HR and link into the processes that exist in the current organization for producing and maintaining role descriptions. Working with HR, identify the key roles and complete a role definition for each, again using the role definition template in Table 8.2. Consider:

- Are any of these key roles 'undoable'?
- Is any role out of kilter with roles above, below, and around it?
- Are there people in the current organization who can do these roles?
- If not, can the organization recruit to fill them; how easy or difficult is this?
- Does the availability of talent affect the timing of the design's implementation?

If the scope of any role makes it undoable or at odds with those around it, loop back and refine your organization chart and the unit and sub-unit role definitions before coming back to the key roles. Similarly if the availability of talent causes an issue you may want to make adjustments too. After making any adjustments, amend and refine the key role definitions where necessary.

As you develop the organization chart start the thinking about the resources needed for the new structure: the numbers of people; their skills; the sources of people. Some of this information can be included on organization charts but that can become unwieldy so it is often better to document it separately at this stage; in an outline resourcing description. For each identified unit or sub-unit capture:

- The size of the unit in terms of numbers of people. Usually in a design outline this is an order of magnitude or a range.
- Any particular skills, educational or training standards needed.
- Considerations and thoughts about how to resource them. For example, the ratios of employed staff to agency staff; the mix of full-time to part-time.

Shaping the Enablers

The segments in the Enablers quadrant are a powerful way of making any chosen design option(s) work. Once you have narrowed down your design then shaping the right incentives and rewards, goal and metrics, and governance is an important part of what will make the design work in practice and they can compensate for the inevitable limitations and instabilities in the organization structures. Enablers are so important they should be designed as part of the whole organization rather than bolted on as an addition after the design has been implemented, as often happens.

In incentives and rewards, the design team work closely with senior HR people and senior management. Together they should think about financial and non-financial incentives and rewards as well as the disincentives and penalties. Incentives and rewards are as relevant for organizations as they are for individuals: so consider the organization and the processes that cascade incentives and rewards through the organization to units and sub-units as well as to individuals. Incentives and rewards are powerful drivers in any organization. People do what they believe they will be rewarded for, either in terms of pay, bonuses, opportunities or promotion. Check carefully that incentives and rewards are really aligned to the organization's purpose, values and strategy. Is there a link to the overriding organization if you are designing a sub-unit? If they start to diverge you may find it hard working collaboratively across the whole organization. In many designs there will be limited or no change to current systems and processes and any changes are more often about the nature and content in this segment. Where the team identifies changes, document the changes needed, highlighting what is new and different from today. Consider:

- What are the major impacts on current systems for performance management, performance appraisal, and reward and bonus schemes?

- Do the current systems, processes, and mechanisms need to change to make the design work?

- Does the design need new systems, processes and mechanisms to make it work?

- Is there a need for dual incentives to focus senior managers on both enterprise and unit goals?

- Is there any training needed to embed the changes; such as, training line managers in new performance appraisal systems?

Goals and metrics are rarely looked at in detail at this stage of design: they are generally picked up in implementation. However, they may be absolutely fundamental to a design, say for a multi-dimensional organization, in which case they may warrant detailed work at outline stage. The processes and mechanisms are addressed if they need to be significantly different from current ones; for instance where they will be tightly tied to how the strategy will be implemented by introducing a particular approach. Sometimes steering committees want a view of what the goals and metrics for the new organization might be; say a draft list of key performance indicators that could apply in the new organization. Make sure these focus on a range of parameters not just financial ones. For instance, are the values and behaviours considered as well as the social impact? Consider a balanced scorecard approach.

The governance framework, structures, processes, and mechanisms ensure that all areas to run the organization 'as a business' and that need to be controlled are controlled. Effective governance does not happen by accident, yet governance is too often an afterthought to organization design and developed piecemeal. We believe governance is an essential part of organization design. 'Good governance is demonstrated by decisions being arrived at after an open debate among a group of people who together have the necessary skills, experience and information. 'Good governance increases the probability that good decisions will be made' (FSA, 2012). During design, the aim is to outline how to make this happen. Tool 8.6 can be used to identify governance.

Tool 8.6 Identifying the governance

To identify the governance framework, structures, processes, and mechanisms needed for the design option(s).

Who to involve

The design team plus others in the organization with know how or experience of setting up governance.

Inputs

The inputs for this are the insight and information gathered during the early steps: the design brief, the current and future state, the change specification, plus the design outline so far.

Hints and tips

- Governance is the preserve of the senior team. The executive will be familiar with the structures, processes and any current arrangements. They know what works and what does not, what they like and dislike. Ask their advice!

- Are there arrangements elsewhere in the wider organization or the existing organization that you are redesigning that can be used as a starting point? Governance is often done well in Finance where regular budget and reporting cycles give them lean well-rehearsed processes and mechanisms for authorizing and cascading that you might learn from. IT organizations too have often worked hard to embed governance and can be a source of advice.

- Is the governance strategic? Check that operational control is done in Work via control mechanisms. Actively design governance around the organization's strategic objectives and performance goals. At this stage you might not know numbers but you will know what needs to get measured.

- Frameworks should relate structures and key roles back to the most senior person in the organization involved (that may be outside the organization being designed).

- Processes that are related should be linked and you should have the fewest number of effective mechanisms possible (governance can become an industry). Aim to assess, improve and reduce the existing number of mechanisms.

- Governance can be temporary, eg for programmes; or permanent.

- Governance often extends beyond the organization being designed. Consider this when you think about the people who need to be involved in structures etc, eg suppliers, clients, and regulators may also need to agree that what an organization has in place for some aspects of governance is fit for purpose.

Instructions

Clarify all the areas that need to be governed; eg the organization, finance, investment, change, architectures, capability, sales, operations.

Clarify the governance objectives and key outcomes for each area to be governed and determine the areas to focus on based on the outcomes.

Outline required governance arrangements: structures and processes:

- Leverage existing governance where appropriate.

- Outline any structures needed, eg meetings.

- For each governance structure include: name, purpose, where authority is drawn from (the individual role or group), attendees (roles rather than individuals), frequency with which meetings are held.

- Clarify how governance structures fit with the other structures or roles in the new organization or beyond in a larger organization.

- Articulate the governance framework to show how the structures and roles relate.

- Identify and articulate key processes at a high level: Produce a list of key processes and complete a high-level process map to document each process.

- Is there any hierarchy that you need to pay attention to in defining governance, eg overriding objectives, values, strategic versus operational importance?

- How dynamic do the governance arrangements need to be?

Note the mechanisms needed to implement the intended arrangements:

- That is, how will the control be put in place, eg through standards, policies, guidelines, procedures, authorities.

- Select the appropriate governance mechanism for the focus area.

- These will be designed later in implementation.

- Consider reporting and escalation mechanisms.

- How will conflict be resolved?

Carry out a sense check:

- Do meetings overlap in remit or personnel?

- Are there too many or too few?

Outputs

- Governance framework.

- Outlines for governance structures, eg committees.

- List of key governance processes.

- High-level outlines for key governance processes.

- List of key mechanisms needed to make governance work.

Compiling and aligning the design outline

In creating the design outline, you have looked further at the Work and Structure quadrants and you have an outline of the Enablers quadrant. Now you bring together all the elements of the design option that you are working on. Design options have outputs from the previous stage subsumed. So a design option may contain elements retained from the current organization as detailed in the change specification (updated where appropriate) plus outputs from elements generated in the design concept and design outline stages. Appendix 4 lists design outputs by level and Compass segment. To unify the design outline review the latest information on the elements and segments you have information on so far, realign the segments, and adjust them as necessary to create a coherent whole. There will be some segments that you have only a little information on at this stage, this is fine. Include all the segments and elements, even if they have not been updated in outlining the design, as they may now need adjusting to align with the additional definition in other segments. Once again, use Tool 8.3 to help you to align the design option.

You now have a completed design outline ready for assessment. Repeat this until you have reached this stage for all the design outlines you are preparing. At that point, you can assess the alternative design outlines.

Conclusion

In this step you have progressed from ideas, to design concepts, and defined chosen designs further to outline level. The first two stages of the high-level design are complete. In the step you have established a number of possible design outlines for the future organization. All the underlying elements and segments have been compiled and aligned to create coherent organizational outlines, which deliver the organization's strategic intent and target capabilities. The design work has captured both soft and hard elements; and while the design outlines are still at a high level, they are much more tangible and people they are shared with will start to see what the future organization could be like. In this step you have produced a lot of outputs: Appendix 4 lists the design outputs produced by level and Compass segment. By the time you complete this step you will have the knowledge to take ideas for organizations and progressively develop high-level designs that meet a design brief. Now we will look at how to assess these; narrowing down the number of concepts to explore further; and getting to a position where an optimal design can be chosen from a number of design outlines. 'All changes are created in a moment – with a simple choice' (R T Gorham).

Assessing the alternatives

09

Greatness is not a function of circumstance. Greatness, it turns out, is largely a matter of conscious choice, and discipline. (JIM COLLINS)

KEY POINTS

Aim:

- To assess and compare design options (design concepts and design outlines).

- To generate insight to improve the quality of designs and inform refinements.

- To narrow down options until you can select the optimal one.

Activities:

- Assessing design options against design principles and criteria.

- Choosing between design options.

- Selecting design(s) to progress.

This step is about conscious choice: it can have a profound impact on how the programme's stakeholders and team view design options. We have seen it change preconceptions, hearts, and minds and get people behind the optimal design. It is simple; yet powerful. The aim of this chapter is to assess and compare design options either at concept or outline level: narrowing down the number of concepts to progress into further design; narrowing down the number of outlines to choose an optimal design. This chapter covers how to assess the design options against the design principles and criteria produced in earlier steps; how to compare the resulting assessments to enable choice between options and when and how to get agreement. The tools and techniques used allow you to review, analyse, evaluate, and bring your ideas to a resolution. They aid the critique of options, individually and relatively: giving you a structured way to present the ideas and if necessary, challenge the brief. This is important because the decision at the end of this step is a huge one for the programme and the organization. It may not be possible to reach all the desired outcomes, but completing this step ensures that you understand the trade-offs or refinements that may have to be made. The outputs provide a measure of success and a basis for dialogues between the designers, the sponsor and/or other stakeholders enabling compromise to be reached between what is required and what can be delivered or afforded. You should gain the knowledge on how you can best select and judge design options you create.

This step is used iteratively with the mapping design options step; normally you will pass through this step twice. This step examines each design option that you are considering against the design principles and criteria defined earlier and then compares the alternative options. Each pass through this assessment step uses the same set of design principles and criteria. In the first pass through, design options produced at concept level are evaluated. The most promising design options are selected for further investigation and/or refinement. You return to mapping out the more detailed options where the designs are progressively developed to create designs at outline level and then cycle back to this step to assess these.

Assessment can help you generate additional insight and lead you to create and explore other options as you iterate, so that you can formulate your optimal organization design. We recommend you take only a few options into design outline level because of the detail and amount of work required to design each option at that level. In the second pass through this step, design options produced at outline level are evaluated. The aim at the end of the second pass is to choose an optimal design.

The assessment process is the same for design options either at concept or outline level. There are two parts to the assessment process. First you assess each design option against design principles and criteria. Then you compare these alternative design options and summarize the evaluations. You may need to pick between close running design options either to narrow down the number of concepts you develop further or to select your optimal design from your outlines. Assessing alternatives is a small step in terms of time and effort: typically this step takes one to two days each time it is performed. The number of people you involve is usually between 2 and 10 depending on how you carry out your tests.

For the vast majority of organization design programmes, the assessment shown in this step will be sufficient. For difficult challenges where the environment is particularly complex, the future, or your organization's future is very uncertain; or if a fundamental change is planned, scenario testing can be added alongside this form of assessment. Scenario testing is optional and used infrequently. This is a different type of assessment from that described above. It is more qualitative and less quantitative and it allows a much deeper level of evaluation. You need sufficient detail in the design to allow a reasonable test, but not so much that you have invested too much time investigating options that will be discounted following the scenario testing. Whether you carry out scenario testing of your design outlines before or after assessment against criteria really depends on your programme; there are reasons for and against carrying them out in either order. You may find it quicker and easier to first eliminate or change some of the outlines as a result of assessing design options against design criteria before turning to scenario testing. In Tom Peters's words, 'test fast, fail fast, adjust fast'. Or if the future is very uncertain you may want to use scenario testing first, if necessary, alter your design outlines before you assess these against design criteria. In Part Three we look at how to use scenarios to explore and rehearse future possibilities and highlight strengths and weaknesses with the design outlines produced and identify unintended consequences of the designs.

Assessing design options against design criteria

Assessing design options against design principles and criteria enables you and others to see the extent to which each design option meets your objectives, identifies constraints, and improves your understanding and learning. The scores and annotated comments help the design team refine their designs, making sure they preserve the aspects that score highly while trying to improve the aspects that scored low. Use Tool 9.1 for the assessment.

Tool 9.1 Assessing design options against design criteria

Who to involve

This can be carried out by a small group as a desktop assessment or by a larger discussion group using dialogue and consensus to score results. The dialogues in both help those involved learn more about the options, enabling more informed scores and annotated comments. It is best not to include people involved in mapping out the design options because they are likely to be too close to the options. As a desktop exercise, involve two to three senior designers from the design team (who can call on expert support if needed). You can include people who developed the evaluation scheme or from your design authority (if you have one). Discussion groups are very useful for building commitment and shared understanding across stakeholders with different perspectives. Here individuals can explain their view on scores allowing everyone to hear different perspectives and see what others value about the options. If a business user group has been established for a programme they can be used. Of course technology can be used to support assessment where time and geographical dispersion necessitates, but we encourage you to use it to facilitate dialogue face to face, if possible, rather than using technology to collate isolated decisions. If you use a discussion group include key stakeholders for a wider set of inputs and so that different opinions can be heard and considered, a good facilitator (preferably someone from the design team) and the design team for support. Whether you use a group or desktop approach the inputs, outputs, and instructions are the same.

Inputs

The inputs for this step were developed in the preceding two steps of the OPTIMAL Way: the design principles and criteria and the design options either at concept or outline level.

Instructions

- Ensure everyone involved has a clear and common understanding of what the design principles and criteria mean and how the scoring system works.

- Complete an evaluation using the design option evaluation score sheet shown in Table 9.1 for each design option.

- You can either score one design option completely across all design principles and criteria or take each criterion in turn across all options and score that way. We find that most groups prefer to work through one design option at a time and work down: as the options are still new it is easier to think them through one at time. Comparisons across models can be made as you assess later options with those already marked to see whether relative scores are 'balanced' or whether you need to make adjustments.

- For each criteria consider the key points of the design option that are relevant to the assessment. Annotate as you go to indicate how scores have been assigned, for information for the design team and so they can be defended or challenged with your steering group. The annotations can be a useful reference to the implementation team later on too.

- Once you have completed the marking of each option a consistency check is useful.

Marking

- Use a four-point rating scale: 1 = poor, 2 = fair, 3 = good and 4 = excellent.

- For a no/yes response: rate no = 1, yes = 4.

- Where a benchmark must be met, eg must operate with a budget of £x million: rate fail = 1, pass = 4.

- When the design is still high-level you may be unable to score all criteria, eg you may be unable to assess costs criteria until later stages of design. Leave these blank or score them zero?

- You may have decided to weight criteria or principles or neither, carry this forward from your marking scheme.

- The overall evaluation score for a design principle is informed by the individual scores and any weighting established when the evaluation scheme was created rather than the sum total of the scores.

Outputs

A design option evaluation score sheet completed for each design concept or outline. Table 9.1 shows the template and Table 9.2 shows a completed example.

TABLE 9.1 Design option evaluation score sheet

Evaluation of option: option name (concept/outline)			
Design principles	**Design criteria with commentary**	**Score**	**Weight**
Design principle 1	Design criteria A • Commentary		
	Design criteria B • Commentary		
	Overall evaluation for design principle		
Design principle 2	Design criteria A • Commentary		
	Design criteria B • Commentary		
	Overall evaluation for design principle		

Scale	**Excellent Yes**	**Good**	**Fair**	**Poor No**	**Not evaluated No info**
	4	3	2	1	No score

In the example shown in Table 9.2, at design concept stage: five options were scored by two people; a senior designer with a design authority representative; six pages of analysis were produced for each option; the assessment (including the comparison of alternatives and summary information below) took two days.

TABLE 9.2 A completed design option evaluation score sheet

Evaluation of option: A : Functional outline		
Design principles	**Design criteria with commentary**	**Score**
Demonstrably delivers the CIO Strategy including the shared service strategy, outsourcing and follows enterprise 'rules'	Will deliver our shared service strategy ● Clear definition of demand, service and supplier management functions ● De-emphasizes current design, build, run model ● Clear step change from current organization	4
	Supports outsourcing of services ● Not clear yet how it helps package and outsource services ● Supports the management of outsourced services	2
	Will not duplicate the demand management function embedded in our client business units ● Partially true, but not all businesses have demand management functions at this stage ● Client relationship function faces demand management in client business units ● Need to manage the size of the client relationship function	3
	Is credible to our clients and to our people ● Clients can easily see and make sense of the structure ● Our people can see the new structure delivers the strategy and hence the rational that design	4

TABLE 9.2 *continued*

	Enables us to not exceed our financial and headcount targets • Difficult to confirm at this stage	
	Can grow, shrink, change flexibly and rapidly as we outsource services • Allows for this in time • In early implementation significant resourcing change implications	3
	Overall Evaluation for Design Principle	3

Scale	Excellent Yes	Good	Fair	Poor No	Not evaluated No info
	4	*3*	*2*	*1*	*No score*

Choosing between design options

Comparing alternatives helps to improve design decisions. It enables you to learn which of the options best meets your organization's requirements. It allows you to assess the alternative destinations/end points. If some of your principles and criteria cover ease of implementation, it can also allow you to assess the relative strengths and weaknesses in the routes to delivery implied by the different options.

Once you have completed the assessment of each design concept or outline, summarize all the evaluations to provide a high-level comparison. Use Tool 9.2 for the comparison. Overall assessment is relative and focuses on priorities for design principles. There are almost always some priorities that an organization regards as more important than others, even when these are not documented. This helps you focus on and critique the relative strengths and weaknesses of the different options. How well does each option meet the principles? Table 9.3 provides a structured way to present this information back to the design team (alongside the more detailed information generated from the individual assessments). The summary with critique is generally all the assessment information most sponsors and steering groups want to see following the assessment of the design outlines.

Tool 9.2 Comparing alternative design options

Who to involve

Even if you have used a discussion group in assessment, the comparison can be completed by one to two people from the design team who were involved in those discussions.

Inputs

The inputs are the completed design option evaluation score sheets for each design concept or outline.

Instructions for comparing alternative design options

- Summarize the analysis from all of the individual assessments using a 'design options evaluation summary'. Table 9.3 shows a completed example.

- Carry forward the overall evaluation scores for each design principle for each option. The overall evaluation score is informed by the individual scores and priorities (even where these are not documented) and any weighting established when the evaluation scheme was created rather than the sum total of the scores.

- Support the summary with a short critique/explanation identifying which option(s) you recommend pursuing and why; which option(s) you recommend dropping and why; and any other steers, for instance, if no option can meet all requirements or a particular combination of features may provide a better result than any one of the options considered.

Outputs

A design options evaluation summary with commentary which covers all the design concepts or outlines assessed.

TABLE 9.3   A completed design options evaluation summary

Design principles	Options		
	A Functional	B Service lines	C Service groups hybrid
Demonstrably delivers the CIO strategy including the shared service strategy, outsourcing and follow enterprise 'rules'	3	2	3
Embeds capabilities required within three years	3	2	3
Simplifies current structure	4	4	2
Broadens spans of control	4	4	4
Simplifies business process	2	4	2
Embeds an ethos which is professional, commercial and values shareholder return focused on service and supplier management			
Makes best use of enterprise's resources	2	2	2
Minimizes implementation impact	3	2	2
Overall assessment of the option	3	2	3

Scale	Excellent Yes	Good	Fair	Poor No	Not evaluated No info
	4	3	2	1	No score

In Table 9.3 we pick up the design option evaluation we looked at in Table 9.2 and show how the relative evaluations at design principle level for three of the five options scored. The example shows clearly how evaluation does not always give you clear direction. Scores of one and four are less common than two and three. Knowing priority principles helps. In this case 'delivering CIO strategy' and 'makes best use of enterprises resources' were critical to this unit and the wider organization. Even though option B had strengths, they were not in most important areas. Options A and C were investigated further.

After completing your assessments and comparison you will be able to reduce the number of options and refine and strengthen the remaining options, but there may still be too many feasible options. To help you pick between close options in most cases, the preferred option(s) will be the ones that:

- have a simpler design rather than a more complex one;
- are more specific about details and assumptions;
- can adapt most quickly to major external changes;
- are expected to be easiest to implement;
- involve least change, eg fewer position changes;
- offer greatest improvements through economies of scale;
- best meet the needs of customers.

OPTIMAL programme considerations

Programme considerations at concept stage

Designers learn from assessment. What have you learnt about your options? Can you get additional insight from others reviewing the designs at this stage? You could also try this for a different take. When you have a selected a few concepts, test them with some stakeholders in the new organization using Word-Concept Association. How? Ask people to associate descriptive words with different design features and concepts in order to show how they perceive or value the issues. Why? Because clustering their perceptions will further help you to evaluate and prioritize design features and concepts.

The outcomes from the concept assessment are reviewed, analysed and evaluated options that can be further explored and detailed in design work. At this stage, to support the design options you have assessed, you will have completed versions of the annotated score sheets for each design concept evaluated, a summary of the design option evaluation with supporting commentary, and have recommendations of options to pursue further or variations to consider. Some steering committees and/or sponsors may wish to be involved in reviewing the selection of the concepts; others will leave this to the programme team.

You may want to review the programme now. Are any risks or issues highlighted? In our experience it is rare at this stage to find any wider impacts on the programme for instance, in terms of other workstreams, plans, budgets, and business case.

Confirming your optimal design at outline stage

At the design outline stage you will have similar output supporting fewer, but more detailed design options. You should be in a position to judge and select the optimal design for your organization. In their excellent book, *Designing Effective Organizations*, Goold and Campbell (2002) suggest nine tests to see if you have a well-designed organization. The purpose of the tests is to raise issues and trigger ideas for design improvements that they may prompt. This insight can help you adjust your optimal design or influence your choice of design. The first four are tests for 'fitness', followed by five 'good design' tests:

- **Market advantage** – Does the design allocate sufficient management attention to the operating priorities and intended sources of advantage in each product-market area?

- **Parenting advantage** – Does the design allocate sufficient attention to the intended sources of added-value and strategic initiatives of the corporate parent?

- **People** – Does the design adequately reflect the motivations, strengths and weaknesses of the available people?

- **Feasibility** – Does the design take account of the constraints that may make the proposal unworkable?

- **Specialist cultures** – Do any 'specialist cultures', units with cultures that need to be different from sister units and the layers above, have sufficient protection from the influence of the dominant culture?

- **Difficult links** – Does the organization design call for any 'difficult links', coordination benefits that will be hard to achieve on a networking basis, and does it include 'solutions' that will ease the difficulty?

- **Accountability** – Does the design facilitate the creation of a control process for each unit that is appropriate to the unit's responsibilities, economical to implement, and motivating for the managers in the unit?

- **Redundant hierarchy** – Are all levels in the hierarchy and all responsibilities retained by higher levels based on a knowledge and competence advantage?

- **Flexibility** – Will the design help the development of new strategies and be flexible enough to adapt to future changes?

The commentary from your assessments around the strengths and limitations of design options will facilitate the tough choices and trade-offs that will need to be made in selection. This is a key decision point in the organization design programme: so the approval for this stage is generally taken by the programme steering committee.

Some organizations and steering committees prefer to see more than one option so they can choose, others prefer designers to provide a recommendation, and yet others prefer to see only a 'final choice'. You should review the programme now. Looking at the option(s) you are taking to your steering committee: consider the wider impacts on the programme in terms of other workstreams, resources, plans, budgets, and business case and the impact of the solution on your organization. Are any risks or issues highlighted? What are the key messages? At this stage take a broad view as you will look at this in more detail for the chosen option in laying out the way forward.

Your steering committee will probably want to see a summary pack to support their decision-making. The contents of this will depend on your organization and its preferences and it will be highly tailored to the nature of the problem and the organization. We have seen organizations where this is only acceptable as a three- to five-page written report and others that want 50+ pages. You will need to judge how much information to take to them for approval. As a guide the pack is likely to include:

- Summary information describing the chosen/recommended option(s).
- The completed design options evaluation summary for the design outlines.
- Significant insight from the assessment process particularly if you need to highlight principles or criteria that cannot be met by any of the options.
- Key risks and issues for the programme and any other programme updates.
- Your recommendation (if appropriate).

In our experience, however much information you take in to a steering committee and whatever the format, the discussion about an organization's optimal design will take time, so allow for an extended meeting. Depending on the organization being designed it may also require final confirmation from more senior decision-makers at executive committees and boards.

Conclusion

This step is reminiscent of Neil Armstrong's saying, 'One small step for a man, one giant leap for mankind.' It is simple and quick, but takes the organization design programme to the next level. As a result of conscious choice and a disciplined approach there is a shared understanding of the strengths and weaknesses of the designs produced and detailed feedback to help make adjustments in subsequent stages of design. There are two passes through the step, iterating back to mapping design options in between the passes to define further detail that in turn can be assessed. In the first pass, the design concepts that need to be defined further are identified and a shared understanding is reached of how these concepts support the organization's strategic intent. In the second pass, the design outlines are narrowed down further so that the optimal design for the organization you are working on can be established. A number of outputs have been produced that provide the basis for buy-in:

Design concept level assessment:

- A design option evaluation score sheet completed for each design concept.
- A design options evaluation summary for design concepts with commentary.
- Recommendations of options to pursue further or variations to consider.

Design outline level assessment:

- A design option evaluation score sheet completed for each design outline.
- A design options evaluation summary for design outlines with commentary.
- A steering committee pack for signing-off the optimal design.

Programme updates (as required).

On completion of this step you will have the knowledge to use an evaluation scheme based on design principles and criteria to assess your design options. Now we turn to finalizing the high-level design and getting ready for implementation.

Laying out the way forward

10

*Organizing is what you do before you do something,
so that when you do it, it is not all mixed up.* (A A MILNE)

KEY POINTS

Aim:

To ensure the high-level design work is finalized and you have
a design blueprint ready for implementation.

Activities:

- Developing the design blueprint:
  - Finalizing the work processes.
  - Describing the operating mechanism and flows.
  - Defining work groups.
  - Compiling and aligning the design blueprint.
- Preparing to appoint people to key positions.
- Preparing for implementation.
- Taking stock of the change required.
- Pacing and sequencing the change.
- Choosing the implementation approach.
- Transitioning from design to implementation.

The previous two steps covered the design and evaluation of a number of options culminating in a choice of an optimal design at outline level to deliver the organization's strategic intent. This chapter is the last step of the OPTIMAL Way and the completion of the design phase of your programme. The aim of this step is to ensure that the high-level design work is finalized and the optimal design concept turned into a design blueprint that can be implemented; in effect the builder's specification is complete and ready to be handed over. This chapter covers how to finalize the design; produce the design blueprint; pass on the design team's knowledge to the implementation team, and make a clean transition from design to implementation. This is important because a clear design shows those that follow it, what is intended for all major decisions. All the structural elements of the Compass framework should be clear; while the design still has latitude for ownership, evolution, and emergence within this. As with a building, where the architect lays out sufficient guidance for the builders (who will carry out some more detailed design); and who in turn will hand over to occupiers who will also design and modify within the whole framework. After completing this chapter you will know how to produce a design blueprint and how to transition from design to implementation. You will be able to do this whether you are designing an entirely new organization from scratch or taking a current organization and redesigning it.

The process for this step is straightforward. So far you have produced the design outline; Appendix 4 has a reminder of the contents of this. First you add to the outline and complete the high-level design. Any feedback from the assessment and the steering committee is incorporated into the optimal design outline; then the additional detail is added to turn it into a design blueprint. To prepare for implementation, you look at the gap between the current organization and the design blueprint and assess the changes needed; identify the design tasks for implementation; and advise the implementation programme on the pacing and sequencing of the design aspects of the change. As you progress from design to implementation, you capture the lessons learned from the design phase; transfer the knowledge base; and say goodbye to the members of the design team who are leaving the programme. Finally you consider the programme plans again and look at the affordability and the do-ability of the programme. This is where you closely examine the risks and the consequences of moving forwards. Whatever route you take there will be both intended and unintended consequences and you test if the organization is prepared for them. You then secure a firm commitment from the organization to implement the new design to deliver the strategy.

In this step you will be working with only one design option – the chosen optimal design. The length of time and effort needed for this step varies with the complexity of the organization that you are designing but as a guide, it typically takes about a third of the time and effort set in completing the previous step.

Developing the design blueprint

How much detail the organization feels comfortable with defining upfront and what can be left until later on to define, are decisions made at the start of the programme. For instance, whether to define the overall shape and allow appointed managers to define the detail they need to at a later step; or whether to be more prescriptive. Now there is additional knowledge from the design phase. Decide again how much more detail to put into the design now and how much you will leave to those that follow. There are pros and cons for the programme team doing more work versus the remaining design being passed on to leaders in the new organization. Essentially, this is a choice between the need for speed of design and control of design elements versus engagement; with its clear-cut advantages of increasing buy-in and commitment to the new design.

Here we present a typical middle course for the mid-sized design programme. In this the high-level design is completed, culminating in the production of a design blueprint. This design blueprint adds important details to the chosen design outline but leaves lower levels of detail to the new organization to develop. The first and minimum step is incorporating any feedback from the assessment and the steering committee. The chosen design outline is updated to document the latest decisions on the optimal design. Now you turn to enhancing the design.

Finalizing the work processes

So far only the top 7 to 10 key work processes have been mapped. In reality there are likely to be many more processes in the organization. This is the time to consider these. Aim to add to the ones that are already defined so that the majority of the work of the organization is covered. The level of formality appropriate to the organization is a useful guide. For a high degree of formality cover more of them while in a less formal situation where processes are emergent then develop less. Aiming for about 80 per cent coverage is a good rule of thumb to apply. Tool 10.1 shows you how to identify and assign responsibility for the additional processes.

Tool 10.1 Identifying and assigning additional work processes

This tool identifies additional work processes; maps them; identifies which units or sub-units will be responsible for them and updates the organization chart.

Who to involve

Include the design team to lead this work, particularly those with process mapping skills, and people from the business unit group to provide business input. Getting a wider range of people involved in providing input here increases the involvement and buy-in to the design process. In addition to the business user group, look at who else in the organization can provide useful input.

Inputs

Inputs are the optimal design outline and the working papers listing work processes identified at the design concept level.

Instructions

Identify additional high-level work processes:

- Use the lists of work processes from the concept stage and the processes and activity maps from the design outline as a reference to earlier thinking to produce a new list of processes relevant to the chosen design. Keep these at the same level of detail as the top 7 to 10 key work processes, identify any other work processes including support processes, add these to the list; eg production processes may be already covered but equipment maintenance processes may not.

- Review the list looking for gaps and overlaps. Refine the list so that it covers most of the processes that the organization will need.

- For each process, complete a high-level process map and record on these: the inputs, outputs, operational controls, and operating mechanisms. You can use the organization's preferred high-level process mapping approach or the one shown in the example in Figure 8.2.

Assign responsibility for the additional processes identified:

- Can the processes be sensibly assigned to units or sub-units already identified? If so, update the role definitions for those units or sub-units adding the additional responsibilities. Add any required accountabilities, competencies and skills and behaviours to the role definitions.

- Identify if new sub-units are needed.

- Consider what to centralize and what to decentralize.

- Consider if there is another unit outside the boundary of the organization being designed that could carry out the process; for example a shared service centre or a third party.

- Complete role definitions for any new units or sub-units and identify the appropriate reporting lines for them.

- Update the organization chart to reflect the new units and sub-units and their reporting lines.

Outputs

- List of work processes.

- High-level process maps of additional work processes.

- Role definitions for all units and sub-units.

- Updated organization chart.

Describing the operating mechanisms and information flows

Completing the Work quadrant of the blueprint needs the support of the organization's IT and operations experts to define the information systems and operating mechanisms. Add to the design work done at the design concept and outline stages and consider what is needed to support all of the identified work processes. Take a view of the whole organization and look at all of the information systems and operating mechanisms and describe the key features of these. The outputs are:

- Description of information systems needed to support the organization.
- Description of operating mechanisms needed to support the organization.

Defining work groups

Usually some parts (but not all) of the structure needs to be explored at a lower of level of detail in the blueprint and we call this lower level of detail a work group. Getting the work groups right is important. In the early 1990s, Barclays Bank took many of its back office processes out its UK retail branch network and centralized them. The processing centres organized around process type, within these work groups were configured as teams, each serving a group of bank branches. The aim of configuring this way was to maintain customer service and personal connections in the branches served. A specialist unit was set up with expertise in taking legal charges for secured loans; eg for mortgages. The original implementation failed to cater for a few highly specialized types of charges, limited to a small number of branches; for example taking a legal charge on precious gems as security on working capital loans. This expertise had developed in branches serving London's diamond traders. Following a review, the main branch-facing structure processing centres were kept and a few specialist teams with niche expertise were established to support all the branch-facing centres.

Tool 10.2 helps you identify work groups. This can be run as one large workshop focused on the whole organization or a series of design sessions each focused on a particular unit or sub-unit or related set of these. The first is preferable where there is high degree of interdependence between the units and sub-units, while the second is more applicable where they are very independent. Physically it is often best done where a large group can work together easily; for example pin boards or post-its; with the design team producing the more formal final documentation for the blueprint.

Tool 10.2 Identifying work groups

The objective is to add detail to the structure.

Who to involve

This is best done as a facilitated, high-involvement exercise. Include members of the design team, particularly those with HR skills and knowledge; people drawn from the business who have knowledge of the work to be done through their current role or with an interest and involvement in the future organization. Depending on the make-up and skill level of the participants you may also need access to additional HR resources to contribute expertise.

Inputs

Optimal design blueprint so far.

Instructions

For each unit or sub-unit, create a process/activity characteristics chart. Figure 10.1 shows a simplified version of a completed chart for a unit performing minor surgery on patients in a private UK hospital. To draw up the chart:

- The columns are all the activities and additional processes (as shown on the unit or sub-unit's role definition).

- The first group of the rows are standard to all charts and they describe attributes of the process or activity.

- The next group or rows are the skills required. Use your own set from the role descriptions.

- The third group is who the process or activity interfaces with; for example this might be other parts of the organization, customer groups or suppliers.

To complete the rows on the attributes, mark each activity with a O or ● to indicate the characteristic, or mark ◉ if in the middle of these two extremes. The row definitions are:

- **Frequent or periodic**: How often is this process or activity performed? Is it frequent, like a bank's bill payment process, which is carried out millions of times per day, or is it periodic, like a month-end report?

- **Quick task or long task**: How long does this process or activity take? Is it a quick task like answering a telephone call, or a long task like implementing a new IT system?

- **Routine or specialist**: To what extent is there a clearly defined way to do this process or activity? Is this a routine task for which there is a defined 'set of rules' or procedures; or is it a more specialized task that requires expertise and personal judgement?

To complete the skills rows, consider what skills are required and mark ● where the process or activity relies on that skill.

To complete the interfaces rows, consider whom the process or activity interfaces with. Judge the strength of the interface by considering its importance to the results, the time it takes, and the amount of information that needs to be exchanged. Mark these as O, ◉ or ● to show the strength of the interface.

When you have completed the process/activity characteristic charts for all the units and sub-units, use them to explore how activities can be combined into work groups. Grouping can be defined in many ways. Use judgement to see which fits best. Consider grouping activities by:

- Common skills.

- Common time cycles.

- Specialization of task.

- End-to-end processes.

- Like activities across all the processes. So if a similar activity occurs in two or three processes, they could be grouped.

- Who they interface with.

In practice finding the right grouping of activities is an iterative process as different ideas are tested. Move between drafts of the groupings and the process/activity characteristics charts a number of times making choices and compromises as you go. Generally consider several ways to group the activities before you settle on the best solution for the situation. Keep amending and refining as necessary.

Once the work groups are decided on, the participants apply their judgement, information from the evidence base and knowledge of the current organization, learning from other organizations, and the sizing estimates in the design outline to estimate the size of each of the work groups.

Outputs

List of work groups with brief description of what they do and which unit or sub-unit they relate to.

Working papers from defining work groups:

- Process/activity characteristics charts.

- Any notes and insight from the workshop.

FIGURE 10.1 A completed process/activity characteristics chart

Unit : Minor surgery

Characteristics of process/activity \ Process/Activity	Create/update patient record	Schedule appointments	Consultation	Schedule surgery and support	Pre-surgery check	Admit as in-patient	Surgery	In-patient recovery and monitoring	Discharge patient	Post op check up	Invoice patient/insurer
Frequent ○ / Periodic ●	○	○	●	⊙	⊙	●	●	●	●	●	○
Quick task ○ / Long task ●	○	○	⊙	⊙	⊙	⊙	●	●	⊙	⊙	○
Routine ○ / Specialist ●	○	○	●	○	⊙	⊙	●	●	●	●	○
Key skills need:											
Administrative	●	●		●							●
Specialized clinical support (eg radiography, phlebotomy)			●		●					●	
Nursing (Ward management)						●		●			
Nursing (Theatre specialism)							●				
Surgery			●				●			●	
Anaesthesia and pain management							●				
Interfaces:											
Patients	○	○	●	⊙	●	⊙	●	●	⊙	●	○
General practitioners	○								⊙		
Insurance providers											⊙

After the workshop, the design team formalize the documentation. They update the organization chart adding the work groups and their reporting lines to the structure chart and produce a role definition for each work group (see Table 8.2) to record:

- Activities and responsibilities of the work group.
- Accountabilities of the work group.
- Competencies and skills needed in the work group.
- Any important behaviour required in the work group if this is different from the whole organization or the level above.

They use the estimates of size and the information on competencies and skills from the workshop to add to the outline resourcing description and produce a resourcing description for the whole organization that contains:

- Estimates of the size of the organization; its units, sub-units and work groups.
- Skills, educational standards or training needed.
- Considerations and thoughts about how to resource the future organization. For example will it be staffed from existing resources or will it recruit new people? What are the likely ratios of employed staff to agency staff or the mix of full-time to part-time?

Preparing to appoint people to key positions

There will probably be some key positions that need to be filled sooner rather than later to make the future organization work. The design outline contains role definitions for key positions already identified. Review these now and add role definitions for any additional key positions you identify. With HR's input consider the scope of the roles and the availability of talent. If the scope of any role or availability of talent makes the role undoable or at odds with those around it, you may want to loop back and refine the organization chart; the unit, sub-unit or work group definitions and then revise the role definition for the key positions. In order to be able to recruit or appoint people to these key positions, you need to turn the role definitions into job descriptions. This involves defining the job size, job scope, and grade. This is the domain of HR and the design team works with HR to link into their processes producing and maintaining job descriptions. Produce job descriptions for key positions.

Compiling and aligning the design blueprint

In creating the design blueprint, you have looked further at the Work and Structure quadrants and you have looked at the behaviours needed in units, sub-units, work groups and key roles. Now you bring together all the elements of the design option that you are working on. Design options have outputs from the previous stage subsumed. So a design option may contain elements retained from the current organization as detailed in the change specification (updated where appropriate) plus outputs from elements generated in the design concept, design outline and design blueprint stages. Appendix 4 lists design outputs by level and Compass segment. To unify the design blueprint, review the latest information on the elements and segments you have information on, re-align the segments, and adjust them as necessary to create a coherent whole. There will be some segments that you still have only a little information on even at this stage, this is fine. Include all the segments and elements, even if they have not been updated in creating the design blueprint, as they may now need adjusting to align with the additional definition in other segments. Once again, use Tool 8.3 to help you to align the design option. You now have a completed design blueprint.

Preparing for implementation

Taking stock of the change required

The next task is a gap analysis of the current organization and the design blueprint. Earlier when taking stock of your change, you did a gap analysis comparing the organization's current state versus the envisioned future state, to produce the change specification. This activity is similar; however, it has a different focus. There you were looking at possibilities and thinking about the extent and direction of change needed for an imagined future organization, now with the knowledge gained and the design blueprint in place, you are examining what the actual change will be and establishing what tasks you need to accomplish it. Tool 10.3 shows how to do this.

Tool 10.3 Defining the change required through implementation

Who to involve

Include all the programme team, the business user group and representatives of functional sections such as IT, HR and Risk. It is led by the programme leader.

Inputs

The inputs are the detailed evidence base and the optimal design blueprint.

Instructions

This is best run as a workshop. In the workshop identify what needs to be done across the organization as a whole and then within the different organization units, sub-units and work groups.

Starting at the top level of the organization chart, compare the current organization to the optimal design blueprint. Use a template similar to the gap analysis template shown in Table 6.2 but amend the rows to ask the questions below for each quadrant of the Compass:

- What elements need changing?
- What new elements need to be built?
- What has to be retained?
- What has to be protected in the current organization?
- What tasks are needed to build, retain or protect these?
- Overall assessment of the amount of change required (none/low/medium/high/complete)
- How difficult is the change to make (not applicable/low/medium/high)?

By starting at the top level, you only need to look at the lower organization levels where relevant or different. For example, for the organization you are designing, the segments of the Enablers quadrant may only need to be specified at the organization level and not for lower-level units and sub-units. When looking at the tasks needed, some may be organization-wide and some may be specific to particular parts of the organization. Appendix 4 shows the design outputs produced at the design concept, outline, and blueprint stages for each Compass segment and in the right-hand column there are examples of tasks you may use in implementation. Use this as an aid to developing a task list.

Pay particular attention to what you need to protect and retain from the current organization. Organizational change can be destabilizing and there may be some areas that you want to ensure do not get harmed; for example is there a particular group of people who you do not want to lose or a critical competency that is in short supply? Aim to be specific about the tasks needed to protect or retain these.

Outputs

- The gap analysis of the current organization versus the optimal design blueprint
- A task list of what is needed to create the new organization.

Pacing and sequencing the design aspects of the change

With the knowledge of what needs to change and what tasks are still to be completed, next look at how to sequence the changes. A business unit group can be very helpful in this exercise as they have particularly relevant knowledge and experience to draw on. Factors to consider in pacing the change include:

- Does the external environment impose any timescales? Information on this is often captured when you outline the brief. Examples include timescales for meeting customer needs, regulatory frameworks, or to deliver a capability before a competitor.

- What else is going on in the organization that may influence the timing? Examples include other change programmes, customer demand and operational peaks that need to be avoided.

- What constraints or limitations are there? For example, availability of finance for the change; risk management; appetite for change; change readiness; or availability of suitable skills to make the change happen. Why, when and how do these affect implementation?

As you consider the sequence, use the Compass to help you decide the order to do things in and to decide which changes you can make before others and which need to be done in parallel. One example of the impact of operating mechanisms driving the sequencing of changes to an organization structure was when the building products group, Wolseley wanted to create a new unified head office structure. Before they could make the organizational changes they had to complete the construction of a new head office building.

As you think through the sequence, focus on the outcomes to deliver the strategic intent and implement the target capabilities. Delivering the target capabilities requires changes across a range of Compass segments and you will need to make progress across them in parallel. Changing one quadrant alone is not effective. Sequencing needs to keep the new organization aligned and make sufficient progress on enough segments for the levers of change to be effective. Think about a crew rowing a boat: they need sufficient strength to row in a consistent direction; they all need to be rowing in the same direction with both sides in balance to make progress. However not all individual crew members need to be rowing at the same strength.

Often changes in one quadrant need a supporting change in another quadrant to make them stick. The Compass helps align each phase of the emerging implementation plan and ensure you take a holistic view of the change. Examples are new work processes with people in place assigned the responsibility for that work; or in a new structure, people with new responsibilities may require refreshed incentives and rewards implemented in parallel. In our experience, for an effective organization change, designers need to look to change at least two quadrants in parallel, sometimes three. Trying to do all four at once can often be too hard to do. Because it is not always possible or desirable to implement target capabilities in one tranche,

FIGURE 10.2   Wave diagram to summarize a change portfolio

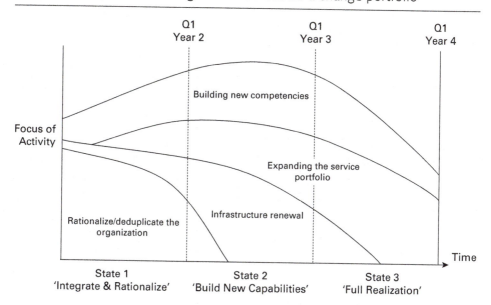

we give you some additional guidance on how to manage this in the chapter on 'How to assess the level of capability maturity of an organization over time'.

The team documents its advice on the pacing and sequencing of the changes. Detailed planning is the domain of the implementation team. Figure 10.2 shows an extract from a pack documenting a portfolio of change. This wave diagram showed the thrust of effort over time. It summarized the much more detailed analysis.

Advising on the implementation approach

There are a number of possible ways to implement. The route to choose depends on what has been learned in the design phase, how large the change required is, as well as how adaptive and emergent an implementation is required. The implementation approach usually comes down to a choice of:

- Establishing a portfolio of programmes to carry out the change. In very complex, large-scale changes, once the design is done the extent and timing of the change means that a number of programmes are required to effect the change. This allows the creation of different ownership for different parts of the change; for example an HR programme for culture change; an IT programme for supporting technology infrastructure installation; and organizational units running their own programmes supporting their own timescales.

- Establishing a new programme for implementation. This is common when the organization does not know ahead of the design phase how far reaching the programme will be and the resulting design requires new skills and approaches.
- Following the design phase of a programme with an implementation phase. A new set of workstreams is defined to move the programme forward, generally with additional people brought in to deliver the changes. This is the most frequent route and the one assumed in this book.
- Closing down the programme and embedding the change as business as usual. Sometimes the team can just hand over the design to business units, operational units, and functional areas to implement over time. Typically where there is a small amount of change required.

All the leaders involved in the design phase of the programme should work with the programme leader to prepare advice for the steering committee on a suitable implementation approach.

Transitioning from design to implementation

Learning from the design phase

At the end of the design phase there is often a review of the programme. This is led by the programme manager and involves all of the programme team including consultants, change managers, HR, finance, risk, and any other specialists. In the review the execution of the programme against the programme plan is examined to learn lessons for the future and to inform subsequent programmes. If you focus on improving future quality rather than performance assessment and create an open environment you will get a richer and fuller assessment. Whether run as workshops, dialogues or interviews, the review seeks to explore:

- How well is the programme performing against its goals and objectives?
- Has anything happened within any workstream or overall to make the programme team deviate from the planned approach? What and why?
- How closely is it running to its plan and to its budget? Where there are variations, why did these happen?
- Are there any improvements to make on the fit between workstreams?
- From a design point of view, what tools and techniques, and design exercises worked well, worked poorly, or could be improved?

- Are there any recommendations for future enhancement or modification of these?
- What advice do you want to pass on to the future training of design teams?
- What has been learned about leading organization design in the organization?
- What overall lessons can be learned for future programmes?

The findings are documented in an end of design phase programme review. This can be used by future design programmes when they are pulling together their programme.

Collating the design documentation

The information gathered during the design will be a valuable resource for many different groups of people during implementation. A good programme office should ensure that documents from every step of the OPTIMAL Way have been kept and are available, but it is still good practice to cross check now that these are complete and accessible before moving forward. It helps to segregate the working papers and discarded design options from the documentation relating to the chosen optimal design blueprint. Include for instance, interview notes, outputs from workshops, draft design documents, and ideas considered and dismissed. This all forms an archive of the rationale, learning and thinking behind the design work. Appendix 3 provides a list of the outputs from the OPTIMAL Way.

Transitioning the design team

It is desirable that as many of the people as possible from the design team during the design phase continue through into implementation. In our experience, it is common for about 60–90 per cent of the team to carry on. Some though will not; for example external consultants, contractors and people seconded from within the organization. For the external people, ensure their knowledge is captured and documented before they leave. Internal people will have acquired scarce, in-demand organization design skills and a good feel for the future of the organization. Usually they are people the organization wants to retain so their transition from the design team needs to be carefully handled. Some people working full-time on the design team will need a new role or may return to their previous role if it still exists. It is worth paying attention to making their transfer run as smoothly as possible as they will be ambassadors for the new design and their enthusiasm counts. Although this may sound obvious, we have seen examples when the obvious has been overlooked and excellent people have been needlessly lost to their organization.

Before the design team disbands, hold a final meeting of all design team members, both full-time and part-time, to review the team's achievements.

This is a chance to celebrate, acknowledge what has been accomplished, identify what has gone well, and reflect on what the team members have learned and can take away from their experience. For all team members it will help anchor the programme as a success for them. For those remaining with the programme, it marks the end of a phase; they can adjust their thinking and shift their focus from design to implementation.

OPTIMAL programme considerations

At this transition point the programme manager needs to draw on all of the other specialist expertise across the programme to look at implementation as a whole not just the design aspects. This includes:

- **Change management:** how to prepare stakeholders for the implementation; the communications messages to all the organization, customer and suppliers and how to deliver these; preparing to overcome any resistance to change; the organization development needs; and the coaching and mentoring of key people.

- **HR:** where resources in the new organization will come from; how the HR policies and procedures will be applied to build the new organization; what learning and development will be needed and how this will be delivered; how talent management can contribute to getting the right people in the new positions; creating the performance standards for the new roles; and how staff and union consultation will be handled.

- **Finance:** financial modelling of the new organization; estimating the ongoing running costs; producing the business case for the new organization; and assessing the likely cost of implementation.

- **Risk:** the risks on the business and on customers during the implementation; the impact of these; and any mitigating actions that the organization needs to be prepared for; projecting the intended and unintended consequences of the new organization and considering if the organization is prepared for them.

The programme manager will collate all of this expertise with the design team's outputs and prepare to take it for approval. The key people to get approval and sign-off from of at the end of this step are the programme sponsor and steering committee. In very large changes you may also need executive or board level approval. The presentation to them should be a summary of all of this expertise; this end of design phase steering committee pack will include:

- an overview of the optimal organization design;
- the business case for the new organization including the estimated ongoing running costs;

- a view of how the implementation will be done and the timescale for implementation;
- an estimate of the costs of the implementation;
- a view of the nature and scale of the risks the organization will face during implementation.

At this stage the programme needs a firm commitment from the steering committee for their agreement to progress to implementation. Implementation typically takes longer, costs more, and carries more risk than the design phase. The organization will devote substantial resources and significant disruption will be incurred from this stage onwards. The steering committee should feel confident that as they take decisions on it, the high-level design has been thoroughly thought through. Their ongoing support and leadership will be a key determinant to the success of the programme going forward.

Conclusion

On completion of this step the design phase of your programme is concluded. All of the steps of the OPTIMAL Way have been carried out and the optimal design for the organization to deliver its strategic intent and target capabilities is agreed. The design blueprint is developed and ready for implementation; the knowledge that has been accumulated by following the approach is available to those that will implement the design; and you should have been given a firm commitment from the steering committee to go ahead. The outputs produced are:

- the design blueprint (detailed in Appendix 4);
- gap analysis of current organization versus the optimal design blueprint;
- task list of what is needed to create the new organization;
- advice on pacing and sequencing of changes;
- advice on implementation approach;
- end of design phase programme review;
- end of design phase steering committee pack.

Working papers from defining work groups:

- process/activity characteristics charts;
- any notes and insight from the workshop.

In this step you have learned how to develop the chosen design outline into a design blueprint and how to prepare for implementation. The high-level design is complete, implementation and realization lie ahead.

Taking the OPTIMAL Way forward

Though pleas'd to see the dolphins play,
I mind my compass and my way. (MATTHEW GREEN, 1737)

We have shown you the OPTIMAL Way to create a high-level organization design. We have given you a Compass to guide you and a map for you to follow step by step. You have the tools to take others with you on your own design journeys to:

- Outline the brief: shaping a design brief so that everyone has a shared view of what is needed.
- Pull together the programme: putting the leadership and team in place, clarifying what is required and how to achieve it; enabling high-level design work to be defined and planned.
- Take stock of the change required: establishing an evidence base for the current state, defining the desired future state and setting out the change required.
- Identify the assessment criteria: identifying the design principles, criteria and an evaluation scheme to select between design options.
- Map the design options: designing concepts at first, then designing selected outlines.
- Assess the alternatives: narrowing down the design concepts first, then choosing an optimal design from the design outlines.
- Lay out the way forward: finalizing the optimal design to produce a design blueprint and preparing to implement it.

If you follow the OPTIMAL Way, you will be able do this with interventions that engage a wide range of people, to seek input and enable dialogues to share the development of ideas. Checkpoints with the steering committee and close linkages with HR throughout will help the design programme keep on track to deliver the desired strategic intent and target capabilities. The OPTIMAL Way allows you to integrate with your existing programme and change management approaches throughout the design work. This will allow you to move forward to implementation with confidence, having followed an approach tailored to each organization design challenge you face.

We have assumed throughout this part of the book that you are taking a leadership role in carrying out an organization design, but at different times, designers assist organizations in many different ways. You may guide others as a:

- catalyst: advising with a vision of what the effective organization might be like;
- instructor: providing knowledge and/or skills;
- partner: working with clients to co-create organizations and learn together;
- contractor: acting as an experienced pair of hands to get the work done;
- facilitator: managing processes, allowing conflicting points of view to surface and be heard;
- counsellor: acting as a sounding board for the client;
- supporter: giving practical advice, assistance and support throughout a programme;
- challenger: diagnosing limitations to growth, challenging preconceptions, creating alternative insight;
- specialist: providing detailed advice on aspects of design work.

Whatever path you find yourself on; we hope the Compass and the OPTIMAL Way will be your design guide; that organization design is no longer filled with mystery and intrigue but mastery and intent.

PART THREE
Dealing with recurring challenges

How to maintain design integrity over time

11

> *Success is a journey, not a destination. It requires constant effort, vigilance, and re-evaluation.* **(MARK TWAIN)**

KEY POINTS

- Maintaining organization design integrity means assuring critical aspects of design are followed and kept aligned.

- A design authority can help maintain design integrity.

- Roles and responsibilities for design authorities are suggested.

- Design authorities can provide assurance, compliance, maintenance and support capabilities.

- Design authorities can aid implementation, operation and future design programmes.

- Design authorities assist maintenance of the design integrity while allowing change.

It takes time and effort to complete an organization design: to ensure that the organizational purpose and strategic intent are clarified and then to define and build a balanced and aligned organization operating effectively as a whole. Organizational design integrity is about prolonging the life and design coherence of an organization so that it continues to deliver its strategy and fulfil its purpose. An organization will undergo many changes throughout its life; to cope with new opportunities, new challenges and adjustments needed. Some changes will be planned, others emergent and some will commence even as the design is being finalized. Over time how do you ensure that you keep the parts of the organization balanced and aligned? How can you use the organization design work that has been done to cope with changes, while continuing to deliver against the purpose and strategy? How do you do this in a way that does not limit the organization?

This chapter aims to show you how to maintain the integrity of an organization's design over time by establishing and using a design authority. It covers what design integrity entails, how a design authority can be used to maintain design integrity; and the roles and responsibilities of a design authority. Design integrity is important because organizations are complex: composed of many interdependent elements which must operate in a way that continues to meet the strategic intent over a period of many years, even decades and yet must allow for continual evolution and adaption. You should gain an insight into the role of a design authority in maintaining design integrity during design, implementation, and operation.

What design integrity entails

In order to maintain design integrity, changes to the design need to be made with an understanding of all the elements of the organization design. These include an understanding of: why the organization has been designed in a particular way; of the assumptions and compromises made by the designers regarding the organization's operation; of the design's component parts, and of the interactions which could impact the strategic intent. The necessary knowledge of the overall design has to be retained in a form that is practically and easily available to the operating organization over its lifetime, ie until the purpose and/or strategic intent change. Failure to retain this knowledge and to control design changes will, over the lifetime of the organization, result in decisions being made without a full understanding of the effect that these decisions may have on the organization. Unintentional consequences are much more likely to occur that could affect the organization's ability to deliver the strategic intent.

When an organization is first built or rebuilt, its design is shared between a team of differently skilled people generally from across many parts of an existing organization(s) and often beyond. Most of the focus is on delivering the strategic intent and design brief. When the organization is operating, much of the detailed knowledge used in the design is transferred to the operating organization through design manuals and other design documentation. Some may be documented as principles, values, behavioural codes, and standards to be followed. The OPTIMAL Way deliberately captures information for this reason. However, the knowledge that is transferred will not be complete. Much of the highly specialized knowledge underlying the design will remain with the original designers, as it is as much about why the decisions were made as what decisions were made. Over the operating lifetime of an organization the people involved in the design will move on and be unavailable to call on. The issue is compounded when interdependencies between changes that are made over a period of time occur. These may affect several areas.

Maintenance of design integrity is understood very well in mission critical situations by some professions, for example, in nuclear power and chemical plants, and some engineering and IT instances. Maintenance of organization design integrity is about assuring that the critical aspects of the design are followed and kept aligned, rather than about ensuring that every aspect is 100 per cent failsafe.

How to maintain design integrity

The impact of change on design integrity can be mitigated by having people involved in the design phase who will subsequently be involved in implementation and operation. However, particularly in operation, their focus is likely to move on from maintenance of the design integrity to their new roles and responsibilities. In addition, all too frequently no single area takes on the role of ensuring design integrity after implementation. A frequent default for design programmes, as with other programmes is to hand over to the operating organization. It is assumed they will somehow adopt the role of maintaining design integrity. Another common assumption is that because it is an organization design programme that HR will maintain design integrity. However, in practice, it often falls to a variety of groups to manage elements of the design in perpetuity because no one area has all the detailed, specialized knowledge required of all the elements in a design. The operating organization or HR may therefore assign responsibilities for aspects to other entities that do have that knowledge. So functional areas with strategic responsibility for design elements inherit parts of the organization design as well. In terms of the Organization Design Compass responsibility may be assigned to a number of supporting areas for different segments, eg Structure and Norms and behaviour to HR, Work to Operations and IT, Enablers to the executive team.

Once this is done, the view of how the design works as a whole and stays balanced and aligned is often lost. It is a recurring challenge, because once this happens, the alignment of the whole becomes degraded over time. Informal and ad hoc handover results in informal and ad hoc results, as the intent behind the design is lost and the different elements drift apart. How do you bring the design together as you review changes? Where is the overall responsibility for the integrity of the design of the organization happening? How is this retained? Somehow you need to retain sufficient knowledge of all aspects of the design to enable those involved to understand the results of the designers' work; and to understand the implications of that work for the rest of the design.

Like strategy, responsibility and accountability for an organization's design and construction to deliver its strategic intent lies with the most senior leader(s), the top team in an organization. Once the design and implementation programme(s) are completed, responsibility for managing the organization as a whole needs to be allocated, ensuring that both the supporting elements and the whole remain aligned as changes happen. It is worth considering how this can be maintained. The key question is where to hand over the design knowledge from organization design programmes to? If this is to several parts of the organization, you will need to think through how to keep the design aligned and directed towards the strategic intent. Entities responsible for various aspects in turn need formal responsibility for maintaining their specialized knowledge of the design and their competence in the detailed design process.

The need to maintain design integrity and to preserve the necessary detailed and specialized design knowledge poses a significant challenge for many operating organizations and HR. They will therefore need to take specific steps to assure themselves that the design knowledge is maintained appropriately. They will need to manage a formal and rigorous design change process so that the actual configuration of the organization throughout its life is consistent with changes to the design, that changes can be made with full knowledge of the original design intent, the design philosophy and of all the details of implementation of the design, and that this knowledge is maintained or improved throughout the lifetime of the organization.

The head of the designed organization needs to set up this formal process as soon as they take control. This is part of their role in delivering the strategic intent. The process of controlling changes to design and accessing design knowledge is not a trivial matter. The amount of data can be vast (see the list of outputs in Appendix 3 and 4 arising from the design phase alone). Further deliverables will come from the implementation phase and added to this many design change issues can be complex. (Software like OrgVue – cited in 'Taking stock of the change required' – can be very helpful here. In particular, OrgVue allows the high-level design information to be married with the detail.) The key question is how to maintain design integrity of the whole as you hand over to various parts of the organization. One solution is to set up a formal design capability within the implementation organization and ultimately, somewhere in the new organization. This solution creates a formally designated entity within the organization that takes responsibility for design integrity. This entity needs to formally approve major design changes. To do this, it must have sufficient knowledge of the design and the design's role in supporting the strategic intent. In addition, it must have access through a defined process to all the underlying design knowledge to ensure that the original intent of the design is maintained. The entity that has this overall responsibility approves design changes and is responsible for ensuring that the requisite knowledge is maintained, is referred to as the 'design authority'. The role is accountable for the integrity of the organization design. Its role is not to 'preserve' the design, allowing no change, but to work with others to maintain the design integrity while allowing change.

The roles and responsibilities of a design authority

The need for a design authority that maintains the design integrity over the operating lifetime needs to be fully acknowledged by the operating organization. The design authority role must be clearly defined and formally recognized. A design authority can be established with many structural forms: as a group, an individual on a team, an 'umbrella function' with delegated responsibilities across the organization, a virtual organization, eg akin to a business unit group. Its remit and responsibilities may cover the enterprise organization, a portfolio of changes, a programme design phase, a programme's implementation, or some elements of the overall design. There can be considerable variability in these roles; so there needs to be clear roles defined and responsibilities and accountabilities set out. The scope and boundaries of the design authority's responsibilities in terms of its assurance role versus its compliance role need to be established, ie over what does it provide advice and over what can it veto.

As design hands over to implementation and operation, a systematic process is needed that takes into account the complexity of the design, the size of the information and allows for the process changing over time. The responsibilities and attributes of a design authority, and the type and nature of the formal responsibilities held needs to be delegated to be developed and maintained over the operating lifetime of the organization. Note that a design authority's remit does not normally cover legal, regulatory or compliance with bodies outside the organization. Table 11.1 provides an example design authority role definition with suggestions for an enterprise-level design authority. The design knowledge that is required within a design authority includes, but is not necessarily limited to:

- the design programme's inputs, particularly the design brief;
- the research knowledge and design exploration and iterations on which the design is based;
- a detailed understanding of why the design is as it is;
- the design outputs (see Appendix 3 and 4);
- analysis of change required;
- change specification;
- design blueprint;
- implications of operating experience on the design.

TABLE 11.1 Example design authority role definition

Role definition – enterprise level design authority

Activities and responsibilities
- Organization design leadership
- Assuring quality of the organization design process and outputs
- Ensuring that an appropriate knowledge base is established, preserved and expanded with experience
- Ensuring that the organization design knowledge is available to all parts of the operating organization
- Assuring quality of overall arrangements for the management, performance, and assessment of designs
- Reviewing, verifying and approving (or rejecting) design changes in scope
- Maintaining (or ensuring that responsible designers maintain) design configuration control by up-to-date records of relevant drawings, specifications, manuals, design standards, calculations, supporting data, systems, structures and elements
- Provision of strategic-level governance and specialist advice

Behaviours required:
- Seeks to understand organization's strategy and purpose
- Consistent with organization's leadership behaviours
- Collaborative
- Use of influence and persuasion
- Operate as a trusted advisor/Non-Executive Director

Accountability: for what and to whom
- This will be organization specific
- For the integrity of the organization design
- For design integrity (the capability and authority to reject proposed design changes that do not maintain the design integrity is a vitally important role of the design authority, or of a responsible designer in its assigned area. The scope and boundaries of this are organization specific)

TABLE 11.1 *continued*

Competencies/skills required:

- Expert in organization design
- Deep understanding of the organization design model and process used in the organization
- Experience in using chosen organization design models and processes and other approaches to design organizations in a variety of situations
- A broad perspective on organization design and organization change theory and practice
- Understanding of the organization
- Specialist element knowledge

The role of a design authority changes at different periods of time and with different remits. There are three distinct differences phases: through the design phase of a programme; through the implementation of an organization design; and in operation. Over the design phase, the design authority can support the design leader providing mentoring and guidance, acting like a senior partner in an architecture practice, to ensure that:

- The design meets any higher level organization's needs; eg when the design programme is part of larger organizational change or when there are organization wide principles, standards or structural rules in place.
- The design aligns with the requirements of the organization's wider frameworks such as its business model, operating models, people strategy, IT strategy and other change initiatives.
- The design process is executed correctly and that all steps are completed to an appropriate depth and quality.
- Relevant expertise is brought in to the design programme as required.
- There is advice and counsel to assist issue resolution or making calls on difficult choices when requested offering wisdom and expertise. They are a voice that can give a broader perspective.
- The final chosen design delivers the capabilities and strategic intent that the organization requires and that it aligns with the original vision.

Once the design phase is complete, the design leader or team can be tasked with a design authority role themselves, acting like architects overseeing the construction. This is equally true whether they are overseeing the implementation phase of a programme, the implementation of a follow on portfolio of change, or implementation delegated to line units. As design authorities, their role is to ensure the integrity of the design through implementation and to provide ongoing advice and oversight to follow on projects as lower level design work is produced.

In operation, the design authority usually takes on a higher-level role often embedded in the enterprise organization. This is akin to the architects replaced by high-level, planning and building regulations and regulators. The concentration here is on major changes, the design authority has a more 'hands off' role and control is primarily maintained by rules, standards and policies, and processes. With subsequent design programmes, enterprise design authorities can help to ensure that the design is constructed within existing broader contexts and utilizes appropriate design inputs. This is the role of the design authority that we have shown throughout Part Two of this book.

Conclusion

A design authority provides an effective means of maintaining design integrity over time:

- during implementation;
- during operation;
- during subsequent design programmes to assure the design is constructed within existing broader contexts and utilizes appropriate design inputs.

The outcome from following this chapter is that you are able to establish how a design authority can be used in your organization. Once you have completed this chapter you will have the knowledge to tailor an appropriate design authority for your organization. You will also be ensuring increased confidence that the organization has the capability to deal with change while ensuring design integrity is maintained.

'The wisest have the most authority' – Plato.

How to choose between design options when the environment is very uncertain

12

It is better to be vaguely right than exactly wrong.

(ATTRIBUTED TO JOHN MAYNARD KEYNES)

KEY POINTS

- Scenario thinking can lead to valuable insight in highly complex or uncertain conditions.

- Scenarios are a great design thinker's tool – using convergent thinking for divergent futures.

- You can use scenarios before or after designing or do both.

- Building scenarios is a skilled craft (a basic outline is shown).

- Scenario planning can help your strategic thinking and inform designs.

- Scenario testing provides insight into how different designs may work.

▶

- Scenario testing supplements the assessments shown in the OPTIMAL Way.

- Tools and techniques are provided for scenario testing.

When the environment in which an organization operates is particularly complex or the future direction for the organization is very uncertain, or a fundamental change of circumstances is possible; there is a greater likelihood of disruptive factors and turbulence derailing any chosen strategic direction. This chapter aims to show you how to increase the chances that the organizational design options you derive and choose can cope; by adding scenario planning and scenario testing. A scenario is a hypothetical story, used to help visualize futures that are not simple projections of the status quo. Scenario thinking is the basis for scenario planning and scenario testing. Scenario planning uses scenarios to help define future strategic visions and priorities, which in turn can influence organization design. Scenario testing assesses a proposed strategy or organization design against the circumstances described in various scenarios.

This chapter provides an overview of scenarios; looks at how to create them; how they can be used ahead of design to help frame debates on requirements and assumptions as well as influence design generation and how they enable the assessment of design options. This is important because uncertainty reduces executives' confidence in their strategic intent and their ability to choose a design that can cope with any potential impact. Turbulence can make it difficult for them to formulate an appropriate strategy and decide whether to invest in the time, effort, and money to design their organization. It can also mean that the time, effort, and money invested in design and changing an organization are inappropriately spent. By using scenario planning ahead of creating design options you will inform their development. By using scenario testing you will be able to understand how your design(s) work in practice so you can select the optimal design. You should gain an awareness of whether to add scenario planning and/or scenario testing to the techniques you use in the OPTIMAL way and know when and how to use them.

Scenarios, scenario planning and scenario testing

Scenarios are not 'the truth', nor factual accounts of what is happening today or forecasts of what will happen in the future, rather they are a combination of analysis and judgment about future possibilities. Scenarios describe different, but plausible, futures and are developed using techniques that systematically gather perceptions about certainties and uncertainties. They are based on what is known to be happening and the application of imagination in order to predict what might happen in future. They need to be provocative to help decision-making and have credibility in terms of their influence and impact. They are a way of thinking about the future based on robust evidence and a set of diverse viewpoints about what could happen in the future. Discussing scenarios with colleagues within your organization can lead to new insight on strategy or direction and can also flag up possible constraints and obstacles that might be encountered in delivering a strategy. A fundamental requirement for good design is good insight. Scenarios can help you think through a range of possible outcomes and the sequence of events that would lead to them. Developing scenarios in themselves generates deeper insight into the particularly powerful drivers of change that matter to a given situation. They allow you to free yourself from 'groupthink' and challenge conventional wisdom by reducing the impact of political constraints to discussions.

> Scenarios expand your thinking ... the exercise is particularly valuable because of a human quirk that leads us to expect that the future will resemble the past and that change will occur only gradually. By demonstrating how – and why – things could quite quickly become much better or worse, we increase our readiness for the range of possibilities the future may hold. You are obliged to ask yourself why the past might not be a helpful guide, and you may find some surprisingly compelling answers. (Roxburgh, 2009).

Scenarios are a great example of a design thinker's tool, as they help you use convergent thinking for divergent futures. Good scenarios have the following key characteristics:

- The scenario is based on a story with a compelling and informative title, a strong human element, important events, and strong plots.
- The story is motivating and it includes information about the motivations of the people involved.
- The story is credible; it could happen in the real world and stakeholders can believe that something like it is plausible.
- The story involves a complex environment and/or captures the uncertainty facing the organization.

Strategic planners have long used scenarios to help define future strategic visions and priorities. They are particularly useful in highly complex and uncertain conditions. Scenario planning has been used by some of the world's largest organizations, including Royal Dutch Shell, Motorola, Disney and Accenture. Scenario thinking assumes that the future can differ greatly from what is known today. It is a useful methodology for strategy development and testing; for organizations or programmes acting in a highly dynamic environment taking complex and often risky decisions. Scenario thinking provides rigour whilst at the same time enabling those involved to draw upon their creativity, resulting in new views and interpretations of the future. It helps you understand the nature and impact of the most uncertain and important driving forces affecting the world. Scenario thinking invites you to explore extremes by pushing thinking beyond 'probable impacts in the near future'. By combining several plausible factors that may shape the organization's future, you are drawn to envisage futures that would otherwise be ignored. Scenario planning was adopted and further developed for corporate planning from earlier work by Royal Dutch Shell in the 1970s. Pierre Wack, head of Shell's planning department at the time described their nature and use in 1985,

> Scenarios deal with two worlds; the world of facts and the world of perceptions. They explore for facts but they aim at perceptions inside the heads of decision-makers. Their purpose is to gather and transform information of strategic significance into fresh perceptions.

A good reference to find out more about scenario thinking is *The Art of the Long View* (Schwartz, 1998).

At different stages in the OPTIMAL Way you can pick up clues as to whether the organization you are designing needs to respond to significant uncertainty or change at this point in time. Scenarios and scenario planning can be particularly helpful as the organization completes its strategic thinking before or while the design brief is outlined. Scenario testing can be used to assess alternative designs; it complements the assessment step in the OPTIMAL Way, but is not a replacement for it. Scenario planning and scenario testing are group processes that encourage knowledge exchange and development of mutual deeper understanding of central issues important to the future of your organization. Scenario planning and scenario testing can either be used together or separately. Using scenarios either before or after design helps you to confirm requirements and assumptions and frame debates. They allow you to bring requirement-related-issues to the surface, which might involve reopening old requirements discussions or surfacing requirements that have not yet been identified. They allow you to test your assumptions and structure dialogue in a constructive and creative way, involve a wider group of people, and test your thinking and designs to circumstances beyond the strategic intent. Scenario planning and testing are creative yet structured approaches.

Building scenarios

In building scenarios you go through the same thinking whether the scenarios will be used for scenario planning ahead of design or scenario testing post design or both. It is possible to use generic scenarios that are available, but these are seldom sufficiently meaningful to justify the cost saving. Typically building scenarios involves the development of visual representations of possible 'different futures', generated from combining known factors, such as demographics, with plausible alternative political, economic, social, technical, legal, and environmental (PESTLE) trends which are key driving forces. Crafting scenarios involves clustering various driving forces and seeking extremes to which they may plausibly be driven. Tool 12.1 covers how to build scenarios that can be used to direct and assess organization designs.

Tool 12.1 Building scenarios

Who to involve

We recommend you use a scenario expert to build your scenarios. Bring one in, if you do not have one in-house. Include the strategic thinkers and senior leaders in the organization. If a design team is in place it may help to include them, so they can understand the discussions for the later steps.

Inputs

The inputs available will largely depend on when the scenarios are built, but include any strategic insight.

Instructions

- Define the time horizon: are you looking ahead 5, 10, 15 years?

- Consider the driving forces acting on the organization. Look for the big forces that will impact the market the organization is in and therefore its shape. For example, globalization of markets and the use of IT will bring significant changes for many organizations.

- Identify the external and internal pressures that have been at play and consider the new pressures that may come into play.

- Construct scenarios by identifying the most critical uncertainties in driving forces (probably three to five).

- Each driving force has an opposing force effectively forming a pair. This will allow you to look at multiple combinations of the most critical uncertainties in two-by-two scenarios (a four-box model).

- Combine the highly correlated ones.

- Discard the ones that are not principal drivers of the scenarios.

- Aim to identify the two important pairs from your insight to become the axes that define the two-by-two scenarios to use.

It is sometimes helpful to construct an 'official future' as a base case.

Hints and tips

- Work from the external environment inwards; market, entity, division.
- Keep it simple.
- Keep it interactive.
- Plan to plan and allow enough time.
- Avoid probabilities or 'most likely' plots.
- Avoid drafting too many scenarios.
- Listen to the mavericks.
- Invent short catchy names for the scenarios (aim for two to four words long).
- Encourage the decision-makers to know and own the scenarios.
- Budget sufficient resources for communicating the scenarios.
- Make the scenarios global enough in scope.
- The scenario should have a reasonable probability of 'catching an error'.
- Factor in scheduled events just beyond your viewing horizon.
- Push extremes of optimism and pessimism beyond what you think is possible.
- Scenarios chosen will factor in risk and probability, but do not ignore significant risks because of low probabilities.
- The most interesting and insightful scenarios may initially seem the most unlikely.

Outputs

Scenarios: Aim for four. Two causes a contrast; three suggests one is best and the other two are extreme; and more than five is too many to manage and understand.

Using scenarios before you design

Scenario planning may have been used in strategy development, before organization design work was even considered. However, if it has not, it can be helpful to do this before design work starts because the results may show that the organization needs to choose a more adaptable structure; one that is more responsive to environmental changes. The knowledge gained from the scenario thinking can influence the design brief and the organization designs generated; for example, you may use it to guide the development of the design principles and criteria. Identify how the scenarios may impact organization design options; for example:

- Do they change the target capabilities required?
- Do they change the nature or volume of the work processes?
- Are there discontinuities for the operating mechanisms?
- Are information flows impacted, eg do you need to change the input mechanisms if volumes change significantly?
- Do they change the choices of structure for the organization, in terms of size and configuration?
- How do you need to adjust Enablers to respond, eg incentives, using goals and metrics to measure anticipated areas against scenario predictions?
- Do you need to adjust Norms and behaviours to respond to possible changes?

Ensure this thinking informs any subsequent design work.

Using scenarios to assess alternative designs

Using scenarios after design enables you to test the robustness of organizational designs. In most instances the techniques shown in the chapter on assessing the alternatives will be sufficient for the organization to choose the optimal design from a number of options. Like the evaluation scheme built into the OPTIMAL Way, scenario testing assesses design options to improve your understanding about them and improve design decisions. As you assess alternatives at outline level in the OPTIMAL Way, it can be very insightful to add scenario testing. Scenario testing is a more sophisticated way of deciding between design options and a different type of assessment from that described in assessing alternatives. It is more qualitative and less quantitative and it allows a much deeper level of thinking. Instead of evaluating design options against the standards defined as design criteria, here they are tested against several extreme but possible futures. This tests the robustness of the options and can give the senior team (and other participants) confidence in the suitability of the proposed design before it is implemented. It can also indicate the limits of the conditions under which the strategy and the organizational design are viable. It provides judgement of how well a design meets your strategic intent under various environmental conditions. The resulting assessment assists learning and can be used for feedback, for decisions on progression, modification or indeed whether or not to pursue designs further. This is more complex than most of the techniques used in high-level design; it takes time and effort to do well.

Scenario testing is optional and used infrequently. While there are many advantages to using it appropriately and executing scenario testing well; it does not provide all the answers. In fact, it usually generates more questions; often questions that have not been asked and for which there is no simple answer. This is why it is qualitatively better than a quantitative assessment. Scenario testing is a more expensive and more time-consuming way of assessing your design options: so use it with caution. Inexperienced users are prone to fall into traps; so do not undertake this assessment lightly; it must be properly planned and resourced to be of value. If you choose to use scenario testing, include it in your planning, so you can start gathering the information you will need when it comes to assessment. Used wisely, however, scenario testing helps executives ask better questions and prepares them for the unexpected. Because of its potential impact on the project, scenario testing and the interpretations of its results demand top management's personal input. Only they can take the responsibility to alter the design or re-schedule the project, if needed.

The main objective of scenario testing is to understand how the design(s) produced are likely to work in practice, but it offers more than that. Scenario testing can also be used to:

- confirm requirements and assumptions;
- frame the debate on assessment;
- understand how the design(s) work in practice;
- learn about the design options:
  - study the end-to-end design;
  - explore and rehearse how things will be handled under future scenarios (in particular the circumstances under which they fail);
  - identify the designs' flexibility and ability to react to developments and challenges;
  - highlight strengths with the designs (in particular those features that are resilient in all scenarios);
  - identify and anticipate potential weaknesses, shortcomings, issues and unintended consequences of the designs including failure to deliver requirements;
  - discuss how problem areas may play out in the new organization;
  - plan creatively for future contingencies: by considering potential issues and situations in a context that allows careful thought and

pre-emptive planning rather than reaction when the weaknesses appear.

- select an optimal design:
  - resolve the controversial issues explicitly;
  - reach consensus if possible, failing which, make clear decisions;
  - facilitate communication of the decision-making process;
  - prepare to modify design options or reconsider strategies.

Scoping for scenario testing should be done when you pull together the organization design programme. There you will need to ask:

- Is the context complex or uncertain or large enough to merit scenario testing?
- What are the questions or issues that need to be addressed?
- What are the objectives of using scenario testing?
- What will it add to the assessment of options?
- What are the key factors that you would like to know regarding the future that scenario testing will help you decide?
- What assumptions will be used for the testing?

The objective of the testing is to understand robustness: 'How well do these design options work out under these scenarios?' Some people call this 'wind tunnelling' and the image of a car undergoing 'wind tunnelling' is a great analogy for what is done here. As each design option is viewed under each scenario, future possibilities can be explored highlighting issues and strengths with the design option, identifying possible improvements, new possibilities, and constraints or risks and identifying any unintended consequences in the designs. The most valuable insight can be used to improve the programme results and the design outcomes. It is best to test using a workshop as this will facilitate dialogue and exploration of what happens with the new organization design options in place under the potential scenarios. Tool 12.2 shows you how to do this and Table 12.1 provides a sample agenda for a scenario testing workshop. In order to run a successful test it is essential to have clearly defined options; we use specifically selected elements produced at the design outline stage. At that stage you have sufficient detail to make the assessment worthwhile. We find it most helpful to focus on the outputs from the Structure and Work quadrants because significant impacts and discontinuities are often seen first in these. Once these are tested you can re-examine and realign the other quadrants following the OPTIMAL Way. Running the workshop usually takes about a day depending on how many scenarios and how many designs you wish to review.

Often in these workshops issues that will come up during implementation are raised. This is very useful data for later and it is wise to capture it. Make sure the facilitator has been given an overview of design option outputs that will be used.

Tool 12.2 Wind tunnelling: Scenario testing designs

Who to involve

Facilitator(s) experienced in using scenarios. Scenario testing is a specialist skill and the people doing the test need to be supported by a facilitator who is an expert in scenario facilitation. Ideally the facilitator will have been involved in compiling the scenarios (and scenario planning if done).

Participants should be people who can work happily with uncertainty and have enough of a stake in making the future work to be honestly critical of the design options presented while still being committed to finding a solution. Consider using:

- The most senior or most insightful people in your stakeholder community as defined in your stakeholder management work.

- Typically heads of business units and board members.

- Not necessarily your steering committee (they will see the results).

- Some people who have not been too close to the design to challenge and who can bring new perspectives.

- People upon whom implementation will depend where their involvement in testing can create a more rigorous test and facilitate a higher quality implementation.

- At least 10 people to allow you to sub-divide groups.

Design team representation – one or more people who understand the options being presented and inputs. They will also need to capture the outputs and the thinking. Ideally include one person from the design team per sub-divided group.

Inputs

The prepared scenarios.

For each design option: selected Work and Structure segment elements; for instance:

- Activity maps of key work processes.

- Outline organization chart.

- Role definitions for units and sub-units.

The design team representatives may need access to any of the earlier documentation and thinking.

Instructions

Using a workshop (see Table 12.1 for a sample agenda):

- Test two design options at most because it is very time-consuming.

- Ensure participants understand the scenarios.

- Engage participants by mixing storytelling, visualization, enactment, techniques. Immersion into the scenario by participants is the best way for potential impact and consequences of it to be experienced.

- Focus on the selected inputs from the Work and Structure segments only.

- Explore what happens under each scenario with the design option in place (break this into groups where each group sees all scenarios for one design option or all design options for one scenario).

- Brainstorm the possibilities, risks and issues.

- Inquire about and rate enabling and constraining factors.

- Summarize the results using Tables 12.2 and 12.3.

Marking Scheme

- You only need a simple marking scheme here that enables you to rank more favourable features higher and to highlight show-stoppers.

Outputs

- Completed Tables 12.2 and 12.3.

TABLE 12.1   Scenario testing workshop agenda

Activity	Who
Introductions (30 minutes)	Facilitator
• Outline of the day and logistics	
• Recap the context	Programme
• Introduce the reason for the design work: its drivers and desired organizational outcomes	sponsor
• Introductions (if necessary)	Participants
• State personal interests/involvement in the programme and hoped for outcomes from the day	
Present scenarios (30 minutes per scenario)	Facilitator
• Explain the scenarios and tell the story of each of them	
Understanding the scenarios (45 minutes in total)	Participants
• Discuss what each scenario means	in groups
• Capture any missing assumptions about the future that need to be made in the scenarios	
• Capture any requested amendments to scenarios	
• Feed back assumptions and requested amendments to obtain agreement	Groups to plenary
Break (During which facilitator will produce amended scenarios)	
Wind tunnel the design options (1 hour for first scenario against first design; max 3 hours in total)	Participants
• Walk through each design option under each scenario	in groups
• Capture findings using Table 12.2 and 12.3	
Review each design (15 minutes per scenario per design option)	Groups to plenary
• Present findings on each design option to plenary	
• Discuss and summarize findings on each design option (updating Tables 12.2 and 12.3 as required)	In plenary
Conclusion (30 minutes)	In plenary
• Vote to get decision on a design option to recommend	
• Is one better than the other at dealing with the different futures?	
• What should the organization do or not do to be successful under these scenarios?	
• Are there aspects of the design that can be amended to improve it?	
• Wrap up and agree next actions	

TABLE 12.2   Scenario test – design option commentary

Scenario	Scenario name
Design Option	Design name
Comments & Observations	
Favourable features	• Description of the aspect and why it is advantageous
Stress points	• Description of the problem, explain why it is a problem, and risk • How resilient is the option?
Concerns	• Description of the problem, explain why it is a problem, and risk
Key Findings	• Include a few sentences summarizing what the future looks like

TABLE 12.3   Scenario test – design element commentary

Scenario	Scenario name	
Design Option	Design name	
Design element	**Commentary**	**Mark**
Design Element	Commentary	Mark

An action plan should be defined from the test results, based on the strengths, and weaknesses identified. The next steps are likely to contain:

- the design team refining the chosen design option, including reviews on the impact on all quadrants on the Compass if necessary followed by a realignment;
- a recommendation to go back to steering committee (as set out in the chapter on Assessing Alternatives).

Following up these actions needs only a few members of the design team with some of the participants from the scenario testing.

Conclusion

Dealing with uncertainty in the organization's environment and complexity is never straightforward. 'The pessimist complains about the wind. The optimist expects it to change. The leader adjusts the sails' – John Maxwell. One way, to 'adjust the sails' is to use scenario thinking before and/or after design. This enables executives to increase their confidence in their chosen strategy, reduce their anxiety about the resulting design and change, and enhance the risk management of their organization. As well as these outcomes, there are a number of outputs from doing this:

- scenarios;
- insight for the design work;
- completed design option commentaries for scenarios;
- completed design element commentaries for scenarios;
- action plans;
- refined design options.

This chapter has shown you how to increase the chances that the design options you derive and choose can cope when there is greater uncertainty by adding scenario planning and scenario testing. Once you have completed this chapter you will be able to assess whether adding scenario planning and/or scenario testing to a design programme will be useful. You will know at what stage in design work to use them and how to apply them.

How to assess the level of capability maturity of an organization over time

13

Maturity is the ability to stick with the job until it's finished. **(ABIGAIL VAN BUREN)**

KEY POINTS

- Capability maturity frameworks aid assessment of progress in implementing designs.

- You can look at capability maturity at different levels of granularity.

- Capability maturity provides a high-level assessment.

- Design maturity breaks capabilities down into their design segments before assessment.

- A framework and process for maturity assessment can be used (one is shown).

- Examples demonstrate how capability and design maturity have been assessed.

Different strategic intents require different capabilities and underlying changes to deliver them. Capability maturity focuses on outcomes: achieving the final state your organization has targeted. Implementing your organization's capabilities well enables it to deliver its strategic intent and is important because it is hard for competitors to match. Although you may require all parts of your organization to reach a consistent final state, they may be unable to do so at the same time because implementation is too difficult or too expensive. Alternatively, you may require different target capabilities and states/levels of these across your organization. Variances may be by area, by groups of people or by levels of seniority, and they may be working to different implementation timetables. In these situations it is important to establish defined states or levels of interim or ultimate achievement, as required: either for the whole organization or for particular areas and groups. Interim levels can be used as a means of measuring progress towards the states over time. If dates are established they can be used as input for planning.

This chapter aims to show you how to assess the maturity of your organization's target capabilities: either at a point in time or periodically. It covers a framework and process for assessing capability maturity at two different levels of granularity with case examples for each of these. These demonstrate two ways in which capability maturity assessment have been used to good effect. You should gain an insight into how you can tailor a capability maturity assessment framework and assess capability maturity.

A framework for assessing capability maturity

Throughout the OPTIMAL Way we have shown you how growing capabilities involves building and developing across a range of aspects. Every capability impacts for instance, the work done, the skills, competencies and behaviour required from your people and/or suppliers and how you measure and reward performance. You can look at capabilities at two levels of granularity: either at individual capability level or if an understanding of a finer level of detail is required, in terms of their design components. For instance, for an organization where a key capability is 'set strategy and focus on outcomes', you can look at this at that level or focus on what that phrase means in terms of the Organization Design Compass segments that need to change in your organization. Say, in Structure, an area with roles and responsibilities for strategic insight and planning as well as in Enablers, goals and metrics and rewards focused on outcomes.

Design maturity is simply a more detailed and specific way of looking at capability maturity, ie the final state required for a capability. The maturity of a capability is looked at the design segment level: this provides greater focus in terms of design implications making it easier to define and take appropriate actions. In this book, we first examined what capability maturity means for an organization when taking stock of the change required. There we looked at the maturity requirements at the design segment level. When you have completed the design phase of a programme you will have a much better understanding of what the design implications for your organization are and what maturity looks like for each capability.

When an organization establishes or re-establishes its strategic intent, it takes time for it to change and develop the required maturity for associated capabilities. A number of tools and techniques have been developed to allow you to measure the maturity levels reached and/or establish interim maturity targets. Some other disciplines have recognized de facto standards for capability maturity models/frameworks and assessments; for example, the Software Engineering Institute CMMI model. So far though, no standards exist in this area for organization design work. Anyone using these types of tools and techniques has to develop their own and therefore there are many variants. Table 13.1 shows a framework for capability maturity assessment you can use. The left-hand side records the capabilities at what level you want to look at them. Across the top the maturity levels are captured.

TABLE 13.1 Capability maturity framework

Capability	Capability maturity levels			
	Level 1 **Name** *Description*	**Level 2** **Name** *Description*	**Level 3** **Name** *Description*	**Level n** **Name** *Description*
Capability name 1				
Capability name 2				
Use Compass segments here if you use this framework to assess design maturity				

How to assess capability maturity

FIGURE 13.1 Process for assessing capability maturity levels

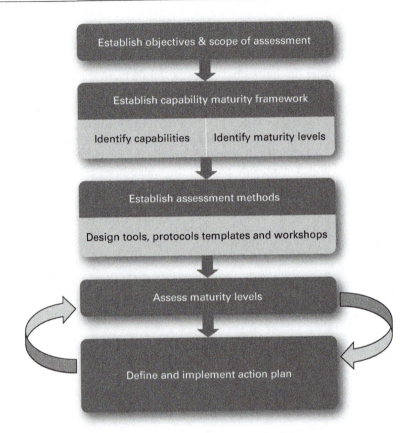

The process for assessing capability maturity levels is shown in Figure 13.1. You start by establishing what you are assessing. What are the objectives and scope for your assessment? What do you need to know and why? What outcomes are you looking to assess? What organization(s) and time period(s) are you going to cover?

Next you want to establish your assessment framework, using Table 13.1 as a template. Identify the capabilities you want to assess and include these on the left-hand side of the framework. If you have been through the OPTIMAL Way, these will probably be your target capabilities. Which capabilities need to be embedded? Do you want to focus on them all or just a subset? How detailed do you need to review them – at capability level or do you want to focus on some capabilities in some areas at design level? They are 'horses for courses': each appropriate at different times for assessing capability levels. Be careful: you may be swamped with too much information if you look at everything at design level. On the other hand you may not have enough understanding for appropriate action in some areas if you use capability level. The second aspect to the framework is considering the maturity levels you want to assess against: four to five levels are typically used. Adding meaningful names and descriptions helps to make them real for the situation you are assessing. A sample from a completed assessment framework is shown in Table 13.3. The framework shows the assessment criteria completed for design maturity for one capability across levels. The case is covered in more detail later in this chapter.

Now you need to look at how you will carry out the assessments and establish the assessment methods you will use in all the organizations being assessed. You will be repeating this across the organization over time: others may be carrying out the assessment, so make it straightforward and consistent. Create any tools and templates to be used, eg workshop designs, interview question sets, questionnaires, analysis proforma/spreadsheets. Set out any protocols to be used, eg written guidelines and instructions about how to carry out the work; instructions on who to involve, how to introduce the work to them, how to gather data, how to assess results, how to report results, who to report results to, when to repeat the assessment. Now the cycle of reviews using your framework and methodology can take place over the time and frequency you have set. After each review the assessed unit should draw up action plans and implement these in any areas that need addressing.

It is straightforward to assess capability maturity either during implementation or embedding an organization design. It takes little time or effort to establish the assessment framework. Typically only one to two days once your strategic thinking is done, with a couple of people involved whatever the size and complexity of your programme. The time taken for assessment depends on how many areas are involved and how many times it is carried out.

CASE EXAMPLE   Assessing capability maturity

In 2005 the UK Government's Cabinet Office established a programme of capability reviews. The objective and scope were a set of consistent capabilities and associated levels to be reached by all central Civil Service departments. It was recognized that across individual departments capability maturity would vary: so the Cabinet Office set out levels against which they could assess each department. The intent was for each department to use the assessment as an organization diagnostic as input to planning and implementing improvements. The Cabinet

Office defined their capabilities around three groups: leadership, strategy, and delivery and identified five levels of maturity. The maturity levels were:

- Strong – good capability for future delivery in place, in line with the capability model. Clear focus on the action and improvement required to deliver transformation over the medium term.

- Well placed – to address any gaps in capability for future delivery through practical actions that are planned or already under way. Is making improvements in capability and is expected to improve further in the medium term.

- Development area – the department should be capable of addressing some significant weaknesses in capability for future delivery by taking remedial action. More action is required to close those gaps and deliver improvement over the medium term.

- Urgent development area – significant weaknesses in capability for future delivery that require urgent action. Not well placed to address weaknesses and needs significant additional action and support to secure effective delivery. Not well placed to deliver improvement over the medium term.

- Serious concerns – serious concerns about current capability. Intervention is required to address current weaknesses and secure improvement in the medium term.

(National Audit Office, 2009)

They also developed the assessment methods: the process to be used, the criteria for each capability, a set of test questions to ask, and marking scheme to be applied in all reviews and the reporting structure. Initial reviews were carried out by a team drawn from within the Civil Service with strong external representation. Typically these review teams have included: two directors general from other government departments, two members drawn from the private sector and one from local government. The reviews consist of a number of activities for the team. They examine documents and surveys produced by the department under review. Over a couple of weeks, they hold challenge workshops, interviews with (mainly senior) staff from the department, their suppliers, and stakeholders, and visit parts of the department. Then they review the information gathered against the criteria, test questions, and marking scheme to ascertain the department's capability assessment. A formal report, approximately 20–40 pages long, is produced containing the assessment and findings for each capability. Table 13.2 shows an example of a summary capability assessment for one department. Following the review, each department then defines their response and action plan; and is responsible for implementing it.

By 2009 the capability maturity of every department had been assessed once and a review of the Capability Review Programme was carried out by The National Audit Office. As result of this, the lessons learned from initial reviews and to reflect the latest strategic thinking, a slightly modified version of the original capabilities was introduced in 2009 for all future assessments. The cycle of implementing planned actions, reassessing capability maturity levels, and defining action plans continued. In April 2013 this was extended from the central Civil Service departments to the whole of the Civil Service and the capabilities plan was revised. The capabilities plan now focuses on four key areas: leading and managing change; commercial skills and behaviours; delivering successful projects and programmes; and redesigning services and delivering them digitally (UK Civil Service, 2013).

TABLE 13.2   Example summary capability assessment

Leadership		
L1	Set direction	Well placed
L2	Ignite passion, pace and drive	Well placed
L3	Take responsibility for leading delivery and change	Well placed
L4	Build capability	Development area
Strategy		
S1	Focus on outcomes	Well placed
S2	Base choices on evidence	Strong
S3	Build common purpose	Development area
Delivery		
D1	Plan, resource and prioritize	Well placed
D2	Develop clear roles, responsibilities and delivery model(s)	Development area
D3	Manage performance	Development area

Capability maturity assessment was ideal for this situation. So far reviews have been carried out on 24 departments, each looking at all 10 capabilities. At this scale, there is sufficient information to take action without getting swamped or the assessment costs exceeding the benefits to be derived. Also the reviews deliberately set out to engage with the leaders of the departments and this was achieved because the focus was limited to a few high level capabilities and a more strategic review. At first sight, the civil service departments are very different; however, a shared framework exposed common gaps enabling the development of shared responses. According to the National School of Government's Sunningdale Institute, 'Capability issues are being discussed more widely and openly, partly because the Capability Reviews process has identified common capability gaps across departments' (Sunningdale Institute, 2007).

CASE EXAMPLE   Assessing design maturity

Here we show an example where design maturity assessment was absolutely the right technique for the situation. The case was a large global corporation setting up an IT and operations shared service centre for their business units and head office functions. They identified that a capability in demand management needed to be in place in eight business units using the new shared service organization. This particular capability was critical to the success of the new organization and yet it spanned boundaries beyond the shared service unit being designed. These future 'customers' of the shared service unit had all been represented in the shared service organization design programme to ensure an optimal design for the whole organization. But in implementation phase, the programme needed a deeper engagement with each business unit to influence how they carried out demand management; while allowing for varying current maturity levels and future maturity targets based on the degree of their use of the shared service centre.

So the objectives for the design maturity assessment were clear. To establish the current, interim, and ultimate maturity levels for demand management capability. The scope of the assessment covered eight business units. The design team then established which segments of the Compass were the priorities for this capability. Seven segments were included: Processes, Information, Structure, Roles and Responsibilities, Resourcing, Incentives and Rewards, and Goals and Metrics. Four levels of maturity were set: skeletal, emerging, mature and advanced.

The framework was completed by defining how each level would be assessed for each segment: 'the marking scheme'. The completed result for some of the segments is shown in Table 13.3. Next the programme team turned to the assessment process, methods, protocols, tools, and techniques. The programme team designed a detailed one-day workshop to be run in each of the business units to complete the existing capability assessment.

With this complete, reviews could start. At each business unit, the workshop was attended by the business unit leaders and people who would be responsible for implementing the demand management capability in that business unit. It was facilitated by members of the design team for the shared service unit. At the workshop, the business unit's team were given an overview of the programme, its objectives, and the Organization Design Compass. They were then taken through a structured question set to analyse their current demand management capability. The question set examined seven processes that contributed to demand management capability:

- demand definition and gathering;

- demand consolidation to service business requirements;

- demand analysis to understand high-level impact on current services;

- demand analysis for impact on new services required;

- translation of business demand strategy into detailed requirements following standardized templates, processes and structures.

The workshop went through an examination of whether the processes were already being carried out and their maturity level in the seven identified Compass segments. The output for each business unit was summarized as a single score; from one for 'skeletal' to four for 'mature' for each Compass segment.

Following the completion of the workshops across all eight business units, the shared service design team (including the business unit representatives), developed a hypothetical target capability maturity for each business unit showing progression over time to enable the shared service unit to achieve its goals. A second set of workshops and dialogues was then held with each of the business units where that theoretical target was refined to take account of the business unit's other change demands. Table 13.4 shows a target timeline for one business unit. Each business unit then developed its own action plan to implement their required capability level in the required timescale. Periodic checkpoints were built into the implementation programme and the assessment was repeated at checkpoints so that the business units and the shared service centre could effectively track and monitor progress. Two major factors drove the timing of these checkpoints: priority to business units with greatest demand on the shared service centre to reach higher levels of maturity for the overall organization to function and the internal drivers within each business unit.

Design maturity assessment was ideal for this situation. It was highly targeted; looking at just one capability. It gave a depth of understanding and guidance by drilling the capability down into the key design segments. The engagement of people from both the business units and shared services unit built a shared understanding across all the areas of the requirements to make the organizations as whole successful. It provided a consistent approach across the eight business units so that they could compare themselves and learn from each other. It allowed for, indeed overtly recognized, the fact that not all business units needed the same level of capability and that they could develop their capability at different times in different ways. By focusing on outcomes rather than tasks it allowed the business units a degree of autonomy, giving them some control over their own destiny and the ability to develop in their way while working in a broad framework.

Conclusion

Capability maturity frameworks provide an effective means of assessing progress towards your organization's strategic intent and the delivery of its optimal design. The outcomes from following this chapter are that you are able to:

- define capability maturity framework(s) tailored for your organization's requirements with appropriate choices of level of granularity (broad or fine) and associated capability maturity levels;

- establish assessment methods, for instance, protocols, processes, templates, and questionnaires so there is a means of repeating the assessment over time where required;

- support organizational units in drawing up action plans and timetables to deliver their increased capability maturity.

You will be able to lead your organization in developing and implementing capability maturity assessments. As Charles Kettering pointed out, 'high achievement always takes place in the framework of high expectation'. These assessment tools are really useful once your high-level design is complete, in implementation, or in embedding a design. Once you have completed this chapter you will have the knowledge to tailor capability maturity assessments for your organization and be able to repeat it over time while helping others understand the outcomes required of them to deliver their part of the organization's capability. You will also be ensuring increased confidence with stakeholders that the organization designs developed are implemented.

TABLE 13.3 Example extract of a design maturity assessment

Compass Segment	1 Skeletal Ad hoc	2 Emerging Not formal, but some regularity	3 Mature Formal: basics are documented	4 Advanced Formal: fully documented, fully functioning, anticipates future needs
Processes	• No process documented and adhered to • Activities and hand-offs done in an ad hoc manner and are 'invented from scratch' each time and in general are not repeated	• A general process followed but not documented and explicitly controlled	• Process is defined and documented • Process targets are defined and monitored	• Process is defined and documented, and reviewed on a regular basis to meet changing business requirements • Deviations are quickly detected and removed before impacting the end customer

TABLE 13.3 continued

Compass Segment	1 Skeletal Ad hoc	2 Emerging Not formal, but some regularity	3 Mature Formal: basics are documented	4 Advanced Formal: fully documented, fully functioning, anticipates future needs
Information	• All requests for information are new • Each request is different from the last • High degree of clerical work to extract and collate information • Group meetings and face to face used extensively to share and understand information	• Information requirements are similar to last time's request • Reuse of forms starting • Quality and timeliness of information may become questioned as level of understanding improves	• People have easy, ready access to the information they need to complete their activities • Group meetings and face to face used for problem-solving and innovation rather than routine information sharing	• Routine documented processes supported by routine automated information systems • Information shared in coherent format across organization boundaries • Future forecasts readily available

TABLE 13.3 *continued*

Compass Segment	1 Skeletal Ad hoc	2 Emerging Not formal, but some regularity	3 Mature Formal: basics are documented	4 Advanced Formal: fully documented, fully functioning, anticipates future needs
Structure	• Structure is poorly defined and staff cannot describe it clearly • Ad hoc task groups are pervasive and take >40% of staff time	• Structure is becoming easier to explain to others outside • Roles and responsibilities and their lines of command are reflected in the business-as-usual structure	• Structure supports effective coordination of responsibilities • More formal processes allow wider spans of control to be implemented	• Effective horizontal linkages with other departments emerging as maturing • Organization no longer needs to channel interface through managed points of contact
Roles & Respon-sibilities	• Roles are missing • No responsibilities • Not documented	• Roles exist • Responsibilities and lines of authority not explicit or do not align	• Roles are documented • Responsibilities and lines of authority exist, but not always aligned	• Roles are documented • Appropriately located • Accountable and with appropriate authority

TABLE 13.4 Sample timeline produced to drive demand management maturity

Demand management capability for business unit A	J	F	M	A	M	J	J	A	S	O	N	D	J	F	M	A	M	J
Segments																		
Processes	1				2					3		4						
Information	1						2					3					4	
Structure		1		2				3						4				
Roles & Responsibilities		1			2				3						4			
Resourcing			1			2						3						4
Incentives & Rewards	3				4													
Goals & Metrics		1					2			3		4						
Checkpoint			1				2					3						4

APPENDIX 1
Skills required in an organization design team

Skills	Level	Reason required
Consultancy skills		
Business consulting	Expert	To analyse and interpret existing policies and procedures, controls, management techniques and human resource management in a company and provide recommendations for further improvements
Facilitation	Very high	To design and run successful workshops and meetings
Organizational auditing	Very high	To analyse a unit in terms of its organization, management, and administration and suggest how to make it more responsive and cost-effective. This covers the organizational assessment and diagnostics
Process evaluation/auditing	High	To evaluate and/or audit business and industry processes in terms of their economy and efficiency. For resources like personnel, property, space: • Looking at effectiveness and efficiency of resource acquisition, management and usage • Identifying causes of inefficiency or uneconomical practices • Identifying compliance with laws and regulations concerning economy and efficiency in the particular industry or business practice

Skills	Level	Reason required
Developing organizational standards and measurement frameworks	Medium	To establish the standards against which organizational performance and conformance will be evaluated and how this will be carried out
Diagnostic and analytical	Very high	To ask relevant questions and interpret responses To get behind the obvious: to understand root causes and establish solutions that are most likely to succeed
Whole system thinking	Very high	To handle complex, multi-perspective approaches
Communication and presentation	Very high	To handle verbal and written communication to a wide range of audiences To surface and manage conflicts

Change management skills

Skills	Level	Reason required
Stakeholder management	Very high	To create positive relationships with stakeholders through the appropriate management of their expectations and agreed objectives
Communications management	Very high	To manage the planning, implementation, monitoring and revision of communications within and outside the organization
Change management	High	To manage the people aspects of change, at organization, team and individual levels

Skills	Level	Reason required
HR specialist and generalist skills		
Resourcing and talent planning and employee selection	Very high	To manage the processes for identification, attraction, integration and development of highly skilled workers and keep them within an organization To select the appropriate candidates for positions within an organization
Role definition/job design	High	To develop effective role definitions and job descriptions
HR policy and procedure developments	High	To develop and implement policies and procedures designed to guide employment/personnel practices
Learning and talent development and training design	High	To determine if existing learning is relevant and cost-effective, and set the direction for future learning including training design and development To effectively design, develop and evaluate effective training programmes including how and where they are delivered
Developing employee performance standards and measurement frameworks	Medium	To establish the standards against which employee performance and conformance will be evaluated and how this will be carried out
Specialist HR skills	Variable	To access to areas like employment relations, employee engagement – depending on the design requirements

Skills	Level	Reason required
Programme and project management skills		
Programme/project management	Very high	To plan, organize and manage resources to bring about the successful completion of specific goals and objectives
Business risk management impact on business and customers • Appraisal/ assessment	Very high	To identify, assess, and prioritize risks from the effect of uncertainty on objectives (whether positive or negative) • Managing the risk of business instability • Managing people and HR risks
Business risk management • Mitigation	Very high	To minimize, monitor, and control the probability and/or impact of unfortunate events
Financial analysis	Very high	To interpret and analyse financial information for management level decision-making and financial planning; including the existing and future costs of running the organization
Financial consulting	High	To provide advice and recommendations for improvement to an organization's financial conditions and outcomes
Cost-benefit analysis	High	To analyse a business decision in terms of its overall benefits, for instance increased income, reduced costs, increased customer satisfaction; compared to its overall costs, for instance resources including monetary

Skills	Level	Reason required
Programme evaluation/auditing	High	To collect, analyse and interpret information about a programme or an aspect of it to determine the way forward for it. For instance: reviewing whether the desired results or benefits of the programme are being achieved; the programme's overall effectiveness, organization, activities; and, whether there has been compliance with the laws and regulations applicable to the programme
Management/ administration	Medium	To manage a contractual business relationship and assess, apply and administer the details and conditions of a contract

APPENDIX 2
Organization designers' typical backgrounds

Background	Involvement in ...
Business consulting	Giving advice to other business people. Either individually, with a small group of independent consultants, or for a large consulting company or in an internal business consultancy within a company
Business process and IT management	Large-scale process or IT changes
Change management	Building consensus and overcoming resistance to change resulting from new innovations and technology, a shift in strategic organizational direction, or managing transitional periods during organizational restructuring, mergers or takeovers. This includes stakeholder management and communications management
Finance	Restructuring
Human resources and training	Recruiting, hiring and training people for various positions within an organization or for other organizations Organizing employee career and professional development initiatives HR people are often the first people that CEOs turn to when restructuring is needed; HR business partners in particular are often in the vanguard of this work
Line management	Running sections that have undergone substantial organizational change, either in establishing a new organization or the restructuring and development of existing sections

Background	Involvement in ...
Organizational development organizational effectiveness	Assessing, coordinating or improving organizational processes, functions, departments, and strategies in order to optimize organizational outcomes including efficiency, productivity and employee morale
	Practitioners in organizational development and organizational effectiveness; either because their job includes elements of organization design or because their work complements organization design in carrying out major transformations
Programme/project management	Execution of small- and large-scale transformation
Strategic planning and implementation	Setting goals and objectives, developing a competitive strategy, providing organizational vision, and devising a plan to implement these measures

Step	Outputs
Outline the brief	Programme leadership: • Programme sponsor, senior HR leader, and the commissioner Lessons from other organizations Design brief: • The shared view of the design and change context • Strategic statements • Annotated target capabilities • Programme brief Working papers: • From the individual interviews – multiple perspectives on the programme and design context • A 'chorus of voices' collating key areas from the individual interviews
Pull together the programme	Design programme leadership and team: • Programme leader, design leader, specialist representatives and steering committee • Optionally design authority and business user group Programme management systems and environment Other programme workstreams (as required) • Cultural assessment (optional) Design workstream: • Knowledge from past organization design work and programmes • Organization design model: the Compass and how it will be used • Design process: the OPTIMAL Way and how it will be used • Toolkit: including methods, tools and techniques • Training materials on organization design, models, process and design brief • Training materials for methods, tool and techniques Programme definition and plan Steering committee pack

Step	Outputs
Take stock of the change required	Working papers from capturing the evidence base: • Master prompt list for establishing the evidence base • Tailored prompt lists for establishing the evidence base • Meeting, workshop and discussion group notes Current and future state: • Evidence base – A summary of key evidence – A detailed evidence base • Current state characteristics • Future state characteristics Internal and external insight Analysis of change required: • Gap analysis • Radar chart of change required Direction for the design programme: • Heat map of change required • Change specification: showing what the programme should change and what should remain • Updated programme definition and plan (and supporting documents) Steering committee pack Working papers from assessing the direction and extent of change: • The current and future organization plotted on: – The environmental complexity and stability framework – The work standardization framework – The classification of operating mechanisms framework • Workshop outputs
Identify the assessment criteria	Design principles and criteria marking scheme

Step	Outputs
Map the design options	Design concepts (detailed in Appendix 4) • Completed design option alignment grids • Insight for more detailed design work Concept level working papers: • Lists of work process identified • Notes from discussions Design outlines (detailed in Appendix 4) • Completed design option alignment grids • Insight for more detailed design work Outline level working paper: • Draft versions of activity maps • Reasons for changes to activity maps of key work processes • Any assumptions surfaced in challenging and refining the activity maps
Assess the alternatives	Design concept level assessment: • Design option evaluation score sheets (one for each design concept) • Design options evaluation summary for design concepts with commentary • Recommendations of options to pursue further or variations to consider Design outline level assessment: • Design option evaluation score sheets (one for each design outline) • Design options evaluation summary for design outlines with commentary • Steering committee pack for signing-off the optimal design Programme updates (as required)

Step	Outputs
Lay out the way forward	Design blueprint (detailed in Appendix 4) • Completed design option alignment grid Implementation preparation: • Gap analysis of current organization versus the optimal design blueprint • Task list of what is needed to create the new organization • List of remaining design tasks to be done during implementation • Advice on pacing and sequencing of changes • Advice on implementation approach End of design phase programme review End of design phase steering committee pack Working papers: • Process/activity characteristics charts • Workshop outputs

APPENDIX 4
Design outputs by level
and Compass segment with
examples of implementation
tasks

Compass	Design level outputs			Implementation tasks
	Concept	Outline	Blueprint	Examples
	Name of the design option			
Work — Processes	• List of top 7 to 10 key work processes • High-level process maps of key work processes	• Activity maps of key work processes	• List of work processes • High-level process maps of additional work processes	• Any detailed, lower-level process design • Develop process that span the organization's boundary
Work — Information		• Description of information systems needed to support key work processes	• Description of information systems needed to support the organization	• Make sure information is accessible – who needs to see what detail • Detailed data and information requirements specification • IT systems specification and build
Work — Operating mechanisms	• List of operating mechanisms for the top 7 to 10 key work processes		• Description of operating mechanisms needed to support the organization	• Specify and commission/install new operating mechanisms • Procedure documentations like standard operating procedures and process manuals

Compass	Design level outputs			Implementation tasks
	Concept	Outline	Blueprint	Examples
Structure	• Named units to two levels down from the top of the organization • Organization sketch of how units link together	• Outline organization chart	• List of work groups with brief description • Updated organization chart	• Drill structure down to lower levels • Build linking mechanisms such as cross-unit teams and communities of practice
Structure Roles & responsibilities	• List of major responsibilities for identified units	• Role definitions for units and sub-units • Role definitions for key positions	• Complete role definitions for all units and sub-units • Role definitions for work groups • Role definitions for all key positions • Job descriptions for key positions	• Role definitions and job description for all positions • Rules of engagement between groups

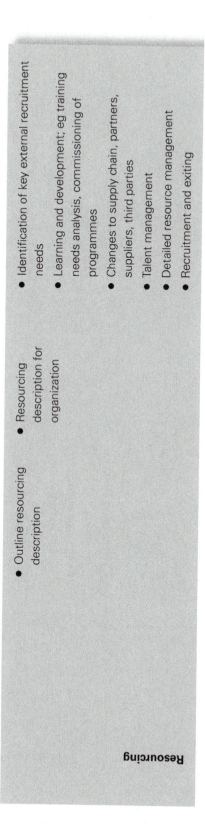

Resourcing

- Outline resourcing description

- Resourcing description for organization

- Identification of key external recruitment needs
- Learning and development; eg training needs analysis, commissioning of programmes
- Changes to supply chain, partners, suppliers, third parties
- Talent management
- Detailed resource management
- Recruitment and exiting

Compass	Design level outputs			Implementation tasks
	Concept	Outline	Blueprint	Examples
Incentives & rewards		• Changes needed to incentives and rewards systems and processes		• Put in place or update organizational performance and conformance management systems • Put in place or update individual performance management systems
Goals & metrics		• Draft list of key performance indicators		• Build performance and conformance monitoring and feedback covering eg risk, compliance, finance, non-financial • Establish processes, mechanisms and content
Governance		• Governance framework • Outlines for governance structures • List of key governance processes • High-level outlines for key governance processes • List of key mechanisms needed to make governance work		• Put in place the structures, processes and mechanisms for governance; eg meetings, standards, policies • Establish risk, financial management and compliance

Enablers

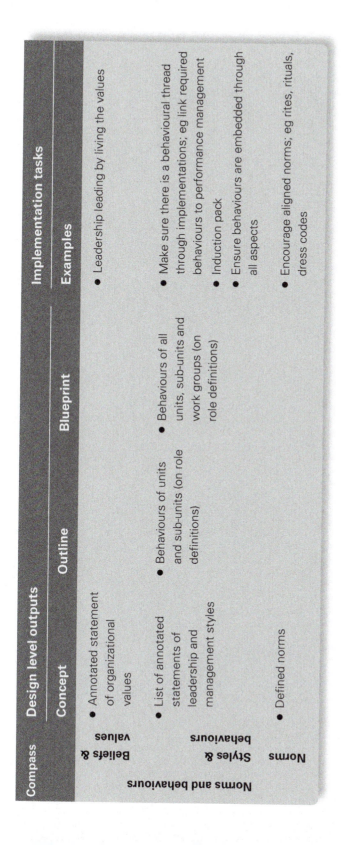

Compass	Design level outputs			Implementation tasks
	Concept	**Outline**	**Blueprint**	**Examples**
Beliefs & values	• Annotated statement of organizational values			• Leadership leading by living the values
Styles & behaviours	• List of annotated statements of leadership and management styles	• Behaviours of units and sub-units (on role definitions)	• Behaviours of all units, sub-units and work groups (on role definitions)	• Make sure there is a behavioural thread through implementations; eg link required behaviours to performance management • Induction pack • Ensure behaviours are embedded through all aspects
Norms	• Defined norms			• Encourage aligned norms; eg rites, rituals, dress codes

Norms and behaviours

GLOSSARY

Archetype   See organizational archetype.

Beliefs and values   A segment of the Compass, part of the Norms and behaviours quadrant; covering what the organization believes in; and the set of assumptions and mindsets held in common and taken for granted by the organization – 'What we stand for.'

Business user group   Senior managers, heads of departments or team leaders who understand the implications design may have on the organization within their area of responsibility and can make trade-offs and difficult calls.

Capability   What an organization needs to be able to do outstandingly well to execute its strategy and win in its environment.

Capability maturity   The level of maturity reached for one or more capabilities.

CIPD   The Chartered Institute of Personnel and Development. The main professional body in the UK and Ireland for those involved in the management and development of people.

Client   The person or organization that commissions and pays for the organization design programme.

Commissioner   A role carried out by an individual or small team at the start of a design programme using the OPTIMAL Way. They establish whether there is a firm basis for a programme to go ahead; shape the design phase; and help to set up the programme.

Compass   An abbreviation of the Organization Design Compass.

Design authority   A role that assures the integrity of an organization design process and/or outputs. It is typically only found on large or complex design programmes.

Design blueprint   The third and final level of design output produced in the OPTIMAL Way. The high-level design to be implemented.

Design brief   Documentation that sets out the client's design requirements: containing the design and change context, the agreed set of outcomes and targets for the programme, and the programme brief.

Design concept   The first level of design outputs produced in the OPTIMAL Way.

Design criteria   The standards used to judge design options. They support design principles and include indicators to look for; and any values to apply.

Design maturity   A more granular level of maturity than capability maturity. The level of capability reached broken down to constituent segments.

Design option   An alternative design produced and assessed in the OPTIMAL Way. Design options are produced at design concept and design outline levels. The optimal option is chosen to create a design blueprint.

Design outline   The second level of design outputs produced in the OPTIMAL Way.

Design principles   Succinct, clear statements describing the guiding set of requirements that you design around. They prescribe what your design must (or must not) include.

Design stage   A stage in producing the design outputs. The first two stages covered in 'Mapping the design options' produce design concepts and design outlines respectively. The third and final stage produces the design blueprint and is covered in 'Laying out the way forward'.

Elements   A generic term for any constituent parts of an organization design model. In the Compass, these are quadrants or segments.

Enablers   A quadrant of the Compass, covering strategic rather than operational performance and conformance; direction and control; and running the organization 'as a business'. The three segments in this quadrant are: Incentives and rewards; Goals and metrics; and Governance.

Evaluation scheme   A means of assessing the extent to which a design meets its objectives.

Evidence base   An information resource collected at a point in time documenting facts and opinions on the organization's relevant history, current state, and existing plans.

Goals and metrics   A segment of the Compass, part of the Enablers quadrant; covering the enabling processes, mechanisms and content needed to set, track and assess organizational and individual goals and objectives.

Governance   A segment of the Compass, part of the Enablers quadrant; covering frameworks, structures, processes, and mechanisms that enable the organization to manage performance and conformance.

Incentives and rewards   A segment of the Compass, part of the Enablers quadrant; covering the processes and mechanisms for setting and operating the organization's systems of incentives and rewards, and disincentives and penalties at organizational level and cascading to individual levels.

Information   A segment of the Compass, part of the Work quadrant; covering the customer and operational data, information and knowledge is needed for the work processes to be completed.

Insight   An understanding that sheds light on what is happening. This can inform what is beneficial or detrimental to a given situation.

Large group intervention   The planning and design work preceding a large group event together with the event itself. A large group intervention is usually part of a bigger change process.

Large group intervention method A framework, technology or set of guiding principles used to create a large group intervention. For instance; The Conference Model ®, Future Search, Open Space Technology and Search Conferences.

Mission Statement See Organizational purpose

Norms A segment of the Compass, part of the Norms and behaviours quadrant; covering the established and approved ways of doing things and the customary rules of behaviour both explicit and implicit.

Norms and behaviours A quadrant of the Compass, part of the Enablers quadrant; covering the values, beliefs, and assumptions that influence how the organization operates and progresses. The three segments in this quadrant are: Beliefs and values; Styles and behaviours; and Norms.

Operating mechanisms A segment of the Compass, part of the Work quadrant; covering the mechanisms used for operational work, together with their support systems and the tools needed.

OPTIMAL Way The OPTIMAL organization design approach. The participative process presented and used in this book to develop high-level organization designs.

Organization Design Compass Also referred to as the Compass. The organization design model presented and used throughout this book. The Compass is divided into quadrants: Norms and behaviours, Enablers, Structure, and Work. Each quadrant is sub-divided further into three segments.

Organizational archetype A commonly seen form of organization. Each archetype has a specific successful mix of operating philosophies, work processes, information flows, operating technology, hierarchy, leaders, membership, control systems, decision-making processes, values and behaviours, styles and norms, that has been well studied and documented.

Organizational purpose A statement that captures succinctly why the organization exists and what it is there to do. (Sometimes called a mission statement.)

Processes A segment of the Compass, part of the Work quadrant; covering the work processes to produce the deliverables for the customer.

Programme brief A specification for a programme capturing important information ahead of the programme definition. It includes for example the goals, objectives, scope, constraints, high-level business case, and resourcing.

Programme definition and plan A detailed specification of how the programme will be executed. It includes information from the programme brief and is more specific about the approach to be applied, workstreams, plans and milestones.

Quadrant A quarter of the Compass; Norms and behaviours, Structure, Enablers and Work.

RACI chart A technique for defining roles by clarifying what the role is responsible for, accountable for, consulted on, or informed of activities and decisions.

Resourcing   A segment of the Compass, part of the Structure quadrant; covering the group of people that make up the organization whether within its internal boundaries or beyond them e.g. partnerships, suppliers, associates and third parties.

Roles and responsibilities   A segment of the Compass, part of the Structure quadrant; covering formal specification of roles and responsibilities of groups and individuals in the organization.

Segment   Each quadrant of the Compass is sub-divided into three segments. These are the twelve aspects of an organization to consider in design work.

Sponsor/programme sponsor   A senior individual from the client organization, who acts a single focal point of contact on the day-to-day interests of the client organization. Their role is to actively champion the change throughout the duration of the programme.

Strategic statement   A succinct description of the core things that an organization needs to exploit its opportunities and avoid threats.

Structure (1)   A quadrant of the Compass; covering the organization's own internal structure and any external arrangements outside the boundaries that are critical to the delivery of services. The three segments in this quadrant are: Structure; Roles and responsibilities; and Resourcing.

Structure (2)   A segment of the Compass, part of the Structure quadrant; covering the formal internal structured, hierarchy of authority and accountability; groupings of people for reporting and the formal mechanisms linking parts of the structure together.

Styles and behaviours   A segment of the Compass, part of the Norms and behaviours quadrant; covering the leadership and management styles and behaviours that significantly impact the way the organization works.

Sub-units   Part of an organization: a sub-division of a unit.

Target capabilities   What an organization needs to be able to do outstandingly well in future to execute its strategy. They cover what the organization must know how to do to execute its strategy and how people in the organization work together to gets things done.

Unit   Part of an organization: the highest level identified in the OPTIMAL Way.

Work   The Work to be done quadrant of the Compass; covering the operation of the organization; and how it produces and delivers products and services to the customer. The three segments in this quadrant are: Processes; Information; and Operating mechanisms.

Work group   Part of an organization: the lowest level identified in the OPTIMAL Way.

REFERENCES

Amit, R and Schoemaker, P J (1993) Strategic Assets and Organizational Rent, *Strategic Management Journal*, **14**, 33–46

Argyris, C and Schön, D (1974) *Theory in Practice: Increasing professional effectiveness*, Jossey-Bass, Hoboken, NJ

Argyris, C and Schön, D (1978) *Organizational Learning: A theory of action perspective*, Addison-Wesley, Reading, MA

Axelrod, R H (2010) *Terms of Engagement: New ways of leading and changing organizations*, 2nd edn, Berrett-Koehler, San Francisco, CA

Axelrod, R H, Axelrod, E M, Beedon, J and Jacobs, R W (2004) *You Don't Have to Do It Alone: How to involve others to get things done*, Berrett-Koehler, San Francisco, CA

Baker, M N (2014) *Peer-to-Peer Leadership: Why the network is the leader*, Berrett-Koehler, San Francisco, CA

Barclays (2013) Barclays purpose and values [online] http://group.barclays.com/about-barclays/about-us/transform/values#sthash.uuZd8BWe.dpuf

BBC (2012) *Which is the world's biggest employer?* [online] www.bbc.co.uk/news/magazine-17429786 (20 March 2012)

Bevan, H, Glenn, R, Bate, P, Maher, L and Wells, J (2007) Using a design approach to assist large-scale organizational change: '10 high impact changes' to improve the National Health Service in England, *The Journal of Applied Behavioral Science*, **43.1** (Mar 2007), pp 135–52

Bijlsma-Frankema, K and Weibel, A (2006) Turning the Tables on Inter-group Distrust: De-entrenchment of borders between judges and administrators in a court of law: paper for EGOS Conference Bergen 2006

Brafman, O and Rod Beckstrom, R (2006) *The Starfish and the Spider: The unstoppable power of leaderless organizations*, reprint edition (2008), Portfolio, New York

Brown, T (2009) *Change by Design: How design thinking creates new alternatives for business and society: How design thinking can transform organizations and inspire innovation*, Collins Business, London

Bryan, L L and Joyce, C I (2007) Better strategy through organizational design, *McKinsey Quarterly*, **2** (May) pp 21–29

Buchanan, D and Huczynski, A (2007) *Organizational Behaviour*, Financial Times/Prentice Hall

Bunker, B B and Alban, B T (1997) *Large Group Interventions: Engaging the whole system for rapid change*, Jossey-Bass, Hoboken, NJ

Burke, W W and Litwin, G H (1992) A causal model of organizational performance and change, *Journal of Management*, **18** (3) pp 523–45

Burns, T (1963) Industry in a New Age: New Society, 31 January, Vol 18, pp 17–20, cited in *Organisation Theory: Selected classical readings*, ed D S Pugh (2007), Penguin, London

Bushe, G R (2013) The Appreciative Inquiry Model, in *The Encyclopaedia of Management Theory*, ed E Kessler, Sage Publications, Thousand Oaks, CA

Capozzi, M, Kellen, A and Smit, S (2012) The perils of best practice: Should you emulate Apple? *McKinsey Quarterly*, September

CIPD (2004) *Reorganising For Success: A survey of HR's role in change*, Chartered Institute of Personnel and Development, London

Cooperrider, D L, Whitney, D K and Stavros, J M (2008) *Appreciative Inquiry Handbook*, Berrett-Koehler, San Francisco

Corkindale, G (2011) *The Importance of Organizational Design and Structure*, HBR Blog [online] http://blogs.hbr.org/2011/02/the-importance-of-organization/

Daft, R (2007) *Understanding the Theory and Design of Organisations*, Thomson South Western, Mason, USA

FSA (2012) Delivering effective corporate governance: the financial regulator's role, speech by Hector Sants, 24 April 2012

Galbraith, J R (1973) *Designing Complex Organizations*, Addison-Wesley Longman Publishing, Boston, MA

Galbraith, J R (1995) *Designing Organizations: An executive briefing on strategy, structure and process*, Jossey-Bass, Hoboken, NJ

Galbraith, J, Downey, D and Kates, A (2001) *Designing Dynamic Organizations*, Amacom, New York, NY

Girod, S J G (unpublished research report, undated) *Revolutionary Processes of Multinational Adaptation: Why organizational restructuring still matters*, Accenture Institute for High Performance, London

Goold, M and Campbell, A (2002) *Designing Effective Organizations: How to create structured network*, Jossey-Bass, Hoboken, NJ

Green, M (1737) *The Spleen* (reproduced 2009), Kessinger Publishing Company, Montana

Handy, C (1993) *Understanding Organizations*, 4th edn, Penguin, London

Henderson, A, Miller, D and Hambrick, D C (2006) How quickly do CEOs become obsolete? Industry dynamism, CEO tenure and company performance, *Strategic Management Journal*, 27, pp 447–60

Heskett, J L (2011) *The Culture Cycle: How to shape the unseen force that transforms performance*, Financial Times/Prentice Hall

Holman, P, Devane, T, Cady, S and Associates (2007) *The Change Handbook: The definitive resource to today's best methods for engaging whole systems*, 2nd edn, Berrett-Koehler, San Francisco

IDEO Method Cards (no date) – 51-card deck to inspire design, William Stout Architectural Books, San Francisco, CA

Katz, D K (1966) *The Social Psychology of Organisations*, Wiley

Leavitt, H J (1964) *Handbook of Organizations*, Rand McNally, Chicago

Maupin, H and Ordowich, C (2012) Adaptive Enterprises at the Edge of Design: An emerging context for design, presentation to the Organization Design Forum in Atlanta April 2012 [online] http://organizationdesignforum.org/wp-content/uploads/2012/05/12Maupin_Ordowich.pdf

McKinsey & Company (2010) *McKinsey Global Survey Results: Taking organizational redesign from plan to practice* [online] www.mckinsey.com/insights/organization/taking_organizational_redesigns_from_plan_to_practice_mckinsey_global_survey

McKinsey Global Institute (2013) *Disruptive Technologies: Advances that will transform life, business, and the global economy*, May 2013 [online] www.mckinsey.com/insights/business_technology/disruptive_technologies

Microsoft News Centre (2013) Transforming Our Company, 11 July 2013 [online] http://www.microsoft.com/en-us/news/press/2013/jul13/07-11memo.aspx

Miles, R E and Snow, C C (1978) *Organizational Strategy, Structure, and Process*, McGraw-Hill Book Co, New York

Morgan, G (1997) *Imaginization: New mindsets for seeing, organizing, and managing: Art of creative management*, SAGE Publications, London

Morgan, G (2006) *Images of Organization*, 4th revised edn, SAGE Publications, London

Nadler, D A and Tushman, M L (1980) A Model for Diagnosing Organization Behavior, *Organization Dynamics*, Autumn

Nadler, D A, Tushman, M L with Nadler, M B (1997) *Competing by Design: The power of organizational architecture*, OUP USA

National Audit Office (2009) *Assessment of the Capability Review Programme*, National Audit Office

Pascale, R T and Athos, A G (1981) *The Art of Japanese Management: Applications for American executives*, Simon and Schuster, New York

Pascale, R T and Sternin, J (2005) Your Company's Secret Change Agents, *Harvard Business Review*, 83 (5 May) 73–81

Pascale, R T, Sternin, J and Sternin, M (2010) *The Power of Positive Deviance: How unlikely innovators solve the world's toughest problems*, Harvard Business Press, Cambridge, MA

Peters, T and Waterman, R (1982) *In Search of Excellence: Lessons from America's best-run companies*, Warner Books, Boston, MA

Pfeiffer, J and Sutton, R L (2006) *Hard Facts, Dangerous Half-Truths and Total Nonsense: Profiting from evidence-based management*, Harvard Business Press, Cambridge, MA

Rosenthal, C (2013) Big data in the age of the telegraph, *Mckinsey Quarterly*, March

Roxburgh, C (2009) The use and abuse of scenarios, *McKinsey Quarterly*, November

Sackmann, S and Stiftung, B (2006) *Success Factor: Corporate culture. Developing a corporate culture for high performance and long-term competitiveness; Six best practices*, Bertelsmann Stiftung, Götersloh, Germany

Salz (2013) *The Salz Review of Barclays' Business Practices* [online] www.salzreview.co.uk

Schwartz, P (1998) *The Art of the Long View*, Doubleday/Currency, 1991; John Wiley and Sons, 1998

Shmulyian, S, Bateman, B, Philpott, R G and Gulri, N K (2010) Art or Artist? An Analysis of Eight Large-Group Methods for Driving Large-Scale Change, in *Research in Organizational Change and Development*, 18, eds W A Passmore, A B Shani and R W Woodman, Emerald Group Publishing Limited, pp 183–231

Sunningdale Institute (2007) *Take-off or Tail-off? An evaluation of the Capability Reviews programme*, National School of Government, Sunningdale Institute

The Economist (2013) Scoop! The Ivory Towers of Ice Cream, *The Economist*, 12 January

UK Civil Service (2013) *Meeting the Challenge of Change: A capabilities plan for the Civil Service*, April 2013

Ulrich, D (1997) *Human Resource Champions: The next agenda for adding value and delivering results*, Harvard Business School Press, Cambridge, MA

Wack, P (1985) The Gentle Art of Re-perceiving, *Harvard Business Review*, September–October

Walls, J G, Widmeyer, G W and E l Sawy, O A (1992) Building an Information Systems Design Theory for Vigilant EIS, *Information Systems Research*, 3(1) (1992), pp 36–59

Weisbord, M R (1976) Organizational Diagnosis: Six places to look for trouble with or without a theory, *Group & Organization Studies*, 1 (4) (December 1976): pp 430–47

Winby, S (2010a) *Adapting to New Realities: The emergence of network organizations and work systems*, White Paper

Winby, S (2010b) *Work Innovation Network: Concepts and practice*, White Paper

Woodward, J (1965) *Industrial Organization Theory and Practice*, Oxford University Press, Oxford

World Economic Forum (2012) *Design Innovation*, Network of Global Agenda Councils Reports 2011–2012

Zeitlin, M (1990) *Positive Deviance in Child Nutrition – with emphasis on psycho-social and behavioural aspects and implications for development*, United Nations University, Tokyo

FURTHER READING

Axelrod, R H (2010) *Terms of Engagement: New ways of leading and changing organizations*, 2nd edn, Berrett-Koehler, San Francisco, CA

Axelrod, R H, Axelrod, E M, Beedon, J and Jacobs, R W (2004) *You Don't Have to Do It Alone: How to involve others to get things done*, Berrett-Koehler, San Francisco, CA

Buchanan, D and Huczynski, A (2007) *Organizational Behaviour*, Financial Times/ Prentice Hall

Bunker, B B and Alban, B T (1997) *Large Group Interventions: Engaging the whole system for rapid change*, Jossey-Bass, Hoboken, NJ

Cooperrider, D L, Whitney, D K and Stavros, J M (2008) *Appreciative Inquiry Handbook*, Berrett-Koehler

Hidden Insights® is produced by Woodward Lewis LLP, see selected organizations and resources below

Holacracy® is a trademark of HolacracyOne LLC, see Selected organizations and resources below

Holman, P, Devane, T, Cady, S and Associates (2007) *The Change Handbook: The definitiver resource to today's best methods for engaging whole systems*, 2nd edn, Berrett-Koehler

Lewis, J (2007) Positive Action, *Quality World*, London, September

OrgVue is produced by Concentra, see Selected organizations and resources below

Pfeiffer, J and Sutton, R L (2006) *Hard Facts, Dangerous Half-Truths and Total Nonsense: Profiting from evidence-based management*, Harvard Business Press, Cambridge, MA

Schwartz, P (1998) *The Art of the Long View*, Doubleday/Currency, 1991; John Wiley and Sons, 1998

University of Westminster (unpublished notes 2013)

SELECTED ORGANIZATIONS AND RESOURCES

Deloitte Consulting, 'As One collective leadership' model, see www.deloitte.com/view/en_GX/global/services/consulting/as-one-collective-leadership/asonearchetypes/

European Organization Design Forum – The European counterpart to the Organization Design Forum in the US, see www.organisationdesignforum.eu

Hidden Insights® is produced by Woodward Lewis LLP, Forum House, Caledonian Road, Chichester, West Sussex, PO19 7DN
To find out more about Hidden Insights®, see www.woodward-lewis.co.uk or contact info@woodward-lewis.co.uk

Holacracy® from HolacracyOne LLC, see www.holacracy.org

Organization Design Forum – The Organization Design Forum builds and advances the community, practice, and leadership of the field of Organization Design and its strategic role in the connectivity to other disciplines, see www.organizationdesignforum.com

OrgVue is produced by Concentra, Thames House, 18 Park Street, London, SE1 9EQ. To find out more about Orgvue, see www.orgvue.com or contact info@orgvue.com

Socio-technical System Round Table – Adaptive Enterprise Team Socio Technical System theorists and practitioners who come together as a professional learning community, see www.stsroundtable.com

The Change Leaders – A community of practice dedicated to the human side of change, see www.thechangeleaders.com

INDEX

CPSIA information can be obtained at www.ICGtesting.com
Printed in the USA
BVOW06s0841041115

425419BV00039B/49/P